IT'S JUST LIFE!
WHY GET YOUR KNICKERS IN A TWIST?

Lennie George Abraham

notionpress.com

INDIA • SINGAPORE • MALAYSIA

ISBN
Hardcase 979-8-89610-282-3
Paperback 979-8-89588-331-0

DEDICATION

This book is dedicated to those who donated that one Sperm and that one Egg which united so beautifully to create the Life that I have been gifted.

To Live, To Experience, and To Enjoy

The Parents

Contents

FACE TO FACE WITH THE BOYS

SELAMAT KEMBALI

GHAR VAPASI

MARHABA AL KUWAIT

AFTER THE WAR

Preface

I wrote this book to spite the offsprings, Zach, Elizabeth, and Rebecca. After having put them through the wringer for the better part of their young lives, I know they are waiting to return the 'favour.' They will never dare to do so in my lifetime, but as surely as the nose on my face, I know that once I'm gone, whenever they get together, I would be their inevitable topic of conversation.

I had often spoken to them about my desire to write and publish a book, and as nothing came out of it for a long time, it soon turned into a family joke.

Should I get a phone call and should they answer, they'd wink at each other, and with laughter lurking in their throats, they'd say in a loud voice to make sure I heard:

'Hang on a minute, I think she's busy with her book.'

And I could be milking the cow!!

Or worse, I would be rebuking them for some misadventure, and they'd say, 'Save your energy for the book, Mother.'

But the cruellest cut of all has been, 'Don't forget to mention us when you receive "The Booker," Momma Bear.'

So even at this late stage in life, I wanted to get it done. By hook or by crook, heck, I'd write my book. Whether it be a winner or otherwise, one thing is for sure – I will not give them the satisfaction of sitting in the lawn after my wake, sipping a cold lemonade, reminiscing fondly, even poignantly, over our lives together, and one of them saying:

'Oi! Remember she wanted to write a book? And how we ragged her about it?'

Then, I know with absolute certainty, that they would collapse into gales of laughter.

Actually, it conjures up the perfect, most beautiful picture – that they should have a laugh when they think of me. I wouldn't want it any other way.

THANK YOU, GUYS. BECAUSE OF YOU RASCALS, IT HAPPENED. EVEN IF I HAD AN ULTERIOR MOTIVE.

MOTHER.

The Three

Acknowledgements

To my young friend Sowjanya. Her patience, wizardry with computers, and flying fingers enabled the creation of this book.

Dr. Priya Mary Jacob, who introduced me to Ms. Anjali Manoj.

Ms. Anjali Manoj, for creating the platform 'Her Trivandrum,' which opened up the vista to exhibit my writing abilities.

Ms. Seena Raghavan, for beta reading my work.

Special appreciation for my 14-year-old illustrator, Jai Saji Panicker.

To each and every one of the delightful ladies of Her Trivandrum, who have been loyal readers and supporters, laughing at my shenanigans and egging me on.

To family members, friends, and others who have knowingly or unknowingly contributed material for filling the pages of this book.

And yet, there will be someone who is going to be miffed that I did not mention them.

C'est la vie!

Introduction

When I decided to pen in earnest, I wondered on the topic until Sibling advised me it was best to select a topic on which I was an authority and was familiar with. That made sense. Whom did I know better than me? Besides, if I wrote about Moi, no one else would have a grouse against what I write, and I definitely have nothing against me.

So, in a nutshell, this book tells my story. When I mentioned this to a friend, she asked me point blank, 'Why would you tell your story? Are you interesting or important enough that anyone would like to know?' And I had the most plausible answer: 'Because I don't know of anyone else who thinks I'm interesting or important enough to do it for Moi. So, the onus is on me. Moreover, I don't think it is wise to write about anything or anyone else. Why get my knickers in a twist?'

In life's vast chase for meaning and want, we can either thrive or die. In the process we create stories and no one can tire of telling these stories, or listening to them, for that matter. Stories keep us amused, awestruck, or terrified and in the telling of them, our hopes, memories even fears are kept alive. Any person, however insignificant, has a story that needs to be said. How it is told makes all the difference, and it is best to keep in mind it doesn't bore the pants off the listener.

In telling my story, I'll be the first to admit that I cannot promise to be kind or nice all the time. How monotonous would that be? Neither will I be malicious or spiteful. On the contrary, the accounts I have contain some harmless teasing, most of them aimed at Moi. I have added the right amount of mischief, compassion, humour, empathy, madness, and cunning to concoct the spicy hotchpotch that is my life. And I think now is the right time to serve it. This book is a journey, beginning from as far back as the fifties, from the backwardness and quaintness of times gone by, to the times of the digital age. I have had the luck to have lived from the times of reading by the light of kerosene lamps to the times of wi-fi.

I began writing from as way back as my schooldays. But sadly, no one saw my potential, if indeed I had any. Also, about sixty years ago, it was a daunting task and not as easy as it is today to write or expose one's capabilities. Nor to find a platform to exhibit one's talents. And yet, Shakespeare and Milton did, you might argue. True, but I'm no genius. So, I stalled, and it never came to fruition. Then I got busy with life and living. Family and profession made great demands on Moi, and my dream was pushed to the back-burner.

Then came retirement, and with the brood having flown the nest, I was left with a lot of time on my hands. I mean, how much of Netflix can you watch or gardening can you do? Also, I'm at an age where I don't have the energy for adventures and am too lazy to start an affair, though I did toy with the idea in the hope that it could make for a great story. But my track record on finding love is so poor that I discarded the notion almost at once. And worst of all, how much conversation can you have with a husband of forty-six years? I can vouch for the fact that we've said all there is to say and more.

At this juncture, two things happened simultaneously. I decided to get back to writing, and I was also invited to transcribe a weekly post for an all-ladies platform on Facebook called 'Her Trivandrum,' which boasted over 15,000 members. I gained support and inspiration from the readers and was encouraged by them to compile my writings and publish a book. Thus, the wheels were set in motion. I've tried to remain as close as I can to the truth, and by that, I mean I've exposed my warts and all, and every bit of the havoc I have intentionally or unintentionally created where ever I went. Some of the more taciturn readers among us might find it distasteful that I'm frank and open about intimate matters that I faced in my teenage and after marriage. Au contraire, it was all a part of my life and I wanted to keep the record straight.

I know of at least twenty people who will definitely read this book. With that confidence, I ventured forth. If, by chance, you are idly browsing through a book stand or where ever, and for whatever reason find yourself flipping through the pages of this book, be adventurous enough to get a copy and read it. You might be surprised.

The Main Players

Father

Mother

Sibling – the late sister

The Husband

The Boy – the firstborn

Elder – the elder daughter

Younger – the younger daughter

Moi (French for 'me,' pronounced 'Mo-wah')

Some names of relatives and others have been changed for fear of repercussions.

THE BEGINNING

Aunt Suzy and the Ponds Jar

Someone once asked, 'So, where do we begin a story?' And a little boy answered, 'Why, at the beginning of course.' Indeed.

I was born in Kerala to a teacher father and a homemaker mother. My childhood was spent in Ceylon. The earliest memories I have of this time, or of life itself, are of the elephant processions in Katunayaka, a quaint little town in Ceylon, where Father was the science teacher. The pomp and grandeur of those majestic creatures must have boggled my four-year-old mind to such an extent that it stays with Moi even today.

I don't know why, but I think for better prospects, we uprooted from Ceylon, and while Father sailed the high seas towards Malaya, he wanted Mother and I to sojourn at our ancestral home in Ayroor, Kozhencherry, to wait for him to settle down and send for us. My story starts there. I spent a short but unforgettable time with the grandparents before leaving to join Father in the new world he was preparing for us.

Seventy years ago, not many would have heard of the Ponds cream. And of the few who had the opportunity to hear of it, I can safely say that only a minuscule number would have actually seen the little white porcelain jar or what it contained. I'm delighted to say that I was one of those privileged few. Not that I owned or used the contents of the jar, but I was an essential, albeit insignificant, part in this narration concerning an incident about the sweet-scented cream. People who had an intimate association with this fragrant salve were a class apart, like my Aunt Suzy. She was an enigma who smelled of red roses and jasmines in bloom, of wild flowers and honey. Sixty-odd years ago, even when I lived on the borders of nowhere, in a quaint little hamlet, tucked away so carefully between the refreshingly green hillocks and winding roads that seem to go on forever, I came into close proximity with this magic portion and lived through the havoc it played in all our lives. That such a little jar, that could easily be accommodated in the palm of a hand, had this magnetic hold on an entire village was beyond reasoning. But that was the way it was. A simple white porcelain jar that did not declare its importance; and yet, when you turned the lid, it would do so smoothly, almost willingly, and when you lifted the lid, it was pure magic. A whiff of the most ethereal fragrance drifted out and engulfed those who were in its mesmerizing presence. I actually saw the cream just once. And I noticed even then that it was just as unassumingly white as the jar itself. So, what was it about this enchanting white jar and its magical white potion that made so great an impression on my four-year-old mind?

Aunt Suzy, from my paternal side, was a beauty in every sense of the word. Anyone could mistake her for a nymph, with her big black eyes – blazing one minute, doe-like the next – curly black hair rippling down her back to well below her waist, and her lissom, svelte figure. Her movements were almost a dance, and her laugh, as she threw back her head and let the tinkling sound flow, could inspire a poet to write a verse. Anyone who came across Aunt Suzy hardly ever paid much attention to anything she said, so lost were they in just watching her vivacious movements and her animated gestures. They just laughed along with her whenever she chose to let out the peals of laughter that always lurked behind her throat. Just being in her presence and to be enveloped by her glorious radiance was enough for us lesser mortals. Whenever Aunt Suzy got into one of her spontaneous frenzy moods, she would play an old beaten-down gramophone and sway her body to some long-forgotten rhythmic music. She would coo deep in her throat in tune with the music, her long cherry-red skirt swishing about her legs, and anyone watching her would fall into some sort of drugged trance. Then the rhythm of the music would gradually change into a crescendo – louder and quicker, and Aunt Suzy would become all arms and legs, a kaleidoscope of twirling colour until finally, this mesmerizing frivolous dance would slow down to the strains of pianissimo. And as the tune finally faded away, the bewitching dancer would bend her head and fold her arms and come to an entire standstill. An enraptured audience, for there was always an audience whenever Aunt Suzy had one of her spontaneous outbursts of anything, which always made me wonder if they were indeed spontaneous, would then burst into loud applause. Aunt Suzy welcomed these adorations as regally as any Queen would. Grandfather and grandmother pampered Aunt

Suzy no end, not so much because she was beautiful, though that did come into account, but more so because she was their youngest child – the baby. The way I saw it, I was more baby than her, but no one else saw the sense in that, and soon, I tired of pointing it out.

It was paramount that Aunt Suzy be kept with a never-ending supply of Ponds, or the sun would set on everybody's happiness. She would sulk and sigh and yet manage to look even prettier, with her red lips in a pert little pout. There would be no laughter, no music, no dance, and grandmother would be all in a dither. The maid would move about quietly in the kitchen, and the farm boy would stop whistling. Even the dog would stop barking, and the house would fall quiet. Even in a house where a death had occurred, there would be sounds of wailing. But here, there would be stone-cold, reticent silence. Thus, it was to everyone's benefit and their collective duty to keep an ever-replenishing supply of Ponds jars at all times.

Although there was a rivalry in my mind as to who was the baby between us, I admit to Aunt Suzy and I sharing a special rapport. I loved the afternoon romps we would take along the green hillocks, following a little meandering brook. The air would be fresh on our faces, and most times, Aunt Suzy would be deep in thought, though she would hum softly to herself. I was satisfied to just walk by her side, skipping along when I fell behind, picking fallen guavas or cashew nuts, throwing stones into the brook, and just being happy to be with someone I loved with no reservations. At times, she would turn to me, smile, tilt her head to the side, and raise her brow quizzically. It was an eternal mystery to Moi, how she did that, but I knew what it meant. Then, we would find some shade, sit down together, and just listen to the birds and watch the butterflies flutter about. Sometimes, as the wind blew, I would catch a whiff of red roses, or were those fresh jasmines in bloom, or the fragrance of wild flowers, or the smell of honey? And the scent would grow stronger as Aunt Suzy bent down to me and gathered me in her arms and told me stories of the village and of the people who resided in it.

However, an incident occurred which, for once, made Aunt Suzy and her Ponds jar take a back seat. It was a telegram from Father and was addressed to Mother. At this point, I would like to say that Mother and I held quite exalted positions in the household on account of Father being brave enough to cross the oceans to seek his fortune in unknown lands. Telegrams were not a common thing those days, and if one should arrive, it was newsworthy. Thus, the arrival of a telegram addressed to Mother created an excitement of sorts. Furthermore, when she announced the contents, there were gasps of incredulity and disbelief. She read out that soon, she would be leaving with me to join Father. This changed things drastically. Mother, and Moi along with her, moved several more notches higher in status. Grandfather was peeved at the turn of events and with good reason too. Logically, being the head of the household, he should have been the one to receive such an important document. He protested vehemently on the unfairness of the situation.

'Am I not the head of this family and have I not steered you all through thick and thin? And now, just because I am a few years older, it is no reason to evade me,' he thundered. 'To think my own son has slighted me thus is unbearable. True, my eyesight is not what it used to be, my hearing frail, and I cannot quite comprehend things the way I used to, but is that reason enough to take me lightly?' But for once no one listened.

Grandfather tried in vain to reinforce the fact that on two occasions, he too had received telegrams, but that information was lost in the midst of the furore that ensued upon Mother making known the contents of her telegram and her plans for departure. And much to Grandfather's consternation, for the first time, no one gave him any importance. As hard as he tried to regain control of the situation, he seemed to have lost his power in the general excitement generated by Mother's news. The admiration she received from the villagers, even as they balked at her bravery to set out into the unknown with a child, all on her own, was noteworthy. We were to prepare to join Father at the earliest.

And so, we began our arrangements for the great departure. Grandfather tried to stay relevant by reminding us he had once travelled to Calcutta to join the university there. He offered us the battered old suitcase he had used and kept advising Mother on how he had packed his box. Grandmother was constantly praying and beseeching God to keep us safe as we travelled into the great big unknown. She kept lamenting that we had enough pepper, coconuts, and paddy fields to feed an army, and so she saw no need for Father to leave home and hearth to seek his fortune beyond the seas, where dangers could be lurking everywhere. She fretted that she had heard of places where people even ate other people! Many expressed doubts if there even was a world outside Kozhencherry. When the day finally arrived, the entire neighbourhood came to see us off. Many of them had even taken a leave from work for the occasion. Mother was pleased to see such a fine turn out to bid her farewell, but the reality was something else. Later, we came to understand that it was more on account of a car that had been specially hired to take us to the railway station. This was a great opportunity for the locals to see the contraption up close, with the added attraction of not having to pay for a bus ticket and go to town to do so. 'And who knew' – they said among themselves – 'if we are lucky enough, the driver might even oblige and open the bonnet so that everyone could get a peek at the engine!' As it happened, the driver was a cocky, boastful fellow who not only opened the bonnet and displayed the machine, but got into the car, switched on the engine, and applied the accelerator. The old Ambassador suddenly roared to life and stayed growling, while the stunned spectators shrieked and jumped back. 'We would not get into it if someone paid us a hundred rupees!' many declared sceptically. And that was not all – the driver enjoyed the bewilderment of the simple village folks so much that he switched on the headlights, then just as quickly, switched them off again, making as if the car was blinking. All in all, the villagers got their time's worth, and they agreed that a leave from work was more than justified in this case.

I was in my pink organdie frock, a dress fit for a princess. To this day, I have never seen another dress that could hold a candle to it. It had a very broad pink satin sash, and on the left side, the most gorgeous rose, also made of pink satin. And of course, there was a pink ribbon in my short, curly black hair to go with the ensemble. For once, I had managed to outshine Aunt Suzy, and this was no mean feat, for I had tried a thousand times before without much success. Finally, goodbyes were said. There was much hugging and kissing and promises made to keep in touch and never to forget loved ones. Grandfather reminded Mother to send him a telegram as soon as we reached our destination safely, probably to make up for the recent one sent to Mother, rather than him, by Father. And Grandmother broke down into great big sobs as she enfolded me into her warm and reassuring bosom; as if on cue, everyone else did the same. When we heard the horn of the car, the entourage began to move with great anticipation; for the real reason that anyone had come was at the gate. I too, was much relieved, for I was beginning to suffocate with all the attention and hugging bestowed on Moi.

We had all moved not a hundred feet when we heard behind us a long, soft moan. Turning around, I was just in time to glimpse Aunt Suzy as she descended on me in a flurry of skirts and arms and streaming black hair. She knelt down beside me, scooped me up in her arms, and folded me to her as if she would never let me go. And for a moment, that was where I wanted to be forever. Then, as if she was forced to do so, she held me back and looked deep and searchingly into my eyes. A mischievous smile lifted the corners of her mouth and with a covert glance at her left hand, she opened her palm. There, to the astonishment of all the onlookers, lay the little white porcelain jar. I'm sure this new twist surpassed the eagerness of the populace to see the car. For anyone could hope to get a glimpse of a car if they went into town, but the content of the Ponds jar was beyond the reach of the plebeians. Aunt Suzy turned the lid of the jar slowly, her eyes never leaving my face. I waited with bated breath to see for the first time, or perhaps, if the Gods favoured me, to use for the first time, this divine cream that played so much havoc in our lives. Her fingers never wavered as she scooped up the cream and lovingly, almost reverently, applied it to my small, upturned, and dumbfounded face. And suddenly, I smelled of red roses and jasmines in bloom, of wild flowers and honey, all things familiar and cherished. My eyes filled up with tears as pictures of afternoon walks and long forgotten tunes on a broken-down gramophone drifted before my eyes. Meandering brooks and evergreen hillocks. Then, I thought of Father and the new world that waited for me. I kissed Aunt Suzy and turned around. Now, I too wore the fragrance from the Ponds jar. I was worthy and ready for a new life. I was prepared to take on the world.

Aunt Suzy

The New World

Of Monkeys and Bees

Once Father sent the telegram and arranged for us to join him, the journey of my life, as I know it, began. We left our ancestral home at Ayroor and made for the railway station at Thiruvella. From there, we were to take a train to Madras. It was a day and a night's journey, and from Madras, we were to board the SS Rajula, the ship that would take us to Father. The journey by train was fascinating. The big mechanical caterpillar huffed and puffed along with much fury and fumes, winding and hooting its way to its destination. People came and went at the many stations that the train stopped at, as if it needed a rest from all the running, and I wondered at how large the world was and how many people it contained. The hustle and bustle were so different from the peace and serenity that I had enjoyed at the Big House and suddenly Ayroor and the village seemed like a dream. Finally, we reached Madras and went to the harbour, where the biggest, most gigantic ship lay docked and waiting for us. It was so huge I thought it could hold fifty of my ancestral homes in it. After we settled in our cabins and had some refreshments, we walked onto the deck and made a few friends. Late in the evening, I heard a loud horn reverberating through the harbour and felt the ship move. We spent seven days on the big vast ocean, the waters so deep that it appeared black. I don't remember much of the journey, but I can tell you this – I slept diligently on my stomach. You see, in case the ship sank, I did not want water entering my eyes. I'm sure Mother would have recognized my brilliance once I explained this strategy to her. I might have overrated myself here, but I'm assuming she being my mother would have. On the eighth day, before the break of dawn, Mother woke me up, and for the first time, I heard excitement in her voice. She led me up the narrow, winding stairs and onto the deck, which was crowded with people. She pointed out to the horizon, and I gasped in amazement. There, far away, a thousand lights twinkled in the darkness. We were reaching our destination.

We settled in Kangar, in the state of Perlis, which shared a border with Thailand. Father was posted as the headmaster of the only English school in that state. The memory that stands out the most about this time is of the copious number of monkeys that lived in the forests behind our quarters. The place was infested with them. I loved watching the monkeys and their antics. Mother would close and bolt the kitchen door to keep them out, but I would secretly unbolt the door so they could come in. They would then raid our kitchen, and many a time, Mother ended up cooking a meal more than once. Mother could never understand how the monkeys came in, and she suggested to Father that the creatures were somehow clever enough to unbolt the door. Father looked at me and smiled, and I wondered for a moment if he had guessed there was a monkey in the house in cahoots with the monkeys outside. I was so relieved no one caught me at my 'monkey business.' Adjusting to the new place, people, culture, and language, not to mention the monkeys and their unsolicited visits any time of day, must have taken a great toll on the parents.

Mother enrolled me in the primary section of the Derma English School. Most of my classmates were Chinese, and the rest were Malays. Except for another Tamil girl called Kamala, I was the only other Indian. It was a wonder to me that there could be other people in the world who did not look like us Malayalees. I thought a lot on why they looked so different from me. I was also worried that my eyes were so huge and round while those of May Ling and the rest of the class had a different shape, which I could not quite describe. Neither could I explain my lips, which were so full and rubbery. In all, I looked so different that it was hard to ignore. I thought that if there had been more of us Indians, it would not have mattered so much. But just two of us in a class of thirty made the dissimilarities all the more glaring. At year end, when we took the class photo, I closed my eyes to slits and bit both my lips inwards into the mouth to make them look thinner in a bid to blend in with the crowd. Everyone else looked beautiful in the picture, and Mother wondered why I looked like a wasp had stung my face, causing it to puff up and look grotesque. I stayed silent because I had an inkling that she would not follow my reasoning or appreciate my ingenuity.

Childr en can be very cruel without meaning to be so, I guess. Once, a boy called Lee Yeong called me 'ape girl,' and I socked him in the face. He was Chinese and must have been tempted to call me so on account of my different look. He must have seen me as a rather large, hairy, dark girl with rubbery lips and huge eyes. Who can fault him? Anyway, the incident caused quite a bit of a stir, as his father was the local policeman. But once things came to a head and it was realised that I was the headmaster's daughter, the affair was resolved amicably. Lee Yeong stayed out of my hair, and I stayed out of his face. But to our surprise, our fathers became good friends. Secretly, Father was so proud of me and kept asking me to repeat the incident. I guess that was the point where my penchant for storytelling began, for with each narration, I embellished a little just to hear him laugh. Soon, I added a kick to the sock. He also bought me two bars of Cadburys to show his pleasure. Unknowingly, he had set a precedent for me for later life.

Much to our chagrin, the natives continued to regard us with some trepidation. However, two incidents turned the tide in our favour. The first concerned a very large beehive that hung at the entrance of the school, terrifying the students and the locals alike. Having been a keen beekeeper at his ancestral home in Kerala, Father identified the queen and moved her to a safe place. Et voila! The swarm followed, and Father was tentatively accepted by the locals.

But what solidified our stance and caused Father to be truly accepted was the second incident. It is well to remember that we lived in a place that had only a small clinic run by an orderly (male head nurse). The doctor visited once in two weeks or a month unless there was an emergency and he had to be called to come in from the adjoining state, Kedah. In the course of his duties as headmaster, Father was also responsible for the health and wellbeing of his students. So, he was gravely concerned when he came across a student who appeared unwell. From the yellow colouring of the sclera of his eyes, Father deduced that the student was jaundiced. He sent for the boy's father. Being an uneducated farmer, the poor man appeared helpless and hadn't a clue as to what to do. And the doctor was not due for another two weeks. Father's family dabbled in herbal medicines, and the land around his ancestral home was overrun with medicinal plants. Being a student of botany and zoology, Father had familiarized himself with various herbs and their uses. After getting permission from the parent of the student, he set out into the monkey-infested forest behind the quarters to look for the herb *Phyllanthus niruri*, commonly called 'seed-under-leaf' or 'gale of the wind' or 'keezhanelli' in Malayalam. I will not claim to know too much about the method of preparation or administration, but I have often heard Father say he ground it to a paste and mixed it in cow's milk, to be consumed before sunrise. All said and done, the boy was soon well enough to go back to school, healthy and happy.

Father became a hero and a Pied Piper of sorts, as people were willing to follow his advice and came to him to solve their problems or just to have a chat. From the title 'Encik' (Mr.), he was elevated to 'Tuan' (Sir/Master) and addressed as 'Tuan Cikgu' (Sir Teacher). As for Moi, whenever I went out with him, I basked in the reflected glory of the adulations Father received and felt like a 'Sultana' (Queen).

We had truly come home, and life was pleasant and peaceful.

Father (in suit) as headmaster

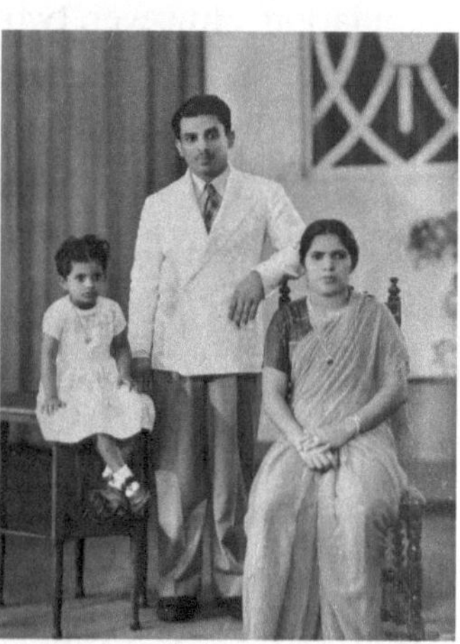

In the new world

How to Catch a Bird

Even if it is so early in the morning that I'm still groggy with sleep, I've never made a cup of coffee in my life without a smile and a trip down memory lane. In fact, I've come to call it 'café nostalgique.' C'est apte.

I'm transported to the headmaster's quarters at the Derma English School in Kangar, Perlis, Malaysia. Perlis was the smallest state in Malaysia, bordering Thailand, or Siam, as it used to be called. Mother would stand in the kitchen, making coffee. In a minute, she'd start grumbling, 'These ants always find their way into the sugar jar no matter what I do.' Then, turning to Father, she'd say, 'Any ideas?' And on cue, he'd answer, 'Have you tried labelling the jar "salt" instead of "sugar"? That should confuse the little creatures.' And the kicker was, every time, Mother would pause to consider the option. I was six or seven years old at that time, so the humour was lost on Moi. In fact, I thought Father had a valid point there. The memory stayed with me, and much later on, I began to appreciate the hidden nuances.

Another memory is of Father placing me on the crossbar of his bicycle and we would go for a peddle in the countryside. Whenever we waited at the crossroads, he would rain a thousand kisses on my head. 'Why do you do that?' I'd ask him, though I blushed with pleasure. He gave me the most sensible answer ever. 'If I kiss the top of your head, sweetheart, it will travel all the way down and cover your whole body.' By George, Mr. George! That made enough sense to keep me in buoyancy for the rest of the day.

Then there were the times we would go out for a Chinese dinner – Father, Mother, and Moi. Sibling was not yet on the horizon. Mother never touched pork, but Father and I relished it. Often, Father would sneak off to the back of the restaurant where the Chinese cook was the parent of one of Father's students. They shared a great rapport. Kind of a quid pro quo agreement – Father imparting his knowledge to the Chef's son in return for the Chef's culinary delights. When Father returned to our table, I'd ask, 'Where did you go?' And he'd answer, 'Just to let the Chef know there is a Princess come to dinner tonight. So, he'd better cook his best dish and get a bottle of "Fanta".' I felt so important and loved.

Once, I was in the garden watching the sparrows twitter and peck about. Father joined me on the grass, and we watched the birds together. He turned to me and asked, 'Would you like to catch a bird?'

'Oh yes, but how?' I questioned.

'It's easy,' he replied.

'What you need to do is get a bit of butter and wait till the bird settles down. After which you slowly creep up and put the dollop on its head. Then wait quietly. When the sun comes up, the butter will melt and run into the sparrow's eyes, and it will be blinded. Now, all you need do is walk up and pick up the bird with your hands.'

It was such a convoluted theory, and the method was beyond my understanding. I was in awe that he knew so much about everything and readily believed him. I was too young and gauche to decode that glimmer in his eyes or his suppressed mirth. And he must have got a real kick out of watching my serious face and imagining my confused brain working in overtime to keep up with his explanations.

Father's cheese and sardine sandwiches were the best I'd ever eaten. A slice of tomato and two pieces of cucumber completed the snack. He made them for Moi whenever there was a school picnic. But more than the sandwiches, I enjoyed the elaborate preparation that went into making them. He told me he learnt the art of sandwich-making from an Englishman, Mr. Peacock, who worked with Father at the school. Before that, Mr. Peacock had worked in one of the biggest hotels in England, Father told me, from where he stole the secret recipe for sandwich making. Much later in life, when I called him out on his bluff, Father laughed out loud and said, 'But didn't that make the sandwiches taste better?' He introduced me to Marmite, a British savoury food spread based on yeast extract. It is made from the by-products of beer brewing and is a vegan source of B vitamins, including supplemental vitamin B12. Sadly, it is a sticky, dark brown paste, with a distinctive salty, powerful flavour and heady aroma. You have to acquire the taste and let it grow on you. It is such that you either love it or hate it. Father and I thrived on it. Mother abhorred it.

When The Beatles took the world by storm, I was like any other teenager. I persuaded Father to buy me a guitar and then started classes. But it was Father who made the most of the instrument. Mother had a hairpiece that she used for church and parties. Father took over the wig, much to her chagrin, and wore it forwards so he had a 'Beatle fringe.' He would strum the guitar and create delightful havoc and amusement. It was also hilarious to listen to him talk in his faux English accent whenever Mother would bother him with household chores. He would tell Mother in an elaborated British accent, 'Darling I have a pine (instead of pain) in my back and need a rest.' Until one day, Mother retorted, 'Why don't you get an axe and cut down the pine?'

But there was no mischief when I was ten and sat with him on the steps of our veranda on that cool, starry night. I listened to him as he gave me strength and confidence to face my life ahead of boarding school. I was petrified at the thought of leaving home, the parents, and all that was familiar. I was wracked with anguish at the perils and pitfalls of facing the unknown. I would be alone.

That's when Father wrapped his arm around me and held me tight. 'Look at the sky, Lennie,' he said. 'Focus on the brightest star. I may be far away, but rest assured I'll be watching it too. And that way, when both of us are watching the same star, you'll be with me.' What utter nonsense was that? But it meant the world for an ten-year-old girl willing to believe anything to put her fears and apprehensions to rest. He spun tall tales all the time. Maybe it was his own escape from a dull and dreary world.

But to me, these little snippets formed such a wealth of memories and stories that I fed my own children with a lot of them. And even today, they never tire of the tales or get enough of them to quench their own curiosity about the people from whom they came to be.

Father and moi

Mother's Day

As a young girl growing up in the fifties, I had never heard of this phenomenon called Mother's Day. Heck, every day was Mother's Day, and I wished like hell that she'd go off somewhere so I could get some peace and quiet. She was always after me like Tom was after Jerry – incessantly, never giving up.

I'd get in for a bath, and she would be right outside, tapping on the door and reminding me to clean behind the ears and between the thighs. Why on earth was it so important to scrub between the thighs, I'd wonder. Who in the dickens is going to look there? Little did I know at seven or eight years of age what a ridiculously important area that would turn out to be in the adult years of one's life! I never knew the concept of privacy either. Everything concerning me was a 'free for all,' particularly for Mother. How else can you explain that I needed to tell her the colour of my urine? I'd never asked her about hers, for pity's sake. 'Drink your water Lennie,' she'd drone on and on, and then scare me to death saying, 'If you don't drink your quota of water, your urine will turn yellow and then…!!' She'd leave the sentence hanging in the air, and I would sit there, petrified at the thoughts I conjured up in my head. I was blessed with a very imaginative mind.

And did she stop there? Never. I'd sneak around the house so as to not remind her of my existence and thus avoid any unwanted attention. But I swear she could smell my presence. 'Is that you, Lennie? Get your algebra book. Let's look at some problems.' I'd scream in my head and refuse, while my legs betrayed me and walked to my room to get the books. The next one hour would be agonizing. The more she taught, the less I understood. What can I say? Perhaps I had a low IQ. She interfered with my eating habits too. What's wrong with potato chips, or chocolates, or toast smeared with butter and sprinkled liberally with sugar? What's wrong with crushed ice-balls dripping with sugar syrup? She'd get in the way of my goodies and tried to stuff my belly with vegetables. Spinach, okra, pumpkin, carrots, and beans. Was I a goat, I wondered. Why was she cruel, I wondered. Why was she big and I so small, I wondered.

Sometimes, I'd sit on the veranda, just listening to the boys in the neighbourhood as they shouted and played, or I'd watch the traffic go by. It would be nice and pleasant, and then suddenly, Mother would appear out of nowhere and occupy the chair beside me.

'What are you thinking, Lennie?'

'Nothing,' I'd answer.

'Ah, don't you know that an empty mind is the Devil's workshop?'

Chr ist, I'd think. *Is the Devil in my head already? Will that show on my face? How does my face look? Are my eyes red? Have I grown horns? Why does Mother keep scaring the daylights out of me? She must really be enjoying this.*

Calmly, she'd go on. 'Rather than keeping it empty, fill it with your multiplication tables. Go on, tell me the table of 9.'

And I'd start: '1x9=9; 2×9=18; 3×9=27,' all the while dreading the moment I'd reach 8×9. For some weird reason, I could never get that right.

And then of course, there was the question of what I wore. I loved skirts. But Mother thought skirts were for bigger girls and believed little girls wore dresses with frills and bows. I don't know if that was the case, but I definitely knew that I wanted to wear a skirt. And I don't need to tell you who always won that tussle. *She is really mean*, I thought. *For once, why can't she like something I liked?*

I have come to sincerely believe that I know the reason why I entered the Dental Profession. Subconsciously, I had a need to find out the truth about teeth. As a child, Mother always scared the bejeebers out of me by detailing how the germs would wreak havoc in my mouth should I go to sleep without brushing my teeth. The germs would creep in, attack, and destroy all the teeth with no mercy, I was told. Imagine lying in bed all night, fearing to close your eyes because if you did, you woke up to a mouth devoid of any teeth. How would I go to school? It was bad enough I had to deal with my big frog eyes and thick lips. Even today, I'm paranoid about germs dancing in glee in my mouth while they break down my enamel and go for the roots of my teeth in their eagerness to uproot them. While Father pampered Moi to no end, Mother was always chastising me, reprimanding me, counselling me, moralising me, and terrifying me. I was continuously at the receiving end of her disciplining. Her eagle eye watched me at every moment. Yet when I was half asleep in the nights, I could feel her presence, gently brushing my hair off my forehead, her lips softly touching my cheeks. Then she would stand by my bed and watch me silently, a strange smile on her face, and I wondered at her behaviour. Adults, and particularly Mothers, are weird, was my conclusion.

By today's standards, Mother's methods might seem harsh. But her intentions were clear. I grew up to be pleasant, obedient, and well-balanced. A girl who brushed her teeth and knew her multiplication tables. What more can a mother do? But the greatest irony of it all was that I followed her methods in the upbringing of my own children and understood then the depth of the whirlpool from which her love sprang forth.

Nowadays, when the kids call me to say 'HAPPY MOTHER'S DAY' and make a hullabaloo of the whole thing, I feel a heaviness and an ache in my heart, unhappy that I had never been able to say the same to my mother.

Monkeying behind mother

Illusions

Ihave nurtured a secret desire to be a writer ever since I could remember. It started when Mother introduced me to Enid Blyton. I was enthralled by the stories she spun. I loved the way she played with words to create stories that took you away to a world of fantasy. Words were the magic that opened doors to strange and wonderful lands. Sometimes, other fancies would overshadow my yearning to be a writer but not quite obliterate it. Writing lurked in the shadows until the latest fancy wore off, and once again, my great passion would come to the fore.

As it was with every other plan that I formulated, I saw the aftermath of it all even before I wrote the first line. I saw the applause, the felicitations, the ceremonies, the interviews, the talk shows, the functions I would attend, and the numerous critical acclaims that automatically followed great writing. I took this decision to be a writer to greater heights when I turned twelve and someone in the family gifted me a diary. It was of the previous year, but that did not dampen my spirits or lessen the value of the gift in my eyes. I was not going to look a gift horse in the mouth. Moreover, I considered receiving a diary as an omen of greater things to come. All I needed to do was record each day's event, and the result would be a book. Naïve as I was, I thought it was as simple as that. Anne Frank had done it, so why not Moi, even if I had not spent a moment in hiding. *Twelve,* I thought, *is a good age to embark on something new.* Twelve. A dozen. It had a certain ring to it.

Before I decided to be a writer, I went through a few other options. At that point of time, each decision had seemed so right. I was perhaps six when I realized for the first time that I would have to do something with my life. I pondered long and hard on various subjects of interest. The milkman caught my fancy, as he visited so many houses and made so many friends. But I was dissuaded as soon as I heard Mother say he started each day at four in the morning. The vegetable vendor seemed another good idea for a while. His colourful array of vegetables pleased me no end. He too had a lot of friends and visited many houses. Then I shifted to my music teacher. She fascinated me for a bit. The way her fingers ran across the piano keys and the exceptional music that drifted out, making an otherwise silent instrument come alive. Our family doctor too set me thinking. His superior knowledge, the way everyone thought he was so clever, his ability to cure the sick, and their gratefulness afterwards made a positive impact on Moi. I had an equal respect for the dhobi and the way he returned our soiled clothes looking impeccably white, stiff, and hygienic. But one job stood apart, and nothing could compete with it.

The ice man was a class apart. I was captivated by him. Don't mistake, it was not ice creams that he sold but ice balls. He had a great big block of ice, which he moved along a grater. He would gather the ice flakes that fell below the grater and roll it into balls. The size of the ice ball depended on the money you had to spare. Once the ball is rolled, with a flourish of his hand, he would execute the 'touches finales' – the final touch. With a twist of his hand, he would smear the ice ball with the syrup of your choice. Pink if you desired strawberry, green if it was lemon, red if rose, and yellow if your wish was orange. And if he was in an exceptionally good mood, you got his ultra special – an ice ball with all the flavours. An ice ball like Jacob's coat, in multi-colour.

But it was when I met Kabir that I took my first pukka decision concerning my future. I had gone for a walk with father on that eventful day. Kabir owned the little shop around the corner. A quaint little place that seemed to have everything from 'paan,' sweet drinks, cigarettes, bread, biscuits, safety pins, hair pins, and ribbons to knickknacks of every kind. To the left of the shop was a small make-shift kitchen where hot 'chaai' and 'vadais' were made. The combined smell of the simmering oil, the chaai, vadai, bread, biscuits, and cigarettes was strange and addictive. Father ordered vadai for me and a hot chaai for himself. He sipped the chaai, savouring each mouthful while chatting with Kabir. To me, Kabir was the luckiest person on Earth. I envied him and his position by the roadside. I wanted to own a shop like his when I grew up. Sit like him, relaxed, puffing on his hookah, laughing out loud, chatting with each customer, and at the same time, deftly dishing out a vadai or chaai for whoever wanted it. Alternatively, he would chew on his paan, then raise his buttocks halfway up, lean out to the side of the shop, and pressing his pointer and middle finger hard against his lips, spit out the longest stream of the brightest red spittle jet I ever saw. That feat mesmerized me. It was the climax point that I breathlessly waited for. He got it correct each time. Same spot, same design. He must have practiced a thousand times to get it so perfect.

Kabir spoke many languages and seemed to know all the news, local and international. He was a good gossip too. His old radio was never switched off. It was always blaring out some Hindi song or the news. At times, as if the din was not enough, Kabir would sing along with some popular number and if there was an audience, he would make a couple of gestures with his hands. When the song ended, there would be a lot of laughs and claps, and Kabir would touch his cap and make a few 'aadabs.' To me, it was a charmed life that he lived. He could eat all the hot vadais he wanted and drink all the sweet drinks in the shop, and no one would ask why. Since it was his own shop, he did not even need to pay! He lived by his own rules. I began to plan my shop. I would include some ice cream and jam rolls, my personal favourites. After each visit, Kabir would offer Father a 'paan' roll on the house. Father enjoyed chewing on it, but I was always a bit disappointed that Father's spittle was never as flamboyant or as long or as red as Kabir's.

However, this scheme fizzled out around the time I turned eight. It was nothing in particular that turned me away from Kabir, but I began to feel he was not suave enough. Especially after I saw Yehudi Menuhin play the violin on TV. I did not know who he was or the name of the piece he played, but I was taken by his look, his poise, his importance, and his confidence. Instinctively, I wanted to be someone like that – not necessarily play the violin, although I had nothing against the notion if it made me charming like him. I rummaged through Mother's iron trunk and found a pair of Father's old pants and a faded coat. They were too big and dull but served the purpose. Next, I went to the garage and found myself a square plank of wood that would serve as a violin. I was inventive and resourceful enough to create what I had in mind. I hammered four nails on either ends of the plank and stretched four rubber bands vertically to resemble the strings on the violin. I got a broken piece of fishing rod, discarded by Father, and it served as an appropriate baton with which to play the strings. The hours I spent in musical ecstasy were numerous. I could hear the claps and applause after each recital, and very often, I found it difficult to separate reality from fantasy. I bowed to my left and then to my right and was always gracious when I waved to the cheering crowd. The bouquets were usually dark red roses. I had not heard of yellow roses, orchids, or anthuriums then. Otherwise, I would have fancied myself a mixed bouquet. The limousines were always white, as I associated black with death. Chauffeur-driven, I would travel to my next concert and once again enthral my audiences with my unblemished compositions. Graciously, I would acknowledge their adulations. Once again, I would be enveloped in the clapping and cheering and hear the calls for encores as the curtains slowly lowered. The fad lasted for about a fortnight; then, I moved on to modelling.

I had a tremendous problem with modelling – I was short and shapeless. Of course, I was not to know that my height was very normal for a child of ten. I did my best with the attributes I had, but somehow, the gait was not quite right, and the sultry look just escaped me for some reason. The pout, so essential for the 'come hither' look, was simply not there. I tried and tried. Again, and again. I practiced 'the walk' in front of the long mirror in Mother's room. I swayed from side to side. I sashayed. I pushed out my lower lip, raised my eyebrows, tried a lopsided smile, tilted my head, and looked from under the lashes, but all to no avail.

Something was missing; something got in the way of the total effect. I was too young to make any sort of professional judgement on this. Yet, with my limited knowledge and devoted scrutiny of the modelling programs on TV, I was able to somewhat pinpoint a defect. I was thrilled with the discovery that my slippers were all wrong. I needed high heels. Stilettos like the ones the models gyrated on. However, as quickly as my spirits rocketed, they plummeted to the depths of despair with the realization that Mother was the simplest of women and the owner of the flattest style of slippers. But nothing gets in the way of a determined missy who was in pursuit of her destiny. In a flash, I knew what I would do. With the ingenuity and perseverance of youth, I created my own pair of stilettos. I simply went to Mother's stitching cupboard and got out two spools of thread. I wore my slippers and then placed the spools under my heels. I was astounded at my genius. Instant high heels. But of course, it did not improve my walk as I had to shuffle along, for whenever I lifted my feet, the spools fell off. But I did not care; I just dragged my feet along, satisfied that I had gained a few inches in height and a certain shift in gait.

But to my vexation, it was not long before another fact hit me in the face like a ton of bricks. I was intently watching a model on TV, soaking up her every movement, when suddenly, my jaw dropped. I realized with horror what I really lacked to make the perfect model. I sadly lacked a cleavage, and I just did not know how I was going to fix the problem. I thought about it deep and hard and finally admitted defeat. I stared long hours at my flat, uninspiring chest, willing it to offer some suggestion but realized that I had no help coming from there. Not even the faintest sign of an encouragement. It was once again left to me to come up with a solution, and true to myself, I did. A brilliant idea hit me. I put on Mother's brassiere. It was a size 38B to my ten years. The prospect of filling it was daunting. Finally, I stuffed the cups with a few of Father's socks. It worked somewhat, but the fitting was still an issue, and somehow, the overall presentation was depressing. I made a careful assessment standing in front of the mirror and came to the sad conclusion that the brassiere was out. It made me terribly sad, because in a way, there was something very feminine and intimate about a woman's relationship with a brassiere, however unfit it was, and even at ten, I had realized it. It was slowly dawning on me that I was in no way remotely associated to my feminine side. I decided to try one final attempt to boost my figure. I got into one of my old dresses, one that had become small for me and a bit tight. Then I went and opened the refrigerator to check out the fruits Mother had in there. Sadly, there was only an apple and an orange. Different kinds of fruits and different sizes. Sighing at the futility of it all, I took them both and pushed them into my dress. They felt cold and uncomfortable. I fixed my 'spool-slippers' and studied the effect in the mirror. It was not bad at all, considering the materials I had to work with. The only thing was, I had to strut about if I had to move, in order to keep the spools from shifting, and relocate the fruits whenever they were displaced. Was satisfied I had a victory of sorts in my endeavour. If nothing else, that was consolation enough. I think the modelling stint was the longest of my dreams. I enjoyed each of my modelling sessions tremendously. I modelled on the sands of the Sahara and on a boat along the backwaters in Kerala. I went to Costa Rica and Kingston town, to Jaipur and Thane. I closed my eyes and heard the photographers click as I shuffled along on my wooden spools, draped in Mother's best Kashmir silk sari. But with the problem of the cleavage taking precedence over everything else, the charm of being a model slowly faded off, and I wandered on to newer pastures.

It was in the 4th grade when I turned ten that Miss Penny Tang entered my hitherto monotonous life. She was my class teacher, and after one look at her, I decided to put an end to any vagrancy concerning my profession once and for all. I was going to be a teacher. She was electric. Even Father became interested in the PTA (Parent Teacher's Association) meetings and regularly enquired if my lessons at school were going well. He kept asking if he was needed to discuss any issue with my teacher. I was confused when he seemed a little disappointed when I told him that I was doing very well at school, particularly since Miss Penny took special care of me. I think Miss Penny had the same effect on most fathers. Our class had the highest turnout for the PTA meetings. Suddenly, fathers were over-enthusiastic in their concerns about their children's education, much to the amusement of the mothers.

Miss Penny's effect on the fathers was understandable. She wore a 'cheongsam,' the traditional tight-fitting, high-necked Chinese dress, mostly in red or other vibrant colours. It was not just with the dress that Miss Penny made a style statement. It was with the length of the slits of her dress on both sides and her 4-inch-high red stilettos. Not to mention her moves and demeanour. She wore red lipstick, which contrasted drastically with her pale complexion and her jet-black page-boy haircut. In all, she was a dynamic package. I saw nothing of all this. I just loved the way she spoke to us – softly and lovingly. She made everything so easy. I wanted to be just like her – dress like her, move like her, and teach like her.

At home, I tried desperately to organize a cheongsam to no avail. No matter how hard I tried, Mother's saris could not take the size and shape of the Chinese garment. I raked my brain until it melted, but I found no solution. The sad thing was that I had collected all the paraphernalia required for teaching; Mother's old handbag to carry as Miss Penny did, an old, used logbook from Father's cupboard to use as an attendance register, pieces of chalk smuggled from school, and a small piece of rattan to use as a pointer. All I needed was the oh-so-important red cheongsam, which was the very essence of Miss Penny. Fleetingly, I would allow myself to think of the things I had, as opposed to those that were totally out of my reach, such as the perfume, red lipstick, nail polish, and red high heels – all very enticing but so totally unattainable. Yet, I believed that if you wished for something real hard, the Gods would relent and grant you your wish. I don't know if that is true, but how could I believe otherwise? The events that followed were testimony to this observation.

Soon, it was Christmas. Mother was busy with sending out Christmas cards, baking the Christmas cake, and doing all the other preparations required for the event. That year, we were having a huge party, as two of my favourite uncles, Koshy and Nair, were coming to spend Christmas with us. They were both young bachelors, full of fun and ready for any game. Since they were unmarried and had no children of their own, they showered me with unconditional love and were always ready to please me. I even had a plan to get Uncle Koshy to marry Miss Penny so she could become a part of the family. *Then, maybe, I can borrow the cheongsam from her*, I thought. Anyway, one day, the uncles took me out to have an ice cream, and during the course of the outing, they asked me what was new in my life. I was already dying to tell them about Miss Penny, so when they asked, I went into an elaborate description of my teacher. I ended by telling them that I had decided to become a school teacher. I told them that I had already started practicing and hesitantly added that some perfume and lipstick would help me in my endeavour. They were delighted by my choice of profession and promised all assistance. As Christmas approached, I made my wish list, as I always did, and placed it under my pillow. I did not look at the list again, as Mother said that brought bad luck. I think this was her cunning way of stopping me from adding onto the already long list. Sure enough, Christmas morning did not disappoint. There was a huge plastic bag filled with all sorts of things by my bedside. I tore it open and emptied the contents onto the floor, impatience getting the better of me. As the contents spilled out, I gasped in sheer delight. My eyes caught sight of a lovely pair of red-heeled slippers and a handbag to match. There were books to read, pens, and pencils. Some drawing books and colour pencils, a stitch kit, and a packet of toffees. There were plastic bangles in four colours, and two beaded chains.

A little apart lay two boxes covered in brown paper. I picked up the smaller box, tore open the brown cover, and lifted the lid. It contained a lipstick, a red nail polish, and a bottle of perfume. I could feel my body heating up, and I could not breathe. The emotions that raced through my being were alien to me. I looked at the larger box and dared to hope of what it would contain. Carefully, I placed the opened smaller box on my bed and reached for the larger box. My fingers trembled as I tore it open. Nestled in the soft tissue papers was a cheongsam in red silk. I stared at it in stupefied wonder. Then, reverently, I removed it from the box and lay it on the bed. It had everything – the high collar, the side slits, and something more. In addition, embroidered across the front was a lovely golden dragon.

It is of little consequence that I did not become a teacher in the end. I went through a lot of phases until I finally reached my destination. But, in all honesty, the journey was an exceptional experience and a means to gather delightful data for the archives of my mind.

Plus One

The year was 1957. I like to think it was September or October when Mother gave me the shocker. I was in grade two. She told me I would soon have a brother or sister. *The heck,* I thought, *how's she going to manage that? If she was going to buy one, from where exactly would she? For that matter, how in the world did she get me to begin with?* Up until then, I had been an only child, and so, I remember a sheltered, lonely childhood. As a result, I played with a lot of make-believe friends; I loved to talk to myself and engaged in monologues. I also enjoyed teaching and talking to the two dolls I had and, more than anything, scolding them as Mother would scold me. I enjoyed school very much and often remembered my friend Norma. She was fair and pretty, which could be one reason I liked her. Who knew? Today, you would call it unconscious bias or some such. But more than that, I loved her side-parted hairstyle. I envied her that. I don't know why, so don't ask me. Perhaps it was because I was denied a side parting. Mother was a middle-parting person and very rigid about her ideas. At every opportunity, I would plot to make a side parting, but I could never get past Mother's eagle eye.

So, it felt really good when she was rushed to hospital one day, say mid-November. My first thought was that she was out of the way, and I could go to school with a side parting the next day. How frivolous it seems today. But that day, there was no masking my joy. With Mother and Father gone and an old Tamil woman in charge, I rushed to the mirror and tried out all the styles. Side parting to the left, side parting to the right. With ribbon, without ribbon. With a slide, with a bow. Suffice to say, I was beside myself with excitement. Finally, I chose a side parting to the left and a blue slide. I found out I could not tie a ribbon, and so the choice was actually made for me by circumstances.

I went to school the next day with my new hairstyle and covertly watched Norma to see if she felt envious. She hardly noticed. By evening, I was disappointed with the side parting. It was a washout and did nothing for Moi. After school, I went home dejected. I felt I had willed Mother to go away so I could indulge myself, and what good had it been? As I dragged myself up the path towards the front door, I'd have given the world for Mother to open it and bend down to hug me. Instead, Father opened the door. He looked tired and sad. There was a sense of hopelessness about him – a distraction. He ushered me into the house, and asked me to have my Milo and biscuits and get ready to go to the hospital. I did not have a clue what was happening. Then he told me Mother was having a baby and I was going to be a big sister. I liked the sound of that. I guess in the midst of all the hullabaloo around settling down in the New World and whatnots, Father must have realised he had not done his due diligence and so had finally worked at producing an heir. I don't know how else I can explain the arrival of a sibling eight years after I had their undivided adoration.

As I mentioned before, we lived in the back of beyond, in Perlis, the smallest state in Malaya. There was just a basic hospital with a senior orderly in charge. He did regular, routine things like tend to cuts and burns, and of course, normal deliveries. A trained senior doctor would come only if there was a dire need, and I'm thinking he would not be a gynaecologist per se, but a general physician. And telephones were rare instruments. The orderly was a Malayalee and a family friend, so he was deeply involved in the whole proceedings. Mother, it seemed, was critical. She had eclampsia. This was a very dangerous situation for both mother and baby. It was hard to get hold of the doctor, though they kept trying. I knew nothing of all this but sensed that everything was not right. Father and I sat on a bench outside the emergency labour room. I did not know what to do or say. I wondered if all this had anything to do with my side parting. How simple is a child's thought process! After what seemed like a million years, the orderly came out to tell Father that they had contacted the doctor, and he would arrive in about two or three hours. As an act of compassion, I think, he left the second part out – that a lot could happen in the meantime. He then sat down beside Father and said with a sigh, 'George, pray with all your heart.'

Father took me by the hand, and we went down the corridor and were soon outside. It was already dark, and we walked about aimlessly for a while. The nearest church was 40 miles away in Kedah, and I guessed Father's need to talk to God. Getting some solace was urgent. The evening call to prayer, Isha'a, at a small mosque outside the hospital gate, broke into Father's melancholic mood. We walked up the steps of the mosque, and in the dark, Father knelt down and cried. I did not know what else to do, so I cried with him. *So much pain for my sin*, I thought. *Never again,* I swore to myself, *will I have a side parting.*

The doctor managed to arrive before it was too late. The baby was removed by caesarean section, but Mother remained critical. We were told 48 hours had to pass before it could be decided one way or the other. I guess the Gods were kind and realised a young girl needed her mother, so they forgave my sin and spared Mother from a dire end. Slowly, Mother revived, and before long, she was home and back to tending my tresses with a middle parting. This time, I was grateful.

Sibling took up all our time. The only thing that bothered me was that she was a bald baby, and I worried if she would ever grow hair. I had actually prayed for a blonde-haired sister with blue eyes, so I considered this indifference to my requirements as gross negligence on the part of God. I had even secretly hoped that if Sibling had a full head of hair, Mother might get diverted and start dressing the baby's hair and leave me in peace to pursue my own style. But the way things had taken such a dramatic turn following my attempts at a new hairstyle left me feeling guilty and afraid. I have never dared to do a side-parting style ever since. *Why test fate?* That was my thought. In my juvenile mind, I did not want to upset a God who seemed severe and unbending in his punishment of those who did not live by His rules.

And, as if to add insult to injury, the new arrival was bonny and fair, and here was me, dark and pudgy. As much as I adored Sibling, I was not blind to the comparisons made by the dogmatic herd of Malayalee women who gathered at church. They were notorious for rating others on the basis of colour. As both my parents were fair, and now Sibling too, well, how do you win this war? The saving grace was that I was too young to care and adored the new arrival.

Sibling and moi

Would You Shave Down There?

The fifties and sixties were austere times for children. It was a time when everything had a rigidly puritanical outlook. Children were not entertained very much. They were seen but never to be heard. Tolerated, mostly. We just flitted from day to day like innocuous, drably coloured moths. No one gave us the time of day or night, to be sure, and no one considered our likes or dislikes. And heaven help us if we had an opinion. It did not matter that a child's sentiment could be hurt by cruel remarks or rebukes. Growing up in those days, especially if you were blessed – or cursed – whichever way you cared to look at it, with a brain that goads you to do the exact opposite of what was the norm, could be very taxing. Especially if your mother, who believed in blending in with the crowd, had a child who would not. And woe betide those little rascals who had a mischievous streak. I thought I was good; though I never knew why, whenever we visited the family in India, my aunts kept their daughters out of my radius, and I was reprimanded a lot by the very same sanctimonious group. Only Grandmother was kind. She understood my need to laugh and talk and have fun. Off and on, I would notice that sometimes, one of the cousins, girls mostly, would stop playing with us and act grown up and coy and whatnot. I never understood the implications of these rigid rules that my older cousins were expected to follow until I began to menstruate much later and also grew a fuzz in the armpits. Then, I realized that I too was becoming an object of interest to the older women of our community and particularly to Mother. I too was asked to stop playing frivolous games, act grown up and behave with discretion. But no one thought to tell me what was happening or why I had to change.

We were in Malaya when I first noticed the subtle changes in Moi, but I did not pay much attention to the details until later. I noticed that whenever I raised my hands for something or the other, Mother would shriek at me to keep my hands down. She stopped me from wearing petticoats when playing outside and insisted that I don't run about and shout. She also stopped making sleeveless dresses for me. This sudden change in her behaviour was a mystery to me. But all was explained when I noticed a sudden hair growth in my armpits, and I was beyond stumped by the appearance of unwanted hair in other unmentionable places too. So, when the fuzz started appearing all over my body, I wondered if I was slowly turning into an animal. It was no fun during school PT classes in the hot, humid climate. Mother was perplexed when I told her about my discomfort and hardly knew how to pacify me. Of course, I never dreamt she could be in the same predicament, simply because I thought mothers were above these sorts of problems. I can't vouch for her dissuasive behaviour, but she seemed uneasy and gave me no solutions. So, I was left to figure out for myself how best to cope.

Having a very fertile imagination can be a bane and a boon, I was to find out. I began to watch Father diligently. He shaved off unwanted hair from his face. First, he would lather the area, then apply the razor slowly, carefully, and smoothly all over the lathered surface, and the result was a hairless, clean, bright face. There it was – the answer. One afternoon, when the parents were having their siesta, I crept into the bathroom and studied the razor. It was no modern-day Gillette Fusion Proglide or a Pearl Shaving Double Edge Safety Razor or a 5-blade Gillette or anything half as fanciful. Father's razor was a real man's razor. He'd turn the screw at the bottom of the handle, and the top head, which held a sharp blade, would open up. He bought the blades in packets, each containing 5 blades. Nacet was his brand. He'd screw in a nice new blade on to the razor and take his chances with the cuts and nicks he made while shaving. Bravery was the key word. And guess who was brave? After making a thorough study of the contraption, I placed it back as I had found it and skulked away. And bid my time.

I knew Father and Mother played a game of cards during the weekend with their friends, the Koshys. They were usually out for about two or three hours. They had an annoying habit of dragging me along, but this time, I stayed put. I had other things on my mind. As soon as they left, after the mandatory orders of 'Don't open the door to anyone' and 'Don't look out of the window,' I sat down to think. Now that the hour was upon me, I was nervous and frightened. The armpits would be easy, but how would one manoeuvre down there? "The Downs" as I decided to call it. I had no one to ask. The only way to find out was to execute the assignment. *No matter how much of theory you know, it is in the practical application that you really find out the truth*, I thought, *and naturally, you need to improvise as you go along.* Having geared up mentally, I made the move before I chickened out and changed my mind. So, I lathered the left underarm and slowly ran the razor. Sacrè bleu! The armpit was as clean as a baby's bottom, and the obnoxious tuft was on the razor. As I had seen Father do, I washed the razor and repeated the procedure in the other armpit. The results were unbelievable, and I was as happy as a monkey with a banana. And confident now. And believe me, confidence in a novice is like dynamite in the hands of a fool.

But of course, there was no time to dilly-dally and gloat over the success of part one of the undertaking. I had to clean up the act before the parents returned. So, I perked up my courage to the maximum and lathered "the Downs" in preparation for part two. The terrain was mighty uneven and tricky, but it was a now or never situation. I guess the soaps those days were not as mild as they are today. They were more caustic and pungent – nothing gentle about them at all. Anyway, I used our bath soap – Lux or Lifebuoy or some such. I'll tell you this, and believe you me, it stung like the dickens. Soap in the intimate crevices can make a lesser person cry. It was a great mode of torture if you really wanted to hurt someone. I thought I'd use the razor quickly, then wash it off, and all would be fine. But how stupid can you be at ten or twelve? As stupid as the stupidest idiot in the world who had a stupid dumbass idea in the first place. *But all is not lost*, I consoled myself. *Only the brave dare, Lennie, so hang in there*, I told myself. That was also when I learnt that the feminine triangular zonal region was one of the most hazardous, perilous, and vulnerable places to tackle. All valleys and curves. I razored, but at what cost? The agony stays with me even today.

When the deed was done, "the Downs" were smarting like hell and bleeding. I could not hold back my tears, and I reproached my weak self. *Even in pain, the brave does not cry*, I told myself. The Brave stood their ground to achieve a mission. Already, my Machiavellian mind was at work to find a solution to my agony. I knew Mother treasured a bottle of Eau de Cologne 4711 somewhere between her saris. She did this to hide it from Father, as he was fond of using it liberally as and when he pleased. So, such exquisite items were always hidden among her saris. I hobbled over to her room and opened the cupboard. I held my knickers in place to stop the blood from the cuts dripping down onto the floor. Then I splashed a liberal amount of the cologne onto my knickers and placed it on "the Downs." The sting was unbearable, and I felt my ears burn. There was an explosion in my head, and I saw a thousand stars. I hopped around and yelped like a whipped dog. I tried not to cry, but the tears came anyway. I was transported to the nether regions, and it took me days to recover. I think I went into an unconscious stupor, and for the next few days, I was a dead girl walking. I was at my wits end, and sadly, there were no more tricks in my bag. It was to my credit that I kept Mother oblivious to my shenanigans. It's not that Mother was stupid. She was very astute and as sharp as a tack. It's just that nobody would think anybody would dare such a hazardous move. That's a time when I really got my knickers in a twist!

These days, I read at the toiletries section of the supermarket about Dove or Oatmeal and Almond. Imagine a whole section devoted to pampering your intimate parts. Why, now the daughters educate Moi and tell me they use a brand called 'Intimate Wash' for "the Downs"!! How intimate is that? Whoever knew!! Not Moi – not even now, I'm afraid. But again, here I am, having survived one of the most catastrophic calamities of my life and the follies of youth, and guess what? The exercise is in fashion today. Now, we have razors with that specific, special need in mind. In pink if you please. With flexible heads.

So, who was a pioneer? See who took the road not less travelled, but never travelled.

DÉJÀ VU

Changing Schools, Breaking Rules

Malaya was under the British rule during those first few years of my life, and so the school followed the Cambridge curriculum. Most of the teachers were British or locals who had done their college education in England. So, a lot of 'Englishness' rubbed onto us too. The lady teachers were all so fashionable and accomplished, and I loved going to school, if for nothing else than at least to watch them and imbibe their manners and social graces. The vibrancy and the diverse cultures brought together by the Malays, Chinese, and Indians to melt in the cauldron that was school created a unique ploy at education. And to be able to live and grow in that petri dish was an exhilarating experience. But soon, Independence, or 'Merdeka,' was declared, and there was talk of changing the education system to the Malay medium. Father was not happy with the idea and so took the decision to pack me off to an English Boarding School in India. I was all of twelve years or less.

Let the heartache begin, I thought!

Needless to say, there was a lot of discussion concerning my move to India. Schools were looked at, boardings were scrutinized, and locations where I would spend short holidays were discussed, among a myriad of other things. It was a Google-less world then. Unmindful of all these goings-on, life was opening up for me and getting intriguing. There was this Malay boy in my class, Shoukat Ali. Seventy-odd years later, and I still remember the name. Whenever he came to class or answered a question or whatever, I felt a zing. No, I hadn't the faintest idea what it was. So, this strange, unnatural urge that I felt – this happiness and breathlessness – I decided to call 'zing.' Perhaps that explained why I was always on the lookout for this boy who hardly knew of my existence. I was even willing to share my sardine and cheese sandwich with him, and I had never had the desire to share it with anyone else before then. It was a revelation to Moi that I was somehow changing.

So, it was with a heavy heart and great sadness that I watched the preparations for the new phase in my life. I was infinitely miserable when I had to bid farewell to my friends at school, but I think zing was the main reason for it. Norma and Aziza were good friends; in fact, we were thick as thieves, and Aziza had given me my first insight into the world of the adults. She had an older sister and so was privy to a lot of things concerning everything. She warned me about kissing a fellow and added ominously that that was how babies were made. Armed with this knowledge and desperate at the loss of zing, I left with Mother for the shores of India and an unknown future for the second time in my short life.

Imagine then, my horror when we were met at the Madras Harbor by Father's younger brother, my Uncle Thomas, who, in his excitement at seeing us after such a long break, scooped me up in his arms and resoundingly kissed me on both cheeks! Holy Maloney, I was petrified. Utterly, thoroughly scared out of my bloomers! I watched myself for a week – time enough for a baby to be made and birthed, I thought, though I hadn't the slightest idea how this would come about or how the baby would get out of my tummy. *From the mouth, probably,* I thought. Because that was the only orifice I could account for. The lower orifices of which I had no great understanding, I did not take into account. Of course, discussing all this with Mother never entered my heard. Such topics were never encouraged. There was an unspoken taboo about all things concerning the private parts of the body. When nothing untoward happened for about a week, I gradually forgot about it.

The school the parents had chosen for me was *The Baldwin Girls High School* in Richmond Town, Bangalore. Built in 1880 with Loyalty and Service as its motto, it was the epitome of all things principled. When Mother left me at the place that was to become my home in the coming years, I felt small and helpless. I can still see in my mind's eye, a little girl so forlorn and feel the numbness of abandonment as Mother made to leave the school after settling Moi. I stood helplessly, holding back my tears until I could no longer, and finally, they spilled over. But as I made to run after the moving car, Matron put her hand on my shoulder and restrained me. This, then, was the place that was to play a big part in the making and moulding of Moi.

As a result of having been in Malaya up until then, my Malayalam was weak, and I had never learnt to read or write the language. I'm not being proud about it; it just did not pan out. In hindsight, I think Father had an ulterior motive when he sent me to India to pursue my education. He had two intentions – one was of education and the other of 'Indianizing' me, more specifically, the 'Malayaleefication' of Moi. It was a 'two birds with one stone' kind of thing – or was that three birds?

School was fantastic, and the boarding gave me friends for life. We laughed, played, cried, studied, and fooled around together. We smuggled food into the dorm, and threw away Matron's slippers, and goofed after lights out. We hung around the back gates of the school, the perfect rendezvous to see the boys pass by and whistled and called for their attention. You'll notice that Shoukat Ali had become a distant memory. We sneaked out of the gates during lunch breaks to buy raw mangoes sprinkled with chilli and salt. If caught in this ultimate act of crimes, it was death by firing squad, for it was a cardinal rule that a boarder was never to leave campus at any time without permission. Why, we had to maintain a distance of a good six feet from the gates. In retrospect, I would not want my kids doing it. But there it was!

Halloween was a big deal. It was always celebrated with gusto. We were allowed to dress up in our garish and grotesque get-ups and frighten the daylights out of each other as well as the juniors that whole evening, while the seniors ripped us apart for supper. It was exhilarating in its grotesquerie.

One Halloween stands out more than the others. Since we had set our hearts on getting back at Matron for all the perceived wrongs that she had done to us, we made a plan. We were particularly buggered with her that week for punishing us for sleeping during study hour. In any case, she regularly punished us for the slightest thing, and we really wanted to annoy her in some way. The regular lights off for bedtime was 8.30 pm, but being Halloween, it was stretched to 9.30 pm. As Matron came in to switch off the lights at 9.30 pm, one of the girls switched it off before she could, and the rest of us pounced on her. It was pandemonium. We pulled at her hands and pushed her backside, and someone gave it a resounding smack, I believe. My personal contribution was a kick in her shin. But it was Sue, who gave her a proper pinch on her arm, who had to pay the price. Being a smart lady, Matron caught hold of Sue's hand, but in the dark, she could not tell who it was. So, she held on tight and would not let go, and Sue, of course, could not call out, as Matron would recognise her voice. When the lights came on, we all stood around sheepishly while she skinned Sue to the bone. Matron complained to the principal, Miss Johnson, explaining how she was pinched and bitten during the scuffle. I seriously wondered who had bitten her, or if Matron had added that little morsel for effect. I would not put it past both parties, the girls or Matron, to have indulged. However, I doubted the bite angle, for in my books, whoever bit Matron would have died of poisoning. Anyway, suffice to say, we have all lived to tell the tale.

Food was never allowed into the dormitory, but this rule did not stop me or my friends, Rachel and Mary. We pooled in some money, bought a condensed milk tin, and smuggled it into the dom. Using the dividers from our geometry sets, we made holes in the tin, then joined the holes to make an opening and sucked out the thick syrup. Once we were sated, we hid the tin in our cupboard for the next night. The next day, after everyone was safely tucked in bed, my friends and I grouped once again in the bathroom. They had their share first, and I was left to finish it off. As I sucked, I felt a small twig in my mouth. I licked on it in order not to waste even a bit. Rachel produced a small penknife that I used to prise open the small hole even further, and as the contents were almost over, I sucked deeply to get it all into my mouth at one go. Suddenly, I felt three or more twigs in my mouth. To get to the bottom of this mystery, we made a few more holes with the dividers. Then, with a pair of scissors and with great difficulty, we joined the holes and forced the lid open to about an inch. We then kept it upside down to drain it. We watched in horror as a pair of whiskers seeped out with the thick creamy milk and then the big, black, winged body of a huge cockroach. None of us reacted, as I think we were already dead on the floor.

Another worthy mischief occurred during the blackouts of ca. 1962, at the time of the Indo-Chinese conundrum. We were all at dinner saying our 'yes pleases' and 'no thank yous,' eating with our forks and spoons and knives and busy being proper, when suddenly, the siren blared and the lights went out. We were plunged into total darkness. For a split second, all was quiet and then, BAM!! All hell broke loose. The beasts that lurked just beneath our veneer of polish surged to the fore, unbridled. I remember the head bearer, Arakaswamy, pleading desperately with the girls to stop pushing him. Then, he was calling out to Matron, while Matron was calling out to the girls. We ran amok all over the dining room, grabbing extra bread and loading up our plates with the meat dish. Some went straight for the pudding. The ruckus we made was so great I'm sure the Chinese would have heard us and ran from our borders. I'll leave it to you to imagine what happened when the lights came on. Matron lectured us for days to come, but none of us cared a damn and hoped for another blackout in the near future.

The girls divided themselves mainly into two groups – those who loved Elvis Presley and those who loved Cliff Richard. It was blasphemous not to belong. I was totally mesmerized by Elvis and his lopsided grin. We had an old beat-up radio on the landing. Whenever one of the favourites came on, someone would yell 'Elvis!' or 'Cliff!' and the girls would scramble in and start clapping, while the nimble-footed ones did the jive or rock n' roll. It was so much fun to move and groove with such gay abandon, not caring if we got the steps right or wrong.

Another incident that makes me laugh out loud even to this day is the case of the hypnotic act. It was beyond hilarious. Mary, my bedside mate, was the perpetrator who thought up the plot and roped me in as her accomplice. I, of course, was game for anything. She told me that she would spread the word that since I came from a foreign land, Malaysia, I knew a bit of magic and mesmerism. I played along. All the girls in the junior dorm were agog with curiosity, and I did my best to conjure up a mystic aura. So, it was decided that on one particular night, I would hypnotise Mary while the others watched. This had to be done under cover of darkness after lights out and after Matron had retired to her quarters. We all lay in bed, alert and eagerly waiting for Matron to switch off her lights. Finally, the hour was at hand. About eight or nine girls tiptoed and grouped around Mary's bed. I stood up and put on my act. Much as I was dying to laugh, I daresay I played my part brilliantly. And Mary was stupendous. While in school in Malaysia, I had memorized some poems and popular folk songs in the Malay classes. I never ever thought they would come in so handy as they did that night. I started the shenanigans in a soft moaning voice, waving my hands over Mary as she lay on her bed, then chanted a popular Malay folk song:

'Burong kakak tua, hinggap dijendela, nenek sudah tua, Gigi nya thinggal dua'.

It was just a silly song and had nothing to do with the occult. Loosely translated, it means:

The old Parakeet bird has landed on the window.

Grandmother is also old and has two teeth left.

Mary and I had an understanding that with this, she would go into a hypnotic state. I then said, 'Mary, lift your right hand.' Hesitantly, she did. The girls gasped. 'Now Mary,' I went on, 'lift your right leg. And she did. I looked around, trying not to laugh. The girls looked petrified. Then I said with a shiver in my voice, 'Now Mary, slowly get up from your bed and stand on one leg and raise both your hands. Then, with one hand, touch your nose, and with the other, touch your head.' That was Mary's stance when Matron switched on the lights and caught us all, mouths agape and out of our beds, breaking one of Matron's uncompromising laws. Matron would have used the guillotine if one was handy.

Every evening after dinner, there was a gathering in Miss Johnson's private room, or boudoir, as she liked to call it. It was not mandatory, but I went anyway on account of the glass of hot chocolate and cookies she served. As restitution, we had to listen to her read verses from the bible and listen to a short sermon. Any one of us could be asked to pray. One day, Matron said we had to pray for Miss Johnson's hearing, and she called for Gillian to lead the prayer. As Gillian sat a little away from Matron, she did not quite hear the topic on which she was asked to pray. 'What was that, Lennie?' she asked me. I replied clearly, 'Miss Johnson has lost her earring.' Gillian then began an ardent prayer that Miss Johnson be able to find her earring at the earliest. She went on to describe the beauty and worth of the ornament and how important it was that whoever found it should return it to its rightful owner. All the girls were stifling with suppressed laughter, and Matron was ready to blow a gasket. Miss Johnson, already partially deaf, was oblivious to the mischief, and with bowed head and closed eyes, remained piously in worship. The only thing I could deduct from the incident was that Gillian too, was losing her hearing – or was it her earring?

Sunday evening service at the Methodist Church was awaited with the greatest anticipation. We would be seated first in the pews, and then, the Baldwin boys trooped in. Theophilus, Alameda, Mafatlal, Francis,

Matthew, Khalil, Paul, Mohandas – were just a few. I had a crush on the whole lot of them. I didn't care if no one reciprocated. My heart would just flip and go Zing! Zing! Zing! During that interim, all was well again. Every evening, after services, there would be a big hubbub over who sent their love to whom, which boy was interested in which girl, who broke up with whom, and all the romantic gossip there was to know. I was just a listener to all the love talk, as I, for one, never received a love letter. Perhaps it was a good thing too, as I was free to love whomever I chose and discard them whenever I felt like it and go after another if it fancied me. You'd not be wrong in thinking I was promiscuous, but who the hell cared? I hadn't even heard of the word. After being a lonely child for so long, and though I had felt abandoned at the beginning, I was now so happy with the friends I had made and totally enjoyed the camaraderie and fellowship of girls my age.

Even then, late into the nights, when sleep evaded, I would cry silently into my pillow. I missed my family and the whiff of the Yardley Rose that lingered whenever Mother kissed me. I wondered if she had forgotten me. It tore me up, and I would settle down only when I heard similar sobs coming from under Mary's blanket. I would reach out for her hand, and she would clasp mine, and we would find some peace and solace in our shared grief.

Baldwin Girls High School

THE OLD WORLD AGAIN

A Strange Kind of Love

It was nearing Christmas, and the boarding school had closed for Yuletide. I was spending the holidays with my grandparents on their farm in the back of beyond. Although I had left this place long ago to join Father in Malaya, I had never forgotten the good times I had enjoyed here. Whenever I spent a quiet moment alone, I would bring them out from the inner recesses of my mind and once again walk in the fields alongside aunt Suzy. So now I was excited to be back to spend the school holidays in my ancestral home, so dear to Moi. The small village had remained stuck in time. Nothing had changed, and the world seemed to have forgotten it and passed on by. I loved and cherished these visits, as they brought back memories of old times and strange tales. During these holidays, I was usually joined by my cousin Rej. He was Tanzanian born and bred, to my Malaysian. At that time, he was boarding at Bishop Cotton's as I was boarding at Baldwin's. True, we were from rival schools, but something about being brought up abroad and being in boarding brought us together in a truce of sorts. And there was no denying the fact that we shared a certain gung-ho attitude in our approach to the events in the village, which caused us to call a ceasefire over school fighting.

We would wake up at the crack of dawn in order not to miss a thing. Our very own personal favourite was Pappan's visit. He was a brash fellow a little over fifty. He always had a smile and a whistle on his lip and was an established chatterbox and charmingly rakish. 'His visit will set the tone for the day,' Grandmother was fond of saying. Now, everyone knew that Pappan was smitten with Pennamma and blindly in love with her. He was like butter with her. She knew how to play him – looking at him covertly, batting her eyelashes, and then widening those huge, hazel eyes. It was a trick with her, to shift from one leg to the other and twirl and twist as if to show off her best side. She was a mistress in the art of bewitching and would flirt like no one ever could. There was an arrogant air about her and there was no denying she was a true beauty. And Pappan was no less brazen. He would twirl his whiskers, swagger up to her, and smack her on her rump all the while cooing out her name a dozen times. In addition, they would end this ritual by snuggling up to each other and rubbing their foreheads.

What made this show of undying affection so unique was that Pennamma was a big reddish-brown Sindhi cow, weighing about 450kg. Or was she Vechur? Or maybe a mix of the two or some other. Whatever her Pedigree or lack thereof, she was unique. She was tethered in Grandmother's huge barn, enjoying all the creature comforts it offered. Pappan came each morning to milk her. After their customary greeting and show of mutual adoration, Pennamma would stand as docile as can be and allow Pappan to squat beside her with his pail. Humming in a low baritone, he would start a tune I recognized as popular in the old days. He would sing….. 'Manasamaine varruuuuuu,' while attending to his chore with religious reverence. Pennamma let the milk flow freely as if she was rewarding a devotee. In about twenty minutes, the job was done, and once again, Pappan would thump Pennamma's rump and call out a few endearments. She would reply to this with a low, gratifying 'mooooo,' and the ritual for the day would be over.

Rej and I were totally fascinated by this bond between them and were always there, watching this strange interaction and wanting so much to be a part of it. But there was no denying the fact that we would be *de trop*. In fact, we felt like dirty voyeuristic outcasts peeping into what was pure, undulating love. There was no place for a third wheel, or a fourth as in our case. This was strictly between Pennamma and Pappan. In fact, Rej lamented over these facts and said with a lot of disappointment how he despaired that Pennamma hardly glanced his way at any time. I guess it hurt his man ego more than it did mine. *In any case, why would she?* I thought silently. Rej was just an ungainly youth of fifteen, whereas Pappan was a well-toned, muscular rascal with a divine, symmetrical body that he flaunted without shame. And he was careful never to cover it with a shirt whenever he was at his job.

But as they say, every dog has its day. Cousin Rej had his before any of us were prepared for it. Pappan's wife came one day to say that he was down with a fever and could not come to milk the cow on that fateful morning. As if Pennamma understood the significance of Pappan's wife's visit, she let out a long moo of anger and frustration from the barn. In any case, the heifer never tolerated Pappan's wife because of the rivalry between them for Pappan's affection.

Rej seized his chance. He persuaded Grandmother that he knew enough about the business of milking a cow, as he had watched Pappan every day. 'Just a matter of pulling at the udders,' he told her. After much cajoling, Grandmother agreed and gave him the pail. We approached the barn gingerly. In a bid to reassure himself rather than to explain it to me, Rej kept repeating the technicalities of the process. Personally, I felt my hands shake a little and my palms get wet. But Rej kept insisting that there was nothing much to the art of milking, and as he said this, he practiced moving his hands up and down. To me, it did not look anything like milking but rather like waving away a horde of crows. But what did I know? As we approached the barn, somehow, it looked forbidding. I'm not superstitions or anything like that, but I felt a premonition. Like someone had touched my shoulder, trying to stop me. I told Rej about my unease and thought that we should abort the project, but he was too committed, too far gone. Like in a trance.

Pennamma stood to our left. She watched us approach with no signs of recognition. There was no batting of the eyelashes or coy looks. Suddenly, Rej tried to whistle. The air just rushed past his lips without any sound. My throat felt dry. Bravely, he kept on. He hit her on the rump, but she rejected the familiarity. He called out her name 'Pennamma,' trying to make it sound friendly. It came out funny – definitely not a low baritone. It was more of a small, tight squeak that emitted from his mouth. The cow shot out her left hind leg in answer, and it caught the pail. In his thick British accent, acquired from the schools of Tanzania and not yet softened by Bishop Cotton, Rej tried to sing. Manasamaine varruuuuuu… the Malayalam song sounded like an eerie, ship-wrecked rendition. It did nothing to soothe or serenade Pennamma as it was meant to do. I noticed a dent in the pail where she had shot out her leg and knew with horrified certainty that if it had been Rej's leg, he would have had a fracture. Cautiously, Rej tightened the rope round her neck while she mooed loudly and shook her head and all of her 450 kilos of muscles, all around and about. Undaunted, he got a stool and sat by her side as he tried to grab at her udders. She waved her tail in his face, and he gasped as the sting was sharp and severe. As she stomped and moved, the udders slipped out of his hand. He tried once more, but she swished her tail a second time, hitting his eye. He was blinded momentarily, and she seized that opportunity to kick out the stool from under him with her left hoof. He toppled and fell. She strained as she turned her head and that brought him right under her. Rej opened his eyes and the udders hung right above him, smothering him. But Rej had no pail and no nerve to proceed. He just managed to crawl out from under her and unsteadily staggered to his feet.

He looked at me and hoarsely whispered, 'My eyes are smarting, and my head is on the verge of exploding.'

I did not answer but looked at him stupidly, my own heart racing. 'And you know what?' he asked me pathetically, 'I can taste blood on my lips and my throat is dry. I feel breathless, and I think I can hear my heart hammering against my ribs'.

He leaned against the barn, aware that every bone ached but relieved and thankful that it proved he was alive. He looked over at Pennamma and she looked right back at him. We read the message in her eyes loud and clear.

'Don't mess with me. I am a one-man cow,' it said. Defeated, Rej turned and left the barn. I followed in silence.

The next day, Pappan came bright and early. The swagger and the whistle seemed so easy. The playful hit on the rump, cooing, and cajoling. The coy looks and the cuddles.

Then the song in low baritone……. manasamaine varruuuuuu………..

Prayer Time at the Big House

Dinner was never served at the Big House without everyone gathering in the main room and offering prayers. It had been ingrained into us that each day was God-given and we had to be thankful for it and had a moral duty to make the most of it in the best way possible. Whoever did not carry out this commandment, which was one of Grandfather's many, had to atone for the heinous crime. In any case, Grandfather argued that during the course of the day, we would have done something or other, knowingly or unknowingly, that was unacceptable in the eyes of God, and it was only natural to ask forgiveness. He stated this point so vehemently, and him being someone we could not trifle with, it was much easier for us to accept, obey, and follow his rules rather than object. Moreover, he would glower down at us from his great height and exclaim that even he would have done something that needed atonement! Grandfather was so upstanding and correct that to think he could have some secret weakness that we did not know about was alarming to Moi. The thought was preposterous, but who knew? Who dared ask? Who could bell the cat? Perhaps everyone had some thing or other that they did in secret and had to account for. That could be the reason why the entire family reluctantly came to the main room at 8 pm, in spite of the thought that it was good time put to waste.

Grandfather demanded a full attendance. No one was exempted, unless of course, they were dead, in which case, the absence was unavoidable. Never mind if there were guests in the house. By 8 pm, they were considered to have overstayed their welcome. Or else, they could join in the congregation. This thought made most of the guests who knew the house rules beat a hasty retreat before the clock chimed eight. If, for whatever reason, any of the inhabitants of the household were out, it was imperative that they meet the deadline of 7.30 pm to return home and prepare for prayers at the set time. In order to maintain the tranquillity of the Big House, everyone kept to the rules. Grandfather saw to it that the rules were followed without fail, every evening of every day of every month of every year.

Prayer time was therefore, an Institute in Perpetuity, when all was said and done. The session lasted for about an hour, during which time there would be an opening hymn at the beginning, and a closing hymn at the end, both with doubtful tunes. In between the hymns, there was bible reading by a family member and a sermon by Grandfather, which went on forever. The closing hymn was followed by a prayer and the benediction. To me, it seemed an awful long time to sit still, but when I watched the uneasiness with which many of the others sat through this agony, my discomfort seemed trifling. There were other rules as well to be followed concerning this religious gathering, so totally in penitence. There was to be no laughter during the entire time we devoted ourselves to this solemn occasion. But we found it very hard to follow this rule as there arose many situations that made it impossible not to laugh. At times, stark raving laughter seemed to come tearing out of us in spite of ourselves, and it would take all of our willpower and more to curb it, only to have a second bout of irrepressible laughter bubbling up from within. And the cause of these episodes of laughter would, at other times, be so insignificant and silly, that it would not even have raised a snigger. Perhaps it was the fact that we were restricted from this act of laughter that seemed to goad us on.

Another rule was concerning sleep. No one was to sleep, doze, close their eyes, yawn, look around generally, or appear to have lost interest. Under no pretext was one to leave the room either. Grandfather never raised his head; he just peered over his spectacles from time to time with his eagle eyes, and should he catch anyone breaking a rule, there would be a second sermon after benediction. That was the best form of punishment he could think of, for the very thought of prolonging the ceremony with a second repetitious sermon kept everyone on guard. But after all, we are human, and to err is human. So, more often than not, we ended up with two sermons. The entire procedure was so monotonously routine that had it not been for the little incidents that kept us in suppressed mirth and merriment, everyone would have dozed off or died of boredom.

Around 7.30 pm each evening, Grandmother would start preparing for the evening prayers. Her every action was done with meticulous precision. She got together her paraphernalia, consisting of her spectacles, prayer books, her mat, and a crisp white cloth with which she covered her head. Grandmother lived by the sayings of the Good Book, and to anyone who cared to listen, she would quote Corinthians 1, Chapter 11, Verse 5: 'But every woman that prayeth or prophesieth with her head uncovered dishonoureth her head'. And while quoting this verse, she would look pointedly at her daughter-in-law, for the latter stubbornly refused to comply, no matter how severe the retributions of her defiance might be. Actually, it was more of an act of insolence against her mother-in-law than anything to do with religious beliefs. After getting her things together, Grandmother would spread out her small mat, which she shared with no one, and with a great sigh, lower her ample self on her seat. She would then cover her head, slip on her spectacles, and bellow a solo rendition of some dubious hymn in an outrageous tune in a voice that was a cross between a bark and a meow and far from melodious. Of note is that this is not the opening hymn but rather a call song or announcement to the household that the time was nigh for evening prayers. Grandfather would be the first to troop in, followed by the others trickling in, until, by 8.15, when the entire household would have thronged in the main room. By this time, Grandmother's bellowing would come to a close. The proper opening hymn for the day would then be chosen, and the entire family would sing as if in one voice, but not quite.

Next on the agenda was bible reading. This consisted of two parts – the reading of the New Testament and Psalm, usually allotted to one of the younger members present, and the religious droning of the Old Testament by Grandfather. Usually, Aunt Suzy read the bible, for it was agreed by all that her voice was loud and clear. But more often than not, she would start one of her giggles, smother it and make it sound like a cough, splutter a bit, then clear her throat and read on. There were many things that went on in this sober gathering that would make a hermit snigger, let alone Aunt Suzy! Take Uncle Thomas, for instance. He always slouched on the mat by the door, half hidden from anybody's eye. And with good reason too. This partially hidden position offered him a place for uninterrupted repose. But sometimes, he got so comfortable that he would doze off and start the different stages of snore. At first, it would be a wheezing, then a gentle snore, which would gradually increase in tempo, much to the amusement of the youngsters and the consternation of the others. Everyone feared a second sermon from Grandfather at the end of prayer in case Uncle was caught, so the entire congregation would then be distracted with the process of waking him up. Someone would nudge Aunt Alice, who usually sat next to Uncle Thomas, and she in turn would nudge Uncle Thomas. But this usually brought no immediate change in the state of affairs. After much prodding and nudging, Aunt Alice would get thoroughly disgusted, and in a last effort, would scratch the sole of his outstretched feet quite hard. This invariably brought on guttural sounds from Uncle Thomas and suppressed guffaws from the rest of us. All this activity would make Aunt Suzy read the verses all the louder, amidst suppressed giggles, in an attempt to distract the grandparents. When Grandfather finally became aware of the situation, he would demand to know the origin of these strange sounds. Cousin Roy would tell him that it was our watchdog Brutus, who might have seen a cat. Whether Grandfather believed him or whether he was just tired of trying to solve the mystery, we never knew, but he always accepted the explanation.

When it was Grandfather's turn to read the Old Testament, we all tried to sit up and look solemn, but invariably, due to his slow, dreary, drawl, there would soon be more than Uncle Thomas in dreamland. Knowing this, Grandfather would peer over his reading glasses and clear his throat loudly in an attempt to bring the audience back to attention. Most times, this brought forth a sudden burst of song from Aunt Grace, who always took the back row and was a light dozer; so, the slightest disturbance woke her up, and no matter at what point of the prayer we were at, she burst into a song. This was just her way of showing us that she was wide awake and attentive, but of course, it gave her away as nothing else would!

In spite of these sporadic outbursts of song from Aunt Grace, which everyone had come to accept, Grandfather went on with his business of bible reading. Nothing ever stopped him from his quota. It is no exaggeration when I say that none of us understood a word of what he read. Most of us were asleep, and even those who were awake hardly appeared to comprehend much of the reading. Even the intellectuals among us – and all the grown-ups claimed to be so – were a little more than baffled by all the chapters and verses. The old testament recorded incidents that happened two thousand years ago and who was interested in that anyway? Whether it was that, or whether no one put in a real effort to pay attention, or whether Grandfather's reading just put them off, was never discussed. For it was an egoistic group that assembled, and who among them would own up to not understanding anything? After what seemed like aeons, Grandfather would come to an abrupt stop in his reading and snap the Good Book shut. I often wondered if he himself understood anything of what he read. He would then close his eyes and settle back in his chair as if he wanted to let all he had read, sink into our hearts and minds. We would all remain thus, suspended in uncertainty, for a while. This small respite would give Aunt Grace enough excuse to get up and go to the kitchen under the pretext of supervising the servants. She would join the group again only when the benediction was being said. This was a smart move on her part because she got to escape the sermon. Aunt Alice had, time and again, tried to manoeuvre herself into this situation of escape, but Aunt Grace always outsmarted her.

The crux of the prayer time, the sermon, came immediately after. Almost always, it revolved around someone who had displeased Grandfather in some way during the course of the day. He would drone on about commitment and responsibility, integrity and gumption, and doing the right thing at the right time. During the entirety of this sermon, each of us would be busy figuring out who was at the receiving end of this monologue. If it was Uncle Thomas, this was wasted effort, for he was blissfully unaware of the proceedings. If it was Aunt Grace, she was absconding, and Aunt Suzy had a glazed look in her eyes, which told us she was anywhere but there. In all probability, she would be wondering how she'd look in a parrot-green skirt she had set her mind on acquiring, and how she could work on Grandmother to obtain the same at any cost.

Aunt Mary in the back row would be busy with her hair. She would be wondering if switching to 'Brahmi Hair Oil' would stop it from turning grey so quickly. She maintained strongly that greying had more to do with oil than age and tried to prove this at every turn.

Cousins Betty and Patsy, sisters aged ten and twelve respectively, always sat behind Grandmother and Aunt Fanny. This blocked them from everyone else's view and gave them the complete freedom that they needed to play a game of 'rock, paper, scissors'. This game was keenly watched by all seated to the left and right of the players. Occasional smothered 'ohs' and 'ahs' could be heard, which denoted a game won or lost.

Aunt Fanny, who always sat in the front row and to Grandmother's right, followed most of the rules governing prayer time. She appeared promptly at 8, took her position next to Grandmother, and joined her in the announcement hymn. She had a breathless, shrill quality to her voice, which hardly got along with Grandmother's grating, raucous noise. They made a formidable duo with their cacophonical contribution, but there's no doubt that it was the best way to declare prayer time. Aunt Fanny was a schoolteacher and an authoritarian. This made her the ideal person to act as deputy to Grandfather whenever he felt under the weather. However, for fear that she would do the job better than him, Grandfather hardly gave her the opportunity. He secretly feared that her surreptitious intentions were to usurp his position if she could. Still, Aunt Fanny appeared punctually, sat in front, covered her head, followed the bible readings, listened attentively to Grandfather's sermons, and intermittently nodded her head too, all in the hope that one day, Grandfather would have to concede defeat.

Sermon over, we would move on to the final section – the prayer and benediction. There were no complaints about this part; in fact, there was a lot of enthusiasm on reaching here. Everyone was more than eager to bend over on their knees, place their head on the floor, and close their eyes in total submissive gratitude that the day's punishment had finally come to a close. The real dark secret behind this readiness was that all present, with the exception of Aunt Fanny, grabbed forty winks in absolute peace while Grandfather prayed and said the benediction. This came to light when no one got up after benediction and Aunt Fanny pointed it out to Grandfather, which made him livid. But for once, Uncle Thomas had his wits about him, probably due to being refreshed and alert after his sound sleep during the arduous time the rest of us had spent in prayer. He was able to mollify Grandfather with the quaintest of reasons. He argued that most of the gathered were so contrite for things done knowingly or unknowingly, that we were taking extra time for penitence. This absolutely stumped Grandfather and pleased him so much that he gave orders that those in extra penitence were to be left undisturbed.

From then on, the entire household has been deeply indebted to Uncle Thomas.

Some of the inmates of the Big House

The Funeral Arrangement

Grandmother was in the throes of agony and had been so for a few days. There was hushed talk of an imminent death in the family. From where I stood, it seemed to me that folks were hovering on the edges of desperation, hoping and pleading silently for one. It had been a long time since we had any sort of a gathering in the Big House, sad or otherwise, and so a funeral or a wedding would be most welcome. Who could blame them for being expectant? At least, there hadn't been one since I came to stay. And with Grandmother so willing to offer an occasion, it was taken for granted that it would be a funeral that brought the great family ramifications together this time. So, as the situation warranted, everyone treaded softly, looked sober, whispered to one another, avoided eye contact, and generally stood around expectantly for whatever it was to happen. Though everyone had an opinion, no one knew what exactly the matter was with Grandmother. A confirmation on the subject was attempted by many of the numerous bearded, grey-haired elders, but they ended up coughing and spluttering and choking on their words whenever they lost sight of what they were trying to say.

Meanwhile, in the inner rooms, the bosomy, thick-waisted matrons struggled to explain the gravity of the situation but dwindled down to lukewarm conclusions.

And as for the dearly beloved who had gathered together for several days now fearing the worst, there was no salvation from this penury, and impatience was growing. Grandmother just refused to make a quick exit, and I secretly wondered if she really wanted to go at all. Her daughters moved about with forlorn faces, as if they were the cause, in some way, for this mishap that had befallen their mother. At intervals though, they would revert to norm and explain to anyone who cared to ask how accomplished each of their children were, or where one could get a certain curry powder, or which washing soap offered the best bargains. The sons, as befitting sons, were busy explaining to the general public that in case it came to the point of having a funeral, the casket would definitely be of mahogany.

It all began on a bright, crisp, Friday morning, and things were right as rain. Not an iota of anything to indicate the storm that was to break. Grandmother had gone about her business as usual, doing minor household chores and generally bossing the servants about. At frequent intervals, she would call out to me just to make sure I was in the vicinity and out of trouble. In the early afternoon, our farm boy Ramu came by with a big jackfruit that he had cut down from a tree on his farm. Grandmother had a great weakness for this particular fruit, though she knew it was bad for her constitution, and the doctors had strictly ordered her against eating any. Perhaps she had a few too many that afternoon – we would never know – for by late evening, she was on the verge of death. It all happened so quickly, and I was truly stumped at the thought of somebody dying in the very house where I ate and slept. In fact, no one had ever died in my presence before, so all this was new to me. Moreover, I loved Grandmother. I wondered if I would be surprised, shocked, frightened, or just curious when the event finally happened. As a result, I keenly observed every scrap of detail, watched everyone, and most of all, watched myself. I had my apprehensions too. Not to mention doubts about if Grandmother would grace us with her esteemed presence whenever the fancy took her, even after her death! After all, she was a wilful lady, and it had been her home longer than anybody else's. By nightfall that day, the house was filled to capacity with grieving relatives, though Grandmother was yet to go.

What really shocked me was that no one really bothered about Grandmother all that much. She just lay on her bed in dire pain, twisting and turning, while everyone around her renewed old friendships and swapped tales. Cousin Mimi had started her postgraduate course in a prestigious college in the capital city, whispered Aunt Mary, who was Grandmother's eldest daughter. She imparted this piece of information to her old friend and rival, Sarah, knowing well enough that Sarah's daughter had dropped out of school and opted instead to marry the local Romeo. Ignoring the warning signs in Sarah's eyes, Aunt Mary went on extolling the virtues of Mimi's academic accomplishments until her friend decided to repay in kind. So, not to be out done, Sarah whispered back that her son, and there was great emphasis on the word 'son', was doing extremely well in one of the Gulf States. This can be noted as a mild chide in Aunt Mary's direction, seeing that she had not been blessed with a son. To this, Aunt Mary retorted that her husband was calling to her and beat a hasty retreat, and Sarah conceded defeat, having been a widow for many years. But had Aunt Mary stuck around, I was sure Sarah would have bounced back with a worthy repartee.

By the window, I noticed a clique of three frivolous young ladies throwing glances this way and that and giggling hysterically whenever it suited them, which was often. They were busy grading the young men who formed a group at the other end of the room. I was astonished to realize that these people were not here due to any sentiments for Grandmother, so why they should bother left me bewildered. Another fellow I noticed was a short, stocky chap who had the strange habit of popping up on his feet, as if in an effort to appear tall. Not that it did him any good. Each time he popped up, like some jack-in the-box, the ladies by the window collapsed into bouts of giggling. Even if it did seem disloyal, with Grandmother fighting for her life, this brought a smile to my lips.

Just then, I realized the older ladies were busy discussing my Aunt Suzy. However vehemently Grandmother denied it, I knew Aunt Suzy to be the flirt she was. In a way, I understood the envy of the other mothers. None of their daughters could compete with Aunt Suzy's beauty in any way. She eclipsed them at every turn. Aunt Suzy appeared to be particularly frisky that day even with Grandmother in a serious condition. She seemed to whirl around continuously among the people almost as if she was on display. Then the thought struck me! Could she be on display? What better place for one to be exhibited than at a wedding or a funeral? This was a cliché I had heard so often, and I felt a fool for not realizing it earlier. No wonder the matrons paraded their marriageable daughters around for all to take a dekko. No wonder they frowned upon Aunt Suzy, for no other girl stood a chance with her gyrating and fluttering about like a butterfly and even hovering around the older men, who themselves seemed in some sort of a trance with her about. I had often heard Grandmother complain to Grandfather that it was time some serious proposals were considered for their daughter. Grandfather seemed to brush aside this urgency, thinking it was not yet time for his daughter to leave the nest. I now suspected that having reached the end of her tether, Grandmother was playing her trump card. And doing it well too, judging by the way the crowd had arrived and the attention Aunt Suzy was getting.

At the other end of the room, a heated discussion was in progress between Uncle Thomas, Grandmother's younger son, and the rest of the elders in the family. The topics varied from the site for burial, the flowers to be used, who should say a word about Grandmother's illustrious life, and all matters concerning the wake. One particular point of note in this discussion was the complete lack of agreement by any two persons on any one point, to bring about a conclusion. The entire lot thrived on being at odds with each other. But things were not as simple as they seemed on the surface, for there were undercurrents and resentments in this group that went deeper than a simple discussion on funeral arrangements.

An elder, Mr. Cherian, objected to the site for burial. He maintained that the site was too near the church boundary and the dear departed would feel a sense of abandonment. 'She would be uneasy and might even be afraid', he argued. This sounded ridiculous to my ears, for I had thought until then that it was the living that feared the dead. And why on earth would a dead person care if she lay by the boundary, and how was she to know if she was abandoned? But had I been older, I would have spotted at once that there was more to this argument than met the eye. That there was a tug-of war going on among the elders for this particular plot of burial ground. It was the ideal place for the final rest. It overlooked the green paddy fields and a flaming, orange-coloured, wild bougainvillea grew by the edge, which gave a vibrancy and vitality to the morbid group that lay there in eternal silence. In fact, Mr. Cherian had long been in discussion with the church vicar over possession of the plot. It was all hush-hush though, and his delay in making the final move was the price. Mr. Cherian thought it too much, but the soft-spoken vicar was adamant for once. And with good reason too. Mr. John, Mr. Koshy, The Mathews Family, and a host of others were willing to pay double for the same plot. It had become a symbolic thing to own the plot by the side of the blazing bougainvillea and overlooking the green paddy fields. But no one ever came close to owning it because there was always one family that outsmarted the other, and this kept the price escalating and the prize more desiring.

Concer ning the wake, Mr. Sam said cupcakes should not be served at a wake. They were cheap, he maintained, and not befitting any dearly departed the likes of Grandmother. At this point, I noticed that Grandmother had already been added to the realms of the departed, never mind that she was still warm and very much alive on the bed inside. Uncle Thomas overruled Mr. Sam's objection, ascertaining that cupcakes were indeed served at many of the wakes he had recently attended and were in fact, pardon the expression, very much in style. He said it triumphantly and looked around for approval. Mr. Sam did not back off even then. He pressed on that cream cakes with an almond and grated cashew topping were more like Grandmother. I wondered how he came to that deduction. I mean, he did not know Grandmother much, and I had known her all my life, and somehow, I never associated her with cream cakes or almonds, though I'll agree she did like cashews. Now, the real issue here was that Mr. Sam had an axe to grind with Uncle Thomas as he believed he had been surcharged for some large amounts of pepper that he had bought from the latter. Knowing Uncle Thomas to be avaricious, I would not be surprised at all by this action. So, Mr. Sam was out to get his pound of flesh.

There was also an essence of intrigue in this argument, a plot within a plot. A 'Bread and Bakery' had started recently at the village, and the owner was Mr. Sam's brother. It was the first of its kind to function locally, and folks were spared the long journey into town to get a loaf of bread or a piece of cake. Should a guest drop in unexpectedly, one was now able to offer them something more with tea. This convenience made everyone turn a blind eye to the fact that, many a time, the bread was not all that fresh or the cake that soft. It was strongly rumoured that Mr. Sam got a commission for every customer that he sent to his brother's shop. And this was no surprise, as it was well known that Mr. Sam did nothing for nothing.

My Aunt Alice spoke only when the occasion required it of her, and when she did, everyone strained to listen, for she spoke just above a whisper. Her words were always clipped and measured. It was almost as if she paid for the words she uttered and hence did not want to waste any. She was very orderly and had a knack for management. So, obviously, she took over the church services and all other arrangements concerning the cortege, such as when it would start the final journey, the route it would take, and such. She was always discussing something or other with the vicar, in undertones.

She decided that two candles should be lit and placed by Grandmother's bedstead and immediately sent someone to go out and buy a few. I stood by and watched as Grandmother protested feebly, saying that she feared her hair would catch fire, but no one heard. Who listened to the dead anyway? And Grandmother was as good as gone. Next, Aunt Alice decided, after a long and laborious discussion with the vicar, that some incense should be burnt next to where Grandmother lay. 'To bring about a correctness to the whole atmosphere', she said. This created so much smoke that Grandmother broke out into fits of coughing, and I feared that she would soon be dead of gagging if nothing else. 'The hearse would be decorated, but not much', Aunt Alice intoned. Jasmines. The vicar nodded and repeated her words monotonously, like a good disciple. There was much nodding and standing around. There would be a band to lead the hearse, it was decided. At that, I thought how Grandmother lived in this world in serenity, but she would leave it with a bang.

Suddenly, out of nowhere, a number of voices broke out into a dirge. This declared that some of the members of the church choir had come. They were notorious for singing off-key, and more often than not, each member tried to out-sing the other. It usually ended in bedlam, and in any case, the congregation usually chose their own tune and ignored the choir. Much the same happened now, and I could see that Grandmother would have done anything to be able to get up and leave the room. If this had been a ruse to get the local boys to see Aunt Suzy, I was sure she regretted it now.

But the coup de grace that took us all by surprise came from the most unexpected quarters – Uncle Thomas' wife. She had been Grandmother's daughter-in-law for well over ten years now and never had a kind word to say to this goodhearted woman. But now, when there was a lull in the proceedings, and everyone seemed to be taking a respite, she let out a slow moan and began to beat at her chest. She tore at her hair, murmured words of despair, lamented that she had lost a dearly loved mother. And her slow moans began to change to loud sobs, then, in anguished frenzy to wails of utter hopelessness at her loss. She seemed so grief-stricken that we wondered if there would be two deaths that night.

This last act really frightened Grandmother out of her stupor. She gasped and struggled into an upright posture. The singing stopped, and so did the wailing. Funeral arrangements and discussions were put on hold. The ladies stopped giggling, and Uncle Thomas rushed to Grandmother's bedside. He was relieved, as he did not have to choose between the cupcakes and the cream cakes. Mr. Sam appeared furious for reasons best known to him. Mr. Cherian made a quick mental note to finalize the price of the funeral plot, once and for all, for his peace of mind. The candles were put out and the incense removed. Aunt Suzy snuggled up to Grandmother, and from over her head, Grandmother smiled at me.

She went on to live for another thirty-three years in perfect health and happiness. When she finally died, she was laid to rest in the shade of the wild, blazing orange bougainvillea, in the plot that looked out onto the green paddy fields.

The grandparents

A Girl Thing

Sixty-odd years ago, the agony of belonging to an insular community was drastic. Topics such as love, marriage, pregnancies, infidelities, relationships, adultery, divorces, and of course, menstruation and menopause, were taboo. This led to a lot of speculation on the part of us children. Those of us blessed – or cursed, depending on how you look at it – with a lively imagination, let our thoughts on the various subjects run riot. The resulting conclusions were either hilarious or frightening. Even thought-provoking in some instances. Cousin Myra was an authority on most things. She was a couple of years older than the rest, and we held her in high esteem. Whatever she said seemed fair to us. In any case, we did not dare to contradict her, as none of us were any the wiser and had no counterargument. She listened in on the grownup conversations, so her knowledge was far superior. She was all of fourteen years, and that was more than any of us were. So, when she stated one day that a woman had to marry a man, in church, before she could be pregnant, we all imbibed that information with total concurrence. I wondered about Aziza's remark about the kiss, but I refrained from airing my knowledge, for even then I knew that where ignorance is bliss, 'tis folly to be wise.

Those were austere times. A humourless time. A time when children were seen and not heard. The elders looked through us rather than at us and told us nothing about life, living, sex, or sexuality. And like any young girl waiting on the wings to maturity, I was filled with a myriad questions on all the 'no-no' topics. It was a time when no one told you anything about anything or prepared you for the onslaught of adolescence. You were out in the open – hung out to dry, so to speak. Alone. Raw. To fend for yourself and find out the bewildering emotions and sentiments that came with the onset of puberty and a surge in oestrogen.

It was also a time when there were no televisions that blared out the goodness of 'Stayfree Supreme' or droned on about the conveniences of 'Always' and 'Whisper', with or without wings. No one was familiar with undergarments either. I wondered if my aunties wore any. Did Mother? And if indeed Grandmother wore one, it would have to be really large, for she was a big woman. And what about Grandfather and the uncles? No one had heard of the 'Frenchie' or the 'Jockey' underwear for men; or being men, were they liberated from wearing any? I had never seen an underwear washed and hung on the clothesline at any time, except mine. Such matters were all shrouded in speculation or on what Myra advised us. No one advertised the facts about stretch brassieres, or about those that hooked up in front, or about brassieres per se. Brassieres were garments that were whisked from here to there and then removed from sight as quickly. Whoever knew you could buy a packet of 'Moods' if you were in the mood? No one knew that pregnancies could be avoided just as they could be planned. Those were times when women would asphyxiate if they witnessed a chat show on television where marriage discords were discussed. Was there such a thing, even? Women simply compromised and complied.

It was during such trying times, three days after my twelfth birthday, that I experienced the horrors of my first menstrual cycle. It goes without saying that I thought I was dying. There was simply no other explanation for it. I could think of no other rationale. One did not bleed for nothing. Or bleed from the privates. I knew bits and pieces from the senior girls at school, but otherwise, I was totally in the dark. Strangely, no one had thought it important enough to mention this landmark event of womanhood to me. I do not know to this day if it was a callous omission on Mother's part or if she thought I would figure it out for myself one way or the other. As she would have done in her time, and her mother before her. Perhaps Mother thought the Matron at the school where I boarded would enlighten me. No matter how hard I have tried to exonerate her for this oversight, I fail to understand where she thought I would pick up the relevant information concerning this subject. Remember those were days when the M-word was unmentionable. In hindsight, it seems to me that if the idea of 'omission to explain' was to frighten the daylights out of an unsuspecting girl so that she would be able to handle anything else that life would later throw at her, then it was a winner of a scheme. If that was the hidden agenda in this lapse, then I salute the pioneer of the 'omission to explain' system. I mean, years later, when I went through the agonies of child birth, I thought back to the petrified girl who stood on the threshold of womanhood not knowing what was happening to her and drew strength from the knowledge that nothing could be worse than that. Since I had survived that, anything else would be a piece of cake.

As I said, my twelfth birthday was a damper. Expect for the usual cake and a couple of cousins getting together to sing 'The Birthday Song' in a loud, shrill voice, everything else was routine. I got the shocker on the third day. I was in the yard helping Grandmother when I felt a queasy wetness between the thighs, followed by a weakness and a cramp in the under belly. I was a reasonably healthy person and never had a sick day in my life, if you can ignore the occasional cough and cold. I headed for the bathroom, stumbled into it, and locked the door behind me. I did not want the maid, Amini, creeping in on me, as she was in the habit of doing. Then she would get into one of her theatricals and go out to announce whatever she had discovered. She was an expert at creating a storm in a teacup, along with the regular teas she made. That was her way of entertaining herself between her dreary daily chores. And who can blame her? The movies were considered a sin – anything fun was a sin, come to think of it. So, everyone found their own entertainment whatever way they could. Hers was stalking and telling on Moi.

After bolting the door, I leaned against it to get my bearings or perhaps to still my beating heart. I did not know what I was afraid of, but I was filled with some unknown panic, a sense of doom. I had a premonition that I was about to discover something disastrous. Hesitantly, I checked myself, and never in my wildest nightmare was I prepared for what I saw. I was bleeding and from the most abnormal of places. In my astonishment and horror, I forgot to breathe for a few seconds, adding to my discomfort. Somewhere, I felt a kind of revulsion too. In its totality, the situation was tragic and pathetic, and what dismayed me even further was that I did not know where to turn for help or advice. I reasoned that if this was something that happened to everyone or something that everyone knew about, then I would have known about it. If this was an 'Oh, by the way,' sort of a thing, I would have heard it in passing, and there would be nothing to worry about.

But if this was an eventuality, then why was I not warned? That on one said anything, said a lot.

Am I dying? was my first thought and concern. Was this the cancer thing that an aunt had recently died of? How long would I live? I wanted so much to live. I had not eaten my fill of ice creams or chocolates. I wanted to write a book. I had never flown a kite or baked a cake. I had not seen the Taj Mahal. What was love then, that an Emperor would build such a monument for his Queen? I wanted to walk on the beach and make a wish as I watched the sun set. I wanted a place to call my own. I wanted to dress up as the grown-ups did and drink tea from dainty cups and saucers. I wanted to wear Mother's pearls and own a diamond ring. I wanted to go to a cinema and find out for myself what was so sinful about it. I wanted to paint my nails and wear perfume. I wanted to visit Bombay and Delhi and England. Would I die before I did all of these things? And if I should die, what happened after? I knew I would miss Mother and Father. And Grandmother. I started to cry silently.

I stood in the bathroom for a good half hour, maybe even longer. I was aware of every aspect of my being during that long wait. I studied myself critically and watched if any part of me was withering away. How else did you die? In all of my twelve years, I had never actually seen a dead person or gone to a funeral. Death was another conjecture with us kids. What was I to think? I hadn't the faintest idea what to expect in case of death. Would it be painful?

Mercifully, at the end of my wait, I continued to remain healthy. I felt no drastic change was imminent. It was hard to explain how relieved I was by that realization. Then another thought struck me. *What if this dying is a slow process? What if it takes a day? Or perhaps a night too? Maybe a week? A month? Maybe I will just bleed to death over a period of time. Will this bleeding ever stop?*

Since there was no sign of immediate death, my thoughts took a turn. I wondered if this was some sort of punishment for something I had done. Did I need to make repentance, like the elders always prayed, to be spared from the fires of hell? There was no other explanation. For the life of me, I did not know what my mistake or sin was, unless you considered my calling Mother a witch or a donkey in my head every time she asked me to do the multiplication tables. I could not confide in Mother about any wrongdoings, as she did not tolerate any form of shenanigans. If I had done any wrong and this bleeding did not kill me, then she would. There was nothing else to do but to try and heal myself, or else live with it, or at the worst, die of it. God sure had a twisted sense of humour, or else why didn't He make us bleed from the nose? I had become bolder and more philosophical, seeing that death was not immediate. I cleaned and dressed myself in the best way I knew and ventured out. I decided to think this through in the presence of fresh air and sunlight.

Finally, I went to my room and sat on the bed. I felt dizzy and lay down. I must have slept, for when I got up, the sun had gone down. I thought back on everything that had happened to me and fervently hoped it was a bad dream, and that, along with the sun, the cause for my anxiety would have also set. It was not to be. Seeing as my luck was such that if I were to kiss a frog, instead of the frog becoming a Prince, I would become a frog, I was not surprised when I woke up to the same predicament and a terrible pain. Yet, there was a bitter-sweetness to the pain. It reminded me that I was alive. In school, when the other girls menstruated and I did not, I had thought something was wrong with Moi. Now, when it did happen, although I was relieved, I did not know what to make of it.

But there were things worse than getting the period? At the boarding, the soiled pads had to be disposed in a place they called 'The Pit.' This dreadful place was in the senior dormitory, the bastion of a battalion of ruthless seniors. Bad enough we juniors had to knock and ask permission, like so: 'Please, may I go to the Pit,' but as we made the long way to the end point, we also had to endure the howling and the hooting and the ragging and teasing. It was like walking the Green Mile only there was no empathy.

I prayed a lot during that time, asking God for forgiveness for whatever I had done without having a clue what I had done. And then, at the end of the third day, I reaped the reward of my ardent entreaties to God. For the bleeding stopped just as suddenly as it had appeared. This time, I cried with relief. The third time this happened to me, Mother got wise. The situation was anticlimactic. She was pragmatic about it all and behaved as if everything was normal. Nothing of what I had dreaded happened. In fact, we hardly talked about it at all. Mother was so complacent, and, I think, relieved.

I could not read her. All she did was put her arms around me and say in a husky voice, more to herself than to me, 'My baby has grown up!' Then she patted me on the back and said in a warning tone of voice, 'Don't be too friendly with the boys anymore. Be careful now that you have grown up.'

I was staggered by this new revelation. Here was a new train of thought I had never imagined to pursue. I had thought of death as an eventuality, but what was this with the boys? Where had that come from? What secrets did the boys hold now? My head was so fumbled with this new conundrum, I started a headache. I did not follow up the conversation with Mother because I could see she was uncomfortable and wanted to get it over with. With that master stroke, she left the room, leaving me flummoxed in an altogether different direction.

I spent a good many days tracing back to any contact I had made with boys. To be sure, there were hugs and shoves and pushes. Do they count? So, what did all that mean? After a lot of soul searching, I decided this was a problem that was too big for my twelve-year-old shoulders. I had an urgent need to unburden myself. I decided to tell Mother everything and face her wrath. It could not be worse than the nightmarish agony I was going through. She remained silent throughout my recounting. A thousand emotions crossed her face, none of which was anger. Strangely though, I saw sympathy and regret. But what startled me most was how she sat in pensive silence, long after I had stopped. It seemed like she was going over everything I had said. Finally, with a sigh, she turned and looked at me for another long moment. I thought I saw sadness in her eyes. Then, she leaned forward, gathered me in her arms, and hugged me tightly. She assured me that I was no sinner and definitely not dying. Then, she told me she was so sorry that I had to go through such a horrifying experience all alone. She said she should have been more sensitive to my needs and should have made me aware of 'the girl thing,' as she put it. In spite of her regrets, she did not enlighten me any further on the subject, though she tutored me on how to handle it best the next time. Next time? How many times? I had a thousand questions, but I could see no opening or invitation for them. Her discomfort was palpable. The shutters had fallen and the subject was once again taboo. That was the way it was. So, I just put my arms around her and told her how much I loved her. She seemed to soften. Then she pulled back and took my face in her hands. She looked at me, smiled, and told me that if ever I was lucky enough to have a daughter, I should share everything with her. 'Everything,' she emphasized, and by that, I knew she meant 'the girl thing.' She need not even have told me that, for I had already sworn to myself that if I had a daughter, I would not want to kill her before she died.

P/S. Many years later, when the time was right, I decided to talk to my daughter about 'the girl thing.' I had so looked forward to it. But as she rushed off to somewhere for something, she called back over her shoulder, 'It's okay Mama, I've got an idea about menstruation and all that comes with it. We girls at school have discussed about it. Actually, I can give you some pointers and modern thoughts on sex and sexuality.'

Good God, I thought, *the shroud had been removed, and I never even knew.*

The Thing About Hibiscus

Ialways got punished at college during my biology classes but not because the teacher had a grudge against me. On regular days, I did fine, but the botany practical classes were my downfall, particularly during the study and dissection of the hibiscus flower. Every time I saw the hibiscus placed on the desk, a sort of wistful listlessness tinged with melancholy and bordering on nostalgia took possession of me, and I could no longer control my senses. And I was utterly useless for the rest of the class. The vacuous, lethargic symptom of this inscrutable illness gradually changed into a dreamy, faraway, sort of hypnotic trance. As much as the teacher tried, she found no rhyme or reason for the definite onset of this malady. Never for a moment did the teacher associate the flower with my apathy to the demands of the class; rather, she thought it was a way of escape that I had devised to get away from something unpleasant. So, she thought that I was being insolent and conniving. God forbid that be true! But once the teacher was convinced that the situation was genuine, she began to really look into what was ailing Moi.

Fate in the form of the monsoons stepped in and took over before the teacher branded me as totally useless. The rains were strong that year, and it was difficult to get perfect flowers, for the pelting downpour would destroy most of them. As a result, that fatal day, one half of the class was given the petunia for dissections, while the other half, the hibiscus. Teacher observed the startling fact that as long as I stayed on the 'petunia side' of the class, I was fine, but as soon as I crossed over to the 'hibiscus side,' I was as good as gone! As long as I stayed away from this dangerous red pathogen, I was fine, but if I so much as looked at it, I was lost. What then, was the secret of the red flower? Actually, this bright red flower was no pathogen; in fact, it was a bewitching and enticing reminder of all that was nice and happy, of holidays and birthdays, of loved ones and long ago. The red flower was so intimately entwined and entangled with memories of childhood that one was not possible without the other. Red hibiscuses did that to me. I would go back in time to the morning I opened my eyes to the most colourful array of these red flowers.

Birthdays are special days for everyone, even more so when you are turning thirteen and on the brink of teenage. Teenage. The word was a mystery and magic. I had heard mother often say that so-and-so had become a teenager. Whether that meant she was good or bad, I had no idea. But I knew for sure that it meant she was different. How so? I was in the dark! Now, I was on the brink, and everything was to change. I would soon find out for myself what this meant. Here I was, on the eve of my thirteenth birthday, all poised and ready to meet whatever it was, head-on. I was hoping against hope that Grandmother would remember the event and make it memorable, for as far as I knew, the thirteenth birthday came only once in a lifetime, and it heralded the oncoming of teenage. I made a special appeal to God on this matter, and I think He too, felt the same way I did.

There was, I noticed, an air of expectancy about the Big House. Grandmother moved about in a hurry, and Aunt Suzy tried very hard to keep me away from the kitchen, where a lot of action was taking place. One thing particularly out of the ordinary was that Uncle Thomas made two visits into town. Both times, when he returned, he rushed in through the back door and carried a number of packets with him. I had a sneaky feeling it had something to do with my birthday. Still, one could never be too sure about these matters, so I kept my hopes neutral. However, at regular intervals, I said a word of prayer and kept my fingers crossed in case God became involved in more pressing matters elsewhere and I was forgotten. *A small gift would be nice*, was all I thought. Mother and Father were still in Malaya, but they had remembered my special day and sent me a lovely frock, in sky blue, with little lavender and white flowers. I just could not wait to wear it, but Grandmother told me it was bad luck to wear one's birthday dress before the actual day. This, I suppose, was the easiest way to prevent me from pestering her to try on the dress. However, nothing stopped me from taking a look at it from time to time or dreaming how I would look when I finally wore it.

By early afternoon that day, Thoyamma walked up to our courtyard. This was an auspicious event, for Thoyamma was associated with everything that was essential for putting together a party. She was a baker and candymaker par excellence, and her confectionaries were known far and wide. There was a 'no nonsense' attitude about her, as she was all business and no play – pedantic about her creations, precise about the job, and sincere to the core. Her mantra was dedication. Getting an appointment with Thoyamma and having her come to cook or bake for a party was as difficult as getting an audience with the Pope. She was always in demand, as there was always a baptism, or a wedding, or a wake, or a thousand other functions for which delicacies had to be prepared. It was rumoured that Thoyamma's reputation had reached such heights that people came from far and wide, and she was forced to turn down a few requests. It was almost a matter of prestige to boast at a party that Thoyamma had prepared the sweets. 'The hands that made magic with pastry,' was a befitting caption for Thoyamma, in case she wanted to advertise. So, it was no small feat to have Thoyamma walk up our courtyard, and at such short notice, for Grandmother had sent for her only the previous day. It is well to bear in mind that Thoyamma had no time for dilly-dallying, and she made no pleasantry visits, so her visit to the Big House had to be with a purpose. I think she can never forget that she was much obliged to Grandmother, for at a time when Thoyamma was out of luck and struggling, it was Grandmother who encouraged her to try her hand at baking and delicacy-making. And Grandmother was also instrumental in getting her many of her initial bakery appointments by putting in a good word for her wherever possible. For this, Thoyamma was eternally grateful and always accommodated Grandmother, no matter how busy she was. I watched from the upper windows as Thoyamma made a hasty entrance into the kitchen. I smiled to myself. Yes, the signs were positive – there was going to be a party for me!

Grandfather decided to have one of his elaborate 'oil baths.' This was another auspicious event. Even if Thoyamma's coming did not confirm my belief that a party was being organized, Grandfather's oil bath did, as he always had one before an important function or meeting or in the event of anything out of the ordinary. He said it got him ready and prepared for anything – he felt younger and thought better. Grandmother always encouraged him when he decided on this elaborate procedural ritual because however inconvenient the ordeal was, it got the old man out of his usual irascible mood and put him in good humour. He would then act with general bonhomie for the remaining part of the day. Better yet, it got him out of her hair. The only person with an opposition to this plan was Ramu, and he had cause for consternation – after all, he was in charge of these 'oil baths.' As a result, Ramu had to spend the better part of the afternoon getting Grandfather's water to the correct temperature and everything else associated with the bath. This is easier said than done, for Grandfather did not believe in anything modern and wanted his water warmed in the traditional way. This meant using firewood to build a big fire outdoors and warming a large container of normal water and bring it to the correct temperature. Boiled water was never added to normal water to bring it to the desired temperature – nothing could be more horrendous. Certain herbs and roots that grew wildly on the farm were also added to ward off joint pains and other minor ailments related to old age. While the water warmed, Grandfather sat on his stool and relaxed, gently dozing as Ramu gave him a thorough rubdown with medicated oil (The making of this oil is a story in itself, better left to be told at another time). Ramu would start these laborious processes with diligence. He was a conscientious worker, and any job he did, however insignificant, he did with reverence. He gave the art of massaging the same respect a surgeon would impart to an open-heart surgery. Maybe more. For Ramu was also an artist of sorts. He started from the head and worked his way, with thoroughness, down to the toes. Yet, in the back of his mind, Ramu resented the fact that he was prevented from joining in the festivities taking place in the kitchen. The only consolation in this painstaking chore came in the form of Amini, who was the love of Ramu's life. She came by frequently to reignite the ebbing cinders under the warming water of Grandfather's bath. Their eyes met and spoke volumes, and neither of them minded how long Grandfather's oil bath took. As far as I was concerned, an oil bath on the day before my birthday was a good sign.

At five o'clock that day, my ears picked up the one sound I always eagerly waited for, birthday or no birthday. It was a badly whistled, unheard of tune that made our dog Brutus growl and snarl. As if the whistling was not enough to irritate, it was followed by a loud and gusty bellow and a cry of 'Rrrrroooti, Butterrrrr buns, Bisket!!!!!' The 'r's of the roti and butter were rolled over the tongue and allowed to drag on for a bit, while the 'bisket' was short and sharp – staccato. This was Varkey Chetan with his special call, signalling his arrival. He was the bread and bakery man. As far as I knew, every child in every home in every village, eagerly awaited his weekly visits. He was a well-weathered, squat chap but spunky and jovial. He had a turban on his head, and on this, he carried a very large basket woven in bamboo. This basket was tautly covered with a faded blue tarpaulin to keep away the crows that seemed to fly above him like some forbidding halo. But his loud, cranky cry kept them at a decent distance. He always came by the back entrance on the kitchen side and called out loudly for someone to help him lower the heavy basket from his head. Ramu always hurried to oblige – anything to get near the kitchen, where Amini could be found – and hung around even after the basket was lowered, until Grandmother gave him one of her 'looks.' We would all gather around Varkey Chetan, who would boast about all the ware he had that day.

'Fresh bread,' he would say, 'fresh from the oven. Why doubt when it is still warm? And the jillabees, dripping with honey. Or try the butter buns,' he would coax, 'or the cupcakes, or scones, or the halwa in three different colours – orange, green, and black.'

As for the biscuits, there were a variety of them to choose from. In all shapes and sizes and tastes. With raisins, with cashew nuts, with cream, with jam! It was a very difficult task making a choice, and I always ended up wishing I could get one of each. While we hovered undecidedly over Varkey Chetan's basket, he would regale Grandfather with his weekly quota of town news. From time to time, he would encourage me to taste a bit of 'this or that' to help me make up my mind as to what delicacies I preferred.

But that Varkey Chetan should turn up that sultry evening, when it was not yet a week since his last visit, made my heart beat faster. Grandmother had sent for him, so something was going on! As Varkey Chetan lowered the basket and removed the tarpaulin, I spied a brown paper packet right on top. Before I could make out what it was, he had removed it and handed it over to Grandmother, with a smile and a wink at me. The message conveyed was lost on me, and for the life of me, however hard I tried, I could not guess what it could be. Then the aroma from the basket hit us full force on our faces, and soon, we were all involved in the bewildering task of deciding if the 'jillibiees' tasted better than the 'halwa,' or if we should buy more of the 'unniappams' rather than the 'achappams.' For once, Grandmother seemed to have loosened her tight grip on her purse strings and allowed us to choose and buy as many delicacies as we pleased. In fact, she herself was uncharacteristically lavish. She bought two big raisin breads and one of Varkey Chetan's specials. This was bread baked with sesame seeds and giving off a whiff of cardamon flavour. It went very well with Grandmother's chicken kurma. But what really stumped me was that Grandfather did not bat an eyelid over all this buying. He was notoriously tightfisted and usually got morose and double-checked everything that Grandmother bought. But that day, he was genial and even suggested that Grandmother had better buy two of Varkey Chetan's specials. Not to be outdone, Varkey Chetan offered one 'on the house.' Meanwhile, things were on the move in the kitchen. Thoyamma's voice would now and then be raised in admonition of something Amini would have done or would not have done. Ramu was called to break the coconuts and scrape out the kernel in preparation for making the 'paisam' or sweet rice, which was a must for any decent birthday celebration. By now, I was confident in my belief that there was going to be a birthday party, and if the gusto with which everyone was going about it was anything to go by, it was to be quite a big party. By evening, Aunt Mary had come over with her daughters, and Aunt Alice was also present. Aunt Suzy and all the rest assembled shortly after, and by nightfall, there was a full house. Since the whole family had gathered, Grandfather was busy deciding on an appropriate sermon for prayer time.

After prayers and dinner that night, I could barely keep my eyes from closing – so hectic had been the day. I kept yawning and dozing until Grandmother coaxed me to retire. She came with me to tuck me in, and that day, she sat by my bedside for a long while. I slept by the window in the room we called 'the wood room' on account of the floor being made of wood. A gentle breeze lifted the lace curtains, and moonlight streamed in and bathed Grandmother's serene face with a celestial radiance. I felt so happy to belong to her. She smiled at me and ran her fingers through my hair. I knew without doubt that I held a special place in her heart. I was the firstborn of her firstborn. Perhaps she thought of her son, so far away in Malaya, and was glad God had given her this little part of him to hold and love. She told me that night that I would soon leave childhood behind with the coming of the new day. I would become thirteen years old and a big girl.

New experiences and new roads to travel. Greater knowledge and greater responsibilities. She said that I should live wisely and always know between good and bad. That God should have a place in my life and that I should be able to offer love and mercy to anyone who needed it. That I should never harbour bitterness or malice. That I should never hurt anyone by word or deed and have the grace to help anyone in need, unconditionally. And most of all, she told me I should never do anything that I was afraid others would find out, for such a thing done in secret would always be wrong. Was this what it meant to be a teenager, I wondered? It sounded like a big job, and it frightened Moi a little. *I will soon find out*, I thought, as I turned over to sleep. I smiled as I felt Grandmother's lips brush across my forehead, and then, I knew nothing more.

I woke up bright and early to shouts of a thousand voices calling out my name. Clapping and laughter followed this. My eyes grew big and round like saucers, and I could hardly breathe as I looked around my room. It was covered, totally, entirely, absolutely, in a burst of the brightest red colour. A thousand splendid red hibiscuses, picturesque, so awesome, totally mind-blowing and overwhelming, filled every miniscule corner of the room. There was not a spot of wall to be seen, so thoroughly and painstakingly had Uncle Thomas and Aunt Suzy camouflaged every inch of space in flaming red. I had prayed to God asking for a small gift, maybe a cake with a few candles. But here I was, blessed with more than anything I had ever dreamed of. I was so humbled by this magnificent gift from the heart, so much more valuable than any material gift. Throughout my life, at each birthday, I would take a moment to stop and recall that unique gift I had received on my thirteenth birthday.

And hibiscuses have always brought those nostalgic yearnings for things long gone but never forgotten.

Conversations at the Big House

The Big House always teemed with activity. There was a hustle and bustle that seemed to make the place come alive. It not only sheltered the people living there but also seemed to take part in every intimate incident of the inhabitants. It seemed to celebrate their happiness and sympathise with their sadness. It stood there, unwavering, a huge granite structure offering refuge, warmth, love, and shelter for those who wanted respite in times of trouble. It was also a happy place to be in. We did a lot of talking in the Big House. The minute anyone returned home from wherever they had gone to, everyone gathered around to get a word-for-word account of all that had transpired during the outing. There was a lot of interest generated in everything that went on. Who came and for what; who went and why; were the cows taken to pasture; did the farm-boy collect the eggs; were the hens in the coop; were the cows milked; were the peppers plucked; how many workers in the paddy fields; who did what, when, where, why, and so on. There was never any time for silence. No matter which corner of the house you went to, there was some business going on, some discussion taking place. It was a house that was bursting at the seams with love and laughter, with heated arguments and scolding, with a lot of teasing and leg-pulling, with a lot of grief and consoling, with crying and cajoling. It was a house that was animated, throbbing, and pulsating with vitality. There was never a dull moment in the Big House. You could wander through the rambling old place, which sprawled over a good area of the land it was built on, and join in any of the happenings that were taking place. I delighted in going from group to group and passively listening to these conversations. There were words of wisdom from the prudish older aunts, who would descend on unsuspecting youngsters grouped together for an afternoon of yarning and chaffing. And should they be caught in the vice-like grip of these puritan womenfolk, then there was no escape for the poor souls, no matter how hard they tried.

Cousin Mathew had just come down for his summer vacation from the University. He was a favourite among the old aunts. As was the custom with young college-going men of that time, Cousin Mathew wore his hair to his shoulders. This was a bone of contention between the two parties. And if he should tie his hair up in a ponytail, then the old ladies would act as if they had witnessed the transformation of a man to a horse. 'But it is so unmanly to trot about, with a ponytail like a stallion,' they would incessantly argue. 'What is the world coming to, when men grow their hair?' was a perpetually repeated question. Cousin Mathew was a good sport and took all this in a humorous vein. He would point out, much to the older ladies' consternation and the other youngsters' delight, that Shakespeare, Buonaparte, Magellan and all the men of the previous centuries wore their hair long. They rode on horseback and fought hand-to-hand combats using swords and spears. They braved the seas and travelled through unknown deserts and crossed great mountains, and proved to be men of valour. 'How would you explain that?' he would tease them. And then he would deliver an indisputable fact and that it was biblical made it all the more worthy. 'And remember Samson from the Bible? His long hair was his strength. It's the least I can do to copy their hairstyle,' he would add with a wink at the others.

Then, Cousin Sara, Mathew's sister, would join the group, and this opened up another subject for discussion, for she was always attired in casual Levis and a t-shirt. The old ladies had an aversion to girls in pants. They would then concede defeat to the case concerning 'men with long hair' and turn their vengeance on Sara and 'girls in pants' with tight t-shirts and nothing shielding the chest. 'Boys are boys and girls are girls and long live the difference,' they'd crackle in unison. 'When there are lovely skirts and frocks for ladies to dress themselves in, why would you want to exhibit yourselves and go around in borrowed feathers? You youngsters vote for comfort, but what is comfort at the expense of decorum? Ladies should look and behave like ladies. One pair of pants in one family is enough or else…,' they'd warn, shaking their heads, finding no words to describe the horrors the world was silently being led to. There was no end to the subjects the old aunts brought up. They found nothing amiss in their thinking that anyone who differed from them in thought or deed was wrong. Their way of thinking was right, period. And they were willing to argue their point of view to death. Most of the young group got tired of the long-drawn-out, senseless arguments, and after a while, they just humoured them by letting them win their point. This only made the ladies bolder and more confident, so the next time they argued their opinion, they became more vociferous.

If you cared to go to the back of the house, where the kitchen was situated, there were a variety of activities to choose from. In the kitchen proper, there would be a hot discussion on the correct number of chillies that had to be added to a chicken curry or on whether black pepper could be added to a fish curry. Aunt Mary thought herself to be a great authority on chicken preparation, and she always declared with finality, 'two for hot and one and a bit for normal.' Everyone present was in acceptance, but the puzzled look on all faces told me that no one understood what she meant by 'two for hot.' Two of what? Two cups, tablespoons, teaspoons? And how much was 'one and a bit'? But if Aunt Grace happened to be in hearing distance, the matter would not rest there. She was a fastidious person and very pernickety. She was prone to questioning everything and everyone until she got the exact meaning of what was said. 'Two of what?' she would question. 'And how much is "a bit"?' Irritated and barely holding on to her temper, Aunt Mary would answer with deliberate flippancy that she meant 'tablespoons, naturally.' To which Aunt Grace would retort that she thought it was 'two cups, naturally.' The thought of two cups of chilies in any curry, and the images of the discomfort of those who were unfortunate enough to have unsuspectingly tasted this, would flit through our minds, and we would start a bout of laughter. This always made Aunt Mary dump the ladle into the cauldron unceremoniously and leave the kitchen in a huff, only to return after a short interval and take up from where she had left off. In the short interval that Aunt Mary was absent, we were given a lecture on the benefits of green vegetables and the harm in overcooking them by Aunt Grace, who was a dietitian and so paid great attention to what she ate. If management of the kitchen was handed over to Aunt Grace, and if she had her way, 'raw, green diet' would be the order of the day, and who can blame us if we gradually got to thinking we were a bunch of cows? Goulash, or meat stew, was another dish on which a lot of time was spent in argument. The seasoned cooks were of the opinion that the meat was added after the herbs were boiled in water, while those who had a degree in home science and followed the more recent trend of 'easy cooking,' were of the opinion that everything could be boiled together, except for the vegetables, which were added last. But if baking was ever discussed, I would move on, for that was a subject on which there was no conclusion. Sometimes, I stood apart and watched all this hustle and bustle and was amazed that anything got cooked at all and served on time. I wondered how a little bit of chilli powder one way or the other mattered so much, or what the great difference was if one inch of ginger or one inch and a half was used, or if three pods of garlic was used and not two. Wasn't there a bit of exaggeration in all this hubbub?

If there was a baby born to anyone, the gathering in that part of the house would be at the maximum. Admiring the baby and congratulating the parents was mandatory. A lot of time was spent on discerning whom the baby favoured – father or mother. 'The forehead is the father's, though the nose is definitely the mother's,' someone would say. 'No, it was the other way around,' a third party would chip in. Then they would go into a detailed dissection of the baby's ears, mouth, eyes, hands, legs, and feet and exhaust themselves in coming to a decision, for the ultimate conclusion had to satisfy both parents. Finally, an agreement of sorts would be reached when one of the participants, bored with the subject, would announce that one can be a hundred percent sure of features only when the baby becomes a year old. Till then, a baby would be like a chameleon, this person would go on, warming up on the subject. Undoubtedly, this statement would make a lot of the gathered gasp in horror. To me, it was mind-boggling, this new knowledge that I had acquired. I had never, in my worst nightmare, associated babies with chameleons; still, the world was full of wonders, and things were never what they seem.

Names were the next favourite item of discussion. A name was a lifelong thing, and a lot of care had to be put into picking the one name that would proclaim the man or woman that the child would grow up to be. Keeping this in mind, a lot of time was spent on details like the origin, meaning, and who else shared the name. Biblical names were preferred, but one had to keep modern names in mind too, in accordance with changing times. So, a parent had to be absolutely sure, and that was not all. If it was a boy, Grandfather expected to be honoured by having the baby named after him. Or was it an honour for the baby to be named after Grandfather? It was too much for my young brain to unravel. Either way, a great privilege indeed! But this was very tricky ground, as Grandfather had a very old-fashioned name, Geevarughese, and no child would grow up to appreciate his own father if he was burdened with such a tongue twister. And if at all the new father conceded to the name due to pressure from powerful corners, he would still have to placate a disgruntled wife who would be thoroughly piqued that her husband had chosen his grandfather's name over hers. What about equal rights? And after all the heated debates they had had over equal opportunities for the sexes! For added measure, she would point out that her grandfather had a better and a more modern name – James or some such. There was no arguing the last point, and a balance had to be kept. Then, there was the question of where the baptism was to be held, who the godparents would be, the number of people to be invited, and the menu. These discussions would go on and on with no end in sight, leading to fights, tears, persuasions, and cajoling, with the new parents and the rest of the family taking sides. To me, it seemed a divorce would take place before the baptism.

A lot of affairs went on in the Big House, and the fun was that they took place right under Grandmother's unsuspecting nose. Grandmother belonged to the old guard that thought that even having a light flirtation, or using a harmless double entendre, was as sinful as committing adultery. Affairs were unmentionables. In fact, it never crossed her mind that such a state would prevail under her watchful eye. No one would dare – not with her around! But the truth of the matter was that Grandmother, not being well-versed in these areas, could easily be hoodwinked, and in many cases, she unknowingly paved the way for these shenanigans. She hardly knew the signs of the beginnings of an affair, even if it stared her in the face. She might be the mistress of the house and other matters in everything else, but as far as affairs of the heart were concerned, she was totally gullible. And that was the reason the affair between the kitchen maid, Amini, and the farm boy, Ramu, reached new heights! He even managed to hold her hand. Had Grandmother known of this, she would have looked upon this with more severity than if a nun had got pregnant. Ramu had had his eyes on Amini from day one. He had tried to entice her in a thousand ways. When Grandmother spotted Amini with twelve glass bangles, all blood red and with fine intrinsic design in gold, she enquired about it suspiciously. But Amini had a ready answer and claimed that it was her step-grandaunt from her father's side, who stayed in Cherthala, who had given it to her for the Onam festival. There was no way Grandmother could verify this claim, and Amini had given so many precise details that the explanation sounded authentic, so she let it go. These glass bangles could be the reason that Amini conceded to let Ramu hold her hands. I fear to think then what could have transpired between the lovers when next, Amini appeared with a new red sari to match the red bangles. No doubt, this really got Grandmother agitated, and she demanded an explanation. Amini repeated her story about her step-grandaunt from Cherthala, but Grandmother was having none of that and told Amini to send for this person. This put Amini in a fix, but she got out of it gallantly by saying that this elusive aunt was away on a year-long pilgrimage. She could not be reached as she could be in any one of the millions of temples across the length and breadth of India. Grandmother knew when she was beaten, but she decided to keep an eagle eye on Gopan, the boy who brought in the laundry. She suspected him because he had a raunchy laugh and dressed rakishly and sported a pencil-thin moustache that turned up at the ends. He flirted outrageously with Grandmother, and though she enjoyed this enormously, she never let him go near Amini. So, the affair blossomed on this side, while Grandmother watched the other side, and both parties were content. The cost of a sari was way above bangles, and if one considered the 'holding of the hand' as reward for bangles, then the reward for a sari would surely be more than 'a hand and a leg' put together. If only Grandmother knew.

The soothsayer was another big attraction. Never mind that none of her predictions ever came true; she still held an exalted position in the Big House. One knew when she approached, for she made a shrill call from way down the valley. It was a unique sound, and we could not mistake it with any other. There were many calls we were familiar with, and each one was distinct and unique. In the old days, I guess that was the only way to get the attention of the people and to inform who was approaching and with what wares. I thought it an ingenious method. There was the call of the fisherman, which went 'meenneh hoo-yeee,' (fish) and there was the call between friends, which went 'hooo-yeh.' Ramu's call when he approached the house was a slow song, more to alert Amini than to announce his arrival, and Gopan always whistled some uncertain ridiculous tune. Then there was the soothsayer's shrill call that went something like 'kaaaeeeeenotum' (palm reading). She took a long time coming up to the house, because many would stop her on the way to ask what their stars foretold. She would finally walk up our courtyard, dressed in an array of colours, her lips red from chewing her betel leaf mix, the stone on her nose-ring sparkling in the sunlight, her hair braided with ribbons of a hundred different colours, silver anklets on her feet, and rings on her toes. In her right hand, she carried a covered box, the inside of which we have never seen, and in her left hand, she carried a bird cage, in which perched the greenest parrot I had ever seen. As she trotted up the courtyard, she would rattle off mantras and gibberish nonsense, which added effect to her act, and then sit down with aplomb and dramatically lay out her paraphernalia. She would coo to the parrot, then admonish it, all in strange gibberish, which left us wondering about a great many things. Still, we were drawn to her like moths to a flame. Suddenly, she would look up and catch Aunt Suzy's eye. A fiendish smile would play on her betel-stained lips, and she would say the time was near when 'a handsome one would sail the seas and come courting.' That was enough to sustain Aunt Suzy till the fortune-teller's next visit. She would dream of her Prince Charming and wait and watch for his arrival. If Aunt Suzy wanted more details on the subject, she would have to place a 'darshina,' or offering, which comprised of Rs. 5 at a minimum. I always took a front seat whenever she came, but I was more fascinated by the parrot than with anything she had to prophesy about my future. Amini had once told me that the bird was actually a little girl who had irritated the soothsayer so much that she had put a spell on her and changed her into a parrot. Sometimes, the sorceress would catch hold of my hand and turn it over, searching the palm. Then she would murmur under her breath, while her body would start to convulse with spasms. I would sit spellbound, hardly breathing for fear that I might break her spell; then, she would leave the house with two parrots! When she opened her eyes, all she would say was 'rosy hands with no break in lines.' I never knew if that was good or bad, and in any case, I was not bothered. I was just waiting to have my hands back. Amini always placed Rs. 5 and held out her palms to be read. She wanted to know for sure if her future lay with Ramu. The soothsayer was sneaky enough to have found out this affair from the locals, who were always willing to gossip, and in truth, that was her source of information. So, she would make snide remarks about a handsome man and go on to describe Ramu. All said and done, when the soothsayer left, everyone's spirits would have rocketed sky high, for she made sure she told each one exactly what they wanted to hear. And I was relieved I was still a little girl.

The conversations dearest to my heart were the ones between Grandfather and Grandmother. Both of them were hard of hearing, but neither realized or would accept the fact. If you spoke naturally, they accused you of whispering, but if you raised your voice, they accused you of shouting and disrespect. Between them, however, there was no problem. They held peaceful conversations on a variety of subjects, hardly raising their voices. How they achieved this was a mystery until one went up close and eavesdropped.

Their conversations would go something like this:

Gf: 'So, it looks like a good day today.'

Gm: 'Yes. Amini makes good bread. That is why I keep her on in spite of that Gopan'!

Gf: 'Yes, yes. I hope it keeps this way in spite of the heat. Then we can spread out the pepper to dry.'

Gm: 'Of course, she will stay as long as I keep her. But her mother might insist on her getting married.'

Gf: 'O! No. I don't insist you spread it out today. Before the rains though, for once the monsoons come, there is no stopping them.'

Gm: 'You're right. There is no stopping these girls once they get it into their heads to get married.'

Gf: 'On his head, did you say? Don't you think that it will be too heavy for Ramu to carry?'

Gm: 'What?! Ramu and Amini? Where did you get such an idea? Look here, now don't go giving the girl ideas. You men are all the same! But I have to watch that girl.'

Gf: 'Right you are! We men are all alike. We think nothing of heavy work. Ramu can carry the sacks on his head.'

These conversations would go on for whole mornings, both content and happy in the knowledge that one was enduring company for the other.

Such was the magic the Big House weaved around those who came in contact with it. It held a thousand secrets and was a witness to innumerable incidents, some good some bad. And without doubt a lot of happiness and contentment.

The doyens of the Big House

The Old Faithful

Appupen was a quaint piece of work. A work of art, nevertheless. The first impression I got when I came across Appupen was that God was in a hurry when He made the blueprint. But on closer examination, I began to marvel at the creation. This was no product made in a hurry or from the regular mould. This was a unique piece. A lot of time and effort had been put into designing this person. How else could anyone account for his strange look? Each bit of him must have been painstakingly mulled over, created, and recreated to get that particular type of perfection. He was not made to be handsome in the regular sense of the word, nor was he made to look ugly. He was not kind-looking or mean-looking either. He did not appear intelligent, and he was a far cry from looking totally stupid. He was definitely not brave-looking, but I would not say he was timid-looking either. Maybe a little macabre, but there was a pathos in his eyes. He was a blend of everything and yet nothing. You might like his face or hate it, but you could never be indifferent to it.

So, there was no doubt about the fact that once I had met Appupen, there was no way I would forget him. It was as if I had seen the Mona Lisa or something equally exquisite – a 'once in a lifetime experience.' It became a face I would trust and cherish forever. If the Mona Lisa was exquisite because of the essence of her mysterious smile, then it would be appropriate to conclude that Appupen was exquisite simply because there could never be another one like him. In any case, anyone could fake a Mona Lisa, as I have seen a thousand reproduced posters and pictures. But there can only be one original in Appupen's case, as none can ever fake his image or reproduce the finer details to perfection or imperfection, if I'm to be pedantic.

Physically, he was a small, withered bit of a man, no taller than five feet. Probably less. Definitely less. Though he was not a dwarf in the real sense of the word, he gave the impression of being one. I wondered if his lack of height could be due to the fact that his body was twisted to the left. His neck though, along with his windpipe and face, were twisted to the right. This forced him to hunch over, and the overall effect was that he appeared to be constantly looking over his right shoulder. This put undue strain on him and made his deep-set eyes bulge out when he attempted to speak, and the general look more grotesque. Sometimes, for no reason, he would start an uncontrollable jerk in his head and shoulders, and in this posture, should he try to speak, the sound came out as a broken, hoarse whisper, and since there would be tremendous difficulty in getting the words out, more often than not, he left sentences incomplete. To anyone meeting Appupen for the first time, it would appear that he was under a lot of stress and was making an effort to straighten himself from this awkward posture. But in reality, he was very comfortable and hardly realized his stance. I sometimes thought he would just crumble down from all the effort.

He could have been anywhere between thirty-five and sixty-five years of age, but that made no difference to his countenance. To begin with, he had a head that was egg-shaped or 'ovalish.' The narrow part of the egg formed the top of the head, while the broader part formed the face. Appupen's eyes were deep-set and shifty. They had a sad look, as if they were searching for someone but had never quite found them. Yet, they were kindly eyes, even bashful at times. Not penetrating or accusing or insolent. Most often, his eyes did the talking. He would just look at me if I asked him anything, and amazingly, his eyes always conveyed a satisfying answer. Once, Appupen had seen a doctor to rid himself of a nagging cough; the doctor told him that he had a twisted windpipe, which is what made talking difficult. He had a big, bulbous nose that sat on a large part of his face. Whenever he endeavoured to speak, stammering laboriously on each word, his huge nostrils would quiver and open and close so comically that those listening to him hardly ever heard a word; instead, they shook in bouts of laughter. This was a very cruel thing to do, and it hurt Appupen deeply, but no one seemed to care. He wore a scanty moustache above thick rubbery lips, which were forever left open as if in a state of wonder. In all, as I said, he was a unique piece of work.

No one knew for sure if Appupen was born with this deformity or if he had acquired it. There were two schools of debate on this, for Appupen was always discussed in detail whenever he passed by the village crowd to run some errands for Grandmother. One school maintained that he was born normal, albeit ugly. It was alleged that his insolence had been his downfall. He was acrimonious in his dealings with the village folks too. A pernicious combination! He would dare the Devil if he could and had no sentiment for anyone's feelings. Being a bitter, hard fellow, he would pick a fight wherever and whenever he could. It was alleged that he was once involved in a fight with five fellows from the neighbouring village over something as trifle as the cost of a hen. However, the number and the size of the fellows were to Appupen's disadvantage, and for once, he was at the receiving end. They broke his body and his spirit, and since then, Appupen was a changed man.

The other school took a more tortuous route and never came to a conclusion. They assumed that Appupen had indeed been born normal, pleasant-looking even. He remained so till about seventeen. Then, he had the misfortune to fall in love, and everyone knows that the path of love is always strewn with difficulties. Even more so in the case of Appupen. He fell in love with Kunjali the moment he set his eyes upon her. Kunjali was all of fifteen years and lived with Ritama, a spinster of very doubtful reputation. Ritama had a vicious tongue that she was not afraid to use. And use it freely and frequently, she did. Ritama claimed to all and sundry that she had found Kunjali as an abandoned baby many years ago. But it was an open secret in the village that she had borne the child herself from her nefarious dealings with the numerous notorious miscreants with whom she kept company and walked with on the wild and darker side of life. Who would dare argue with Ritama? It was also said, sotto voce, that she knew a bit of witchcraft and voodoo and even practiced black magic. No one knew the truth of all this, and Ritama seemed to encourage the talk for it gave her an aura of darkness and mystic, however misplaced. She even willingly added spice to these morbid rumours by threatening those who displeased her with dire consequences and evil spells.

Anyway, when Appupen fell in love with Kunjali and the girl seemed to reciprocate, Ritama felt threatened. She realized that she was going to lose an unpaid servant and her only companion. And most of all, Ritama was saving Kunjali to be introduced to the village elite so she could generate a significant income form the young girl's services. No one ever visited Ritama, and she preferred it that way, for then, her secrets remained secrets. Ritama warned Appupen repeatedly with a volley of threats and curses to leave the girl alone. But the more vociferous Ritama's curses became, the more adamant was the young lover to win his lady. Until one day, goaded by Ritama's never-ending bitching, Appupen dared to walk up to the old witch's door and ask for the girl. This so incensed the cantankerous hypothetical necromancer that she supposedly sprinkled some magic powder and uttered the ultimate magic formula. Everyone in the village remembered that Appupen lay at death's door for two weeks after this incident. And when he returned to the village after his tribulation, he looked grotesque and old. He had lost his bravado. His eyes were shifty, his skin weather-beaten, and his voice a croak. And of course, he had acquired the frightful dwarfish posture.

No one seemed to know when Appupen came to work at the Big House, for he seemed to have been there for ever. And Grandmother always began one of her innumerable stories with, 'Appupen, do you remember...' which put him with the very beginning of time. Nor did anyone have an idea from where he came. It was as if he was just there. Moreover, who on earth would hire such a strange-looking fellow to work as a domestic? Grandmother was that way with lame-dogs and lost souls, and perhaps that was why she accepted Appupen the way he was when he drifted to the Big House. Her large, kind heart never saw his abysmal looks but rather saw his need to be accepted, and that was what she did.

However much Appupen stared into a cracked mirror he hung by his table, he had to accept the fact that he was bald except for the tuft of hair making a circular border around the back of his head. Still, he was proud of what little hair he had and wore it like a crowning glory. He even grew it to well below his shoulders and combed and cared for it better than any woman would. There were sprinkles of grey in between, which he vainly tried to hide. On two occasions, I caught him trying to manipulate the scanty tuft into a hairstyle that would hide some part of his baldness. He must have thought through this scheme thoroughly before executing it, for the idea in itself was not bad. It was creditable, but the snag was that the amount of hair available for this 'hairdo' was too little to make a success of it. Painstakingly, Appupen would oil his hair and then comb all of it forwards (as opposed to letting it hang limply down his shoulders) and plaster it over the baldness. The ends formed a sort of fringe on his forehead. To say he looked preposterous was putting it mildly. Still, none of us ridiculed him or made any unwanted grimaces for fear of hurting him. Perhaps he wanted an opinion from me, for he would stand around long after I'd told him about some chore Grandmother wanted done. When he saw that I was not forthcoming, he would ask to see her. Grandmother shared a special rapport with Appupen and humoured him no end. She would spot the new style as soon as she came out. She'd pretend to look about and asked me where Appupen was. I thought Grandmother had taken leave of her senses, what with Appupen standing smack in her face. But this was one of her many games, and she was having a joke at Appupen's expense. Appupen, being the gullible soul that he was, would then let out his usual breathless guffaw and declare himself, whereupon Grandmother would pretend to inspect the person before her. She would then act amazed and question if indeed the handsome fellow before her was Appupen. I do not know if this fooled the fellow, but he was always pleased, though sheepish, at such compliments. Perhaps he knowingly let himself be fooled because in his world, compliments were a rarity, and he was hungry for a word of appreciation. Or he was an old fool who considered the compliments genuine.

However, this hairstyle fad of which I spoke earlier did not last long because whenever Appupen wore this style and ran his usual errands in the village, the wind would play havoc and blow his hair back from his forehead and have it standing up on ends. While this made him look taller, the overall effect was appalling. It had all the village boys running after the old man, teasing him and calling out 'Appupen motta thala, Appupen motta thala,' (bald-headed Appupen) in a singsong chorus, and no matter how hard the old man tried to chase them away, with curses or rebuffs or rebukes, they kept doggedly after him with their song. It was all that Appupen could do to keep the tears away.

Yet, when I watched Grandmother closely as she complimented Appupen, it was without malice and with such sincerity that I asked her about it. She told me that sometimes, we have to look beyond the external beauty. 'To be able to see the inner beauty, characterized by integrity, loyalty, kindness, and simplicity, you have to look beyond the person. Then,' she added, 'you will see the beauty that I see in Appupen.'

Appupen slept in the shed by the barn. It was a nice, warm place, and he kept it clean and neat. He did not have a lot of worldly possessions, though

I saw that what little he had was dear to his heart. There was a bed with a mat in one corner, and under this bed was an old rusty tin trunk in which he kept all his precious things. A big padlock hung from this box. By the side of the bed was a table and a chair. On the table was a wooden crucifix that he had crafted with his own hands using his precious penknife. An old, worn-out bible was neatly placed next to it. One good point, which had probably won over Grandmother in the first place, was that he was a devout Christian and a regular churchgoer. If ever there was a Sunday morning, Appupen would dress in his best clothes and make the journey to church. Neither hell nor high water kept him from his weekly Sunday mass. He always wore his blue oversized shirt, washed, starched, and ironed with meticulous care, a crisp white 'mundu,' and a 'kavini' or shawl on his left shoulder. He wore no slippers. He carried the old worn-out bible, which I doubted he could read due to weak eyesight and illiteracy. Still, anyone could see the Holy Book was a great source of comfort and confidence to him. Every night, he would open the Good Book and sit by the candlelight and look at the pages. I always asked Grandmother why he stared at the Bible if he could not read it. She would smile and tell me that we need not read for God to know what was in our hearts.

Once in a while, as if to break the monotony of living, Appupen would get offended by something of the least consequence, said or done by any one of us at the Big House. This was a strange thing because he would overlook bigger slights and insults, yet get hurt at the least expected of things. At such times, he would go missing for two or three days but would turn up without fail before Sunday, because he was not one to miss church. It was a rule that when he turned up, he would offer no explanations, and Grandmother would ask for none. It was as if he had just gone to the village to buy a packet of sugar.

Though Appupen helped with odd jobs in the kitchen and drew water from the well nearby, he was mainly responsible for looking after the cows. He knew them by name and spoke to them as one would to a friend. He bathed them and took them out to pasture. They knew the sound of his steps and mooed in sadness whenever he neglected them or delayed their meals. There was an enviable intimacy between man and beast that could not be lost on anyone watching them. Sometimes, when Grandmother needed a nap and a respite from my chatter, Appupen took me along when he drove the herd to the fields. He would let me use the stick that he kept to guide them the right way. Intermittently, he would call out 'Pai, Pai' (slang for cow) and I would imitate in kind. Usually, on reaching the grazing grounds, I would sit some distance away and watch the cows, while Appupen would hunch over and start collecting fresh grass to feed them at night. He pulled them by the roots with his bare hands, all the while telling me that fresh grass brought more milk than dry hay ever would. Whenever we were together, he would go into an incomprehensible rhetoric on each of the cows, and when he told his stories, he would stammer with gay abandon and hardly cared.

'It was one June monsoon night, when three of the mud ridges in Cheriachen's paddy fields broke down due to the torrential rains, that Kunjumol was born,' Appupen would say. 'Everyone ran to mend the ridges, but I never left Ammu's side. And a good thing too, for it was a difficult labour and a miracle that Kunjumol was born unharmed. And Kutty, the big brown beauty that gives about 6 litres of milk? Her pain, when she had a broken leg, was devastating. But I nursed her back to health with devoted care.' And he would pause a moment to look at the cows grazing together peacefully. Then his eyes would fall on Kochupennu, a young black heifer with one big spot of white on her forehead. Her ears were pierced and she had rings in them, and around her neck, she wore a chain that looped four bells so that she made music wherever she went. Appupen had bought these ornaments especially with Kochupennu in mind. I think she knew that she was a beauty and that Appupen had a special place in his heart for her because every time she spotted him, she would moo out a call. Appupen would let out his hoarse laugh and shake his finger at her and tell her it was time she paid a visit to the neighbour's place and met with 'Kittu,' a handsome virile bull known for his sexual prowess and a fit mate for the lovely black heifer.

Though I remember Appupen for a lot of things, I remember him most for saving my life. As usual, I had followed him to the fields that day. He had collected baskets of grass for the night and was busy picking up firewood. On an impulse, I gathered a fistful of the grass and walked towards Kochupennu and held it out to her. She came to me and started eating out of my hand. For a while, we stood like that, enjoying each other. Then, out of the corner of my eye, I saw something moving fast and furiously towards me. It was that big burly bull, Kittu, from our neighbour's field. He had broken free from his tether, jumped across the small canal that separated their land from ours, and was charging straight on at full speed. I was numb with fear and stood rooted to the ground. Maybe Kittu had got tired of Kochupennu's teasing and was coming for her in a big way. Whatever it was, the ground shook beneath his advancing hoofs, and he looked so frightful and menacing that I swooned. Appupen gave a shout of horror, dropped the firewood, and scrambled his way towards me. Every step was an effort because of his deformity, but nothing held him back. He came to me in the nick of time and half carried, half dragged me to safety. But not before he was gored, right across his back, both horns making deep, open wounds. By then, there were shouts from all over, and people rushed up to take control of Kittu.

Appupen lost a lot of blood and was in the hospital for a long time. He was unconscious for two days and had twenty-one stitches put on one wound and twenty-five on the other. A total of forty-six stitches. It was enough to make him a hero in the village. He had risen to the occasion and acted like a warrior! He even became the envy of the macho men in the village. The young boys who used to tease him now asked to be shown the scars on his back, proof that he was valiant. And Appupen, who wore the scars on his back like a king wore his crown, was ever obliging and even allowed the boys to run their fingers on it. Often, when the fancy took him, he would recount the events of that horrible afternoon when he acted without thought for his safety or his life. As usual, he would stammer and stumble through the sentences, but no one sniggered or laughed. They saw the goodness and the bravery of the man. I am always filled with awe and gratitude when I think of the courageous and selfless heart that beat inside the twisted and deformed body. Here was a man who was ready to offer the ultimate sacrifice to save another life. Few men would have been that gracious or magnanimous.

I then understood what Grandmother meant by 'a beauty that surpasses the conventional kind.'

FACE TO FACE WITH THE BOYS

The Malayalification of Moi

Things were not going as Father predicted. While in Malaya, I was an Indian-Malay-Anglo combo. You could even throw in a bit of Chinese. It was an ambiguous mix, to say the least. Father had actually sent me to India to sort this out. Instead, I turned out to be totally Anglicized. I'm not saying this as an accomplishment but more as an eventuality to the circumstances I was exposed to. Bangalore was more English than England at that time, I think. More is the pity, since it hampered Father's plan. And as if to add fuel to the fire, the Beatles took the world by storm. Elvis and Cliff took a back seat. The girls at school went crazy, and I with them. I cut my hair, knowing it could kill Mother. My hair, being curly, did not quite resemble a Beatle cut, but that didn't matter. The important thing was getting into the spirit of Beatlemania. We sang *Hard day's night* and *I wanna hold your hand.*' But my all-time favourite secretly remained Elvis and *Jail house rock,*' and the two were etched deep into my heart forever.

School went on as expected, boring us to death. Piano lessons were frightening on account of Mrs. Fewkes always being one step ahead of us. The boarding though, was a riot, even if Matron was a killjoy. We went to the Methodist Church and did everything but pray during Sunday services. Life was great. Towards the end of term, a slow, pulsating excitement would begin somewhere in the pits of our stomachs and reach a crescendo with the coming of our trunks into the dormitory. The happiness of going home for the holidays became a reality. Tickets were booked, trunks were packed, and goodbyes were said. The Kerala Batch, the Bombay Batch, the Delhi Batch, and the Madras Batch were the four main batches that left at respective times for their destinations. We'd leave the school in uniforms, so we would stand apart from the general crowd and so that Matron could keep an eye on us. But once the train moved and Matron became a blur, we'd jump up and shriek as we threw off our restricting uniforms and got into our summer dresses. It was, of course, the rule that we were to reach home in our uniforms and to maintain perfect decorum so as not to disgrace school and uniform. Who made these silly rules anyway, and for what? And in any case, we thought the greatest rule of all was that rules were made to be broken.

'Shirt, skirt, blazer and tie.

Shoes and socks, and don't ask why.' Courtesy Matron Ray. Meh!

The journey was fun. And guess what? The Baldwin boys were in the adjoining compartment. We were all young, carefree, and looking for an adventure, at the threshold of embarking into young love – any type of love. The shenanigans that followed are best left to the imagination of the reader.

Holidays were a very jarring experience. I was already an amalgamate of three different cultures. Coming to my roots in rural Thiruvella in the early sixties really threw me. I was a misfit from the get-go. No one understood me, and I understood no one. But I was too naive to protest. Besides, Grandmother adored me and shielded me from the negative forces, so I did not care or complain. I had a sneaky feeling the aunts found me too forward and headstrong and reported this to Father. But Father, of course, was wound tightly around my little finger. All I had to do was say 'Apacha' (Father) in a faux British accent, and that was that. Once, the aunties asked me why I took French as a second language, and in a bid to shock them, I replied that it was in order to marry a Frenchman. I watched the righteous aunts turn pale at my answer. I'm sure they saw me as a danger to their good little daughters, and they would have concluded that I was really wicked if I should harbour such thoughts as marriage at so young an age. Who knows what else I thought about? To think of marriage, let alone speak of it, made them think I had a worldliness well beyond my age. The sanctimonious aunts discussed the incident with Grandmother and were incensed beyond belief when she just smiled at me indulgently and didn't rise to the bait. I was the child of her precious firstborn son. I knew I could get away with anything, even murder. During the long summer vacations, I visited the parents in Malaysia, and I think Father was appalled at my slow but gradual transformation into something so alien from the good Malayalee girl he had in mind. I was no better at the language; I did not conform to the dressing chic; and the short curly hair styled à la Beatle was a far cry from the long, luxurious black hair of the average Malayalee lass. Cutting the hair was the straw and it mortified Mother to such an extent she could not speak for a few days. So, it was left to Father who took a firm decision. I was to be moved to a school in Kerala before any lasting damage could be done to Moi.

Thus, I found myself at St. Roch's Convent, Trivandrum, in the middle of my ninth school year. I was very wary of the whole situation, but since no one was asking me what I wanted, I made the best of my predicament. It was run strictly by Belgian nuns, and as they were good to me, it was easy for me to be on my best behaviour. The boarders were also not a wild bunch like at Baldwins, and as there were no distractions in the form of boys or Sunday church, I excelled academically. And the nuns were tight – Sr. Francine and Sr. Britto brooked no nonsense and no hanky-panky. But much to my horror and bewilderment, here, I encountered a different sort of 'phenomenon,' for want of a better word.

There was this girl in my class. She was from a very affluent family and was beautiful. I actually wanted to befriend her. But much to my amazement, she refused to talk to me, look at me, or even give me the time of day. I wondered how I had offended her. Much later, I was told that it was on account of her intense love and adoration for me that she refused to talk to me. What the heck was that? It was explained to Moi that I was her 'piri' (or was she my piri?). I was dumfounded and totally bamboozled until it dawned on me that she felt a zing where I was concerned, much like the zing I had felt for Shawkat Ali so many years ago. For the life of me, I could not figure out how to handle it. Nor could I reciprocate.

On graduating from High School, I enrolled at Mar Ivanios College, a co-educational institution. My intention was to finally face up to my challenges. First, I joined the second group with an idea to pursue medicine – not that I wanted to, but the parents decided for me. Theatre was more my thing, but who was listening to me? The second and more crucial reason was to settle a matter that needed attention and caused grave concern to Moi. In spite of all my bravado, I had never been up close and personal with any of the boys. I had just watched them from afar. So, I hadn't a clue as to what manner of behaviour one should adopt if one came face to face with one of the species. This second, more pressing issue needed careful analysis and execution.

Until then, I had worn only dresses or skirts. I also had this trick of folding the waist band of the skirt so that it stayed above the knee. Sacrilege!!! No girl worth her salt exposed her legs in college in Kerala. They had to be covered. So, the dilemma my aunts faced concerning my attire to college was serious to all but me. They wanted me to be dressed like a puritan, what with the boys and all. Again, no one thought to ask me. I was rather large-framed and well-muscled (read that as fat. I'm just being kind to myself), and so it was decided that long skirts and blouses were out of the question. A salwar kameez set I had was ruled out, probably because it had not yet been introduced here in God's own country in the sixties, and I would look like an oddity. The aunts were scandalised at the thought of my gyrating in a co-ed college dressed like they do in the Hindi movies, though I doubt they had ever seen one. My teenage mind just could not comprehend their anxiety, and I didn't know why they made a mountain out of a molehill. Finally, they settled on the sari, which was six yards of material that I was going to wrap around Moi without having a clue how to go about it. Tenacious as the aunts were, they went all out teaching me how to wear it. I never found out what it was that they had against me or why they were so vindictive where I was concerned that they would burden me with and bury me in six yards of material. Probably, it was the Indo-French alliance that I was working on that they resented. Whatever it was, they derived some sort of Machiavellian glee at my discomfort. And I'll tell you this, I looked huge and stupid, what with a whole lot of pleats tucked into my skirt, giving me a big potbelly. Another irritating thing was that the pleats, tucked into the skirt, were so long that they dangled between my legs up to the knees. So, in a moment of enlightenment I tucked the freaking lot of pleats into my under wear. That really got my knickers in a twist. I think I'll leave it at that. The whole thing was a farce, and I, an unwitting victim. Even today, I sweat all over and especially between the legs when I recall those days of torture.

The last, but not the least in my list of misfortunes, was that I had made friends with this wee petite girl with whom I walked to the college that first day. The hoots and howls were like none I'd ever heard before or ever since, except maybe when I walked to the 'Pit' at Baldwins. It felt like I had been cocooned thus far in life and then thrown to the wolves. *Welcome to being a proper Malayalee girl,* I thought, with a bit of sadness and a whole lot of fear. You would think there was nothing more that could go wrong. Well, think again. The college was situated on a small hilltop. There were two ways of entry. The first was a long, winding road used by the college bus, private cars, and motorcycles. The other means of entry was a narrow pathway made up of steps, about seventy-two or more. It was a daunting task, navigating them, with the boys ever so willing to push and shove as you did your breathless best to reach the top. I would drag myself and the sari up all those steps, and on reaching the top, I'd have always stepped on the pleats and they'd have come off the skirt and would be trailing behind. You can conjure up the rest of the scenario. By lunch, I was the most infamous girl in college and the talk of the campus. The boys took to calling me 'maidanum' (playing field), but it did not hurt since I did not have a clue what that meant. Much later, I found out I had to thank my trapezius muscles, which formed my broad shoulders, for this moniker.

The French classes were the best. Thirty-six boys and one girl, Moi. I thought that without any competition, I finally stood a chance of snagging a fellow. But the idea turned out to be a big disappointment, for there I was in my hideous sari and Beatles' hairstyle and hardly able to converse, since almost all the boys spoke in Malayalam. I was at a college where no one had the foggiest idea who John, Paul, George, or Ringo were or that my hair was a Beatle style. The saving grace was that I thought the boys looked scrawny and ugly and did not hold a candle to the chaps at Baldwins. I soon had a volley of monikers in French, none of them complimentary. But I was made of sterner stuff, and thought, *To hell with it all. I'll remain Moi till the day I die.*

A Catholic priest, Fr. Puthusherry, taught us French. He was adamant that we should only parlay in the language during class. It was hilarious, with the boys incorporating Malayalam words when they were at a loss for the French equivalent. Once day, during class, a helicopter hovered rather low by the window, creating havoc. The boys clamoured to the window, with some of them climbing and hanging onto the bars and waving frantically. The Priest kept shouting, 'arrête ça' (stop it) till he was blue in the face, but no one listened to him. Then he changed his command and shouted out, 'asseyez vous' (sit down), but again, no one gave a damn. In all probability no one understood him. Finally, he bellowed in Malayalam, 'Iriyada thandekile! Ninda oka thandhe paranjyal madhi' (Sit down, you rascals! Your damn parents are to blame for this). The response was magical. Shell-shocked, the boys just gaped at him, then silently went to their seats.

Ah ha! I thought, as I quickly scribbled down those magical words in my note book. There! The next time someone yells 'maidanum,' I knew just how to retort. That week, I wrote to Father and mentioned how I was picking up some Malayalam. It was no lie either. Well then, my dears, with that I guess I had arrived.

The Truth About Tooth

Two years in Mar Ivanios, due to all the limitations imposed by the nuns in the hostel, seemed like an eternity. I was trapped in a place that was least congenial to my way of thinking and behaviour. It drained the joie de vivre out of Moi. Of course, I told the parents that I was fine and thriving. It was rather ironic that when I finally had the boys at arm's length, I found them most unattractive in behaviour and looks. Agreed, I'm no great looker myself, but heck, I don't mind having a few good ones around to admire and pass the time of day. What else was a person to do, but study? That was the intention of joining this circus in the first place, wasn't it? So, I did it with gusto and with a vengeance.

Now, the hostel I stayed in during this time was run by Roman Catholic nuns belonging to some strict order. They were a different kettle of fish altogether. While we had had a cosmopolitan bunch of nuns at St. Roch's, courtesy of the European nuns, the bunch at M.T. Hostel where I was put up were hardcore Malayalees with a bridled outlook on life. They were angry with themselves with each other and with the rest of the world. Need I say more? They were a seriously empty (M.T.) bunch. See the pun? They walked around sanctimoniously with pious faces, hiding their malicious and vindictive hearts beneath their nun's habit. If I said they were brazenly spiteful, malicious, and bitter, no one would raise an eyebrow. It was as if those traits were part of their religious vows. They had this strange, dogged aversion to any part of a woman's body, particularly the breasts and umbilicus. Even the outline or shape of a breast under the dress would send the pious nuns into an epileptic fit. Why, even a bit of undergarment, like the strap of a brassiere on display, made them froth with rabid madness. And exposing the umbilicus, that bit which used to be the lifeline between mother and child, 'would get you a reservation in purgatory,' they preached. It was the ultimate sin if anyone, and by that, they mean the boys in college, caught a glimpse of either of these items. Oh! The umpteen sermons we have had, of said parts. I'd take the fires of hell any day to their monotonous, sanctimonious monologue. Sometimes, I feared it would induce a mass suicide in the hostel. I just concluded that they were perverts who got satisfaction from talking about a women's private parts and lacked diversion. Probably, no one had loved them or wanted to marry them, so they joined the convent. That was my final diagnosis.

Two years passed without any serious glitch – except, of course, for the hooting, howling, and snide remarks in the college proper, tiptoeing around the nuns, and hiding one's umbilicus in the hostel, everything else was routine. The final exams came and went. Once they were done and dusted, I packed my bags, bid farewell to all, and went home to the parents in Malaysia for some much-needed reprieve from trying to be a Malayalee girl.

During that break, I did a typewriting course, procured my driving license, and joined a traditional Malay dance class, specifically, the 'joget' dance.' I thought I would meet some boys, that sort of thing, but where's my luck? If I had to rectify the situation, I had to shed a few pounds I thought, and in order to do so, I decided to diet. I also took up bike riding with Father. My main purpose was the slimming down of my trapezius in a bid to look more feminine. But diet was an uphill task because I was so weak and vulnerable at the sight of mee goreng, ayam percik, or rendang. And satay? Let's not even go there. I only had to think of food to gain a few pounds. Father, of course, was of no help because this was one area where he was weaker than all of us put together. The end result was that in spite of all my efforts to erase the 'maidanum' moniker, I fear I only increased it to 'vishala maidanum'(broad playfield). Some people are just that way, I decided – born unlucky. I also contemplated a lot on what made me attractive to the same sex and not to the opposite. Was I mannish? That 'piri' incident at school had unnerved me, and the boys in college barely noticed me, probably because they saw me as competition. What a ghastly notion. There were several other culprits to add to my muscular framework. Oh! Didn't I mention it? My squint, the left eye, and of course, the constant reminder to put on some powder in a bid to look fair. A good, unbiased look at the mirror told me my moustache was also looking very promising, and my biceps were certainly well-developed and something to be proud of. But sadly, the more I tried, the more I failed. Mostly, I was not to know that my fight was against the onslaught of puberty and the hormones that surged into my system with a vengeance, causing all the unwanted hair growth, body odour, and acne. I was so dejected that in the end, I threw in the towel and decided to let myself be. There were too many issues to address, and I knew they were some pretty serious issues, too. The good thing was that I never cared enough or stayed depressed long enough. I was too busy living.

Then, the exam results were out, and I had excelled. Personally, like I said, I wanted to join the theatre. Who knew, I could have been another Ratna Pathak or Dolly Thakore. Hell, they would have tried to be another Moi. But Mother reminded me sternly that we were a family of teachers. We could be teachers or break away and become doctors. That was that. I was accepted at the Dental School. Encouraged by my dentist in Malaysia, who seemed to enjoy putting the fear of God into his patients, I joined up ecstatically to a whole new world of problems and experiences. I was on the way to terrorising some innocent souls. Nothing seemed more enjoyable. I was discovering myself and that I had a malicious streak in Moi. A bit of schadenfreude on the side but a lot of kindness too. I was pleased. I liked me.

I had never thought about Mother as an attractive woman before then. I just thought she looked better than most other mothers I had met. In fact, I was actually proud of her genteel manner and soft voice. But I was perplexed and even a little peeved at an incident that occurred at the medical examination, which was mandatory before enrolling at the Dental School. Mother had accompanied me for the medical check because we had heard that new students were always bullied by seniors during this time. As we waited our turn, a group of mean-looking older fellows (heavily moustached cowboy types) who were loitering nearby sauntered up to us. One had this old, torn, ragged coat casually flung over his shoulder. The other two wore their coats of equal description unbuttoned, letting them flap like the wings of an albatross. Note that during my period of reprieve with the parents in Malaysia, I had taken to reading Westerns, and Rawhide was my favourite TV show. Clint Eastwood made me go Westward and zing like no tomorrow. So, it was only natural that I graded men on a scale of ten in comparison to Clint Eastwood at ten. Coming back to the medical checkup incident, these seniors, whom I graded at 3, 4, and 4.5, respectively, sniffed out that I was a fresher and approached me like a cat would a mouse.

They enquired if the lady sitting on the bench a little away was my mother. I nodded, as my mouth was too dry to speak. I think I saw an evil grin begin on their lips. They bent down and whispered in my ear, 'In that case, you had better go home and leave her here to study.' It took me a while to understand the implications of the insult.

And thus, the ragging began. And boy! Was I the perfect prey. Sacré bleu! I was more than perfect. I was there, just begging to be ragged. Big-built, cockeyed, defiant, not in conformity with the general crowd, somehow an oddity at every turn. However, I think between the raggers and Moi, they got the raw deal, but not because I was brave. The reason I remained uncaring and unabashed and that no amount of insult fazed me was that whatever they said flew right over my head. Yet, they were persistent in their torment, hoping to wear me down some time or the other. But Christ on a bicycle! It amused me to think that as time passed, I began to enjoy these skirmishes and even kept a look out for my tormentors, missing them if they did not turn up. My friends thought I was becoming a looney tune. I also did the next best thing – I kept a smile on my face, which only infuriated and provoked them further. I was such an alien, and they needed to break me, or else they feared they would lose respect. The word spread. The thing with these chaps were that they hunted in packs, looking for the lone victim. But sometimes, even more dangerous than the pack was the lone hunter with a threatening purpose. But this I say with sadness – even more unbelievable was that some of the hunters were in our ladies' hostel, which was supposed to be our shelter and refuge.

The Dental School per se was not that bad. Of the thirty students in a batch, fifteen were Central Govt. selection. So, we were a mixed bunch, and as a result, some amount of civility was automatically incorporated into our general behaviour. There were others like me, who were not completely local bred and therefore had peculiarities and behavioural patterns that were alien to the general bunch of students. Have you ever noticed that it's the little things that make the biggest sound? While I was with the parents, I had gotten my hair cut into a pixie hairstyle, or something to that effect, much to Mother's horror. Now, at the college, I found out that the lady students were expected to put up their hair in a bun. My new friends told me that my short hair could cause a controversy and I might appear defiant or arrogant. Short hair was not befitting a Malayalee girl. In a serious bid to help me, they tied up my hair with a rubber band and fixed a false bun that we acquired from the Ladies Store, a shop in Statue, at the heart of Trivandrum. The whole thing looked like the backside of a hen, much to my dismay. But I did not want to appear churlish, so I went along with it. I had yet to purchase my distinct white doctor's coat, that which would set me apart from the common person and make me noble, reverent, and relevant. As the college store was closed, I could not get my coat on time.

My guardian was a senior professor in the Oral Pathology Dept. She was also a cousin of Father's. She reassured Mother that she would resolve the coat issue as well as see to all my other needs. Reassured thus, Mother returned to Malaysia. So, when my guardian saw my predicament concerning the coat, she offered me her coat instead. And that was the first of the many muddy puddles that I would put my foot into. How was I to know that a fresher's coat was to be bright-white, unused, tight, and short? Stitched so as not to fit a person decently. An ugly, awkward coat, probably stitched by a tailor who was hand-in-glove with the senior students to make the unsuspecting fresher look gawky and ludicrous. Now, the coat my guardian offered was her own coat – old, worn out, torn, and knee length. No buttons, so it was left open to flap about. This was her 'coat of arms' in a manner of speaking, that I had usurped. Distinctive. A professor's coat. Earned through years of toil and struggle. When she gave me her coat and told me to use it, I did so. I like to believe she did not know she was offering me as sacrifice at the highest altar. Now, this here, this impersonation of a professor by way of wearing an old, beaten-down, buttonless, torn coat, was blasphemous. It was taboo. There was no previous case of such an incident, of such arrogance in the history of the Medical College. I was the first to do it.

I walked into my class, heavy set, coat flapping, odd-looking hairdo. Totally inappropriate. The students jumped to their feet and stood respectfully. It took me a moment to realise that they thought I was the lecturer. When I got over the shock and went to sit with them, they, in turn, were shocked out of their eye sockets and gaped at me with suspicion. I have never understood who was more shocked. Moi or them. After this incident, even the pseudo polite seniors at the Dental School felt an unnecessary need to rag me whenever I crossed their paths. The die was cast for the rest of the year. But it said something about me too though I could not put my finger on it. For it was an irrefutable fact that I too enjoyed this sadistic ritual, this aggression, and even began to look forward to it. Had they known this fact, I'm sure the seniors would have stopped the harassment, for what joy was there to be derived in harassing a person who enjoyed it? That was an absolute anomaly. Did they not realize it is not wise to wrestle a pig in the mud, for the pig enjoyed it? Poor sods!

But then, as I mentioned earlier, a lone hunter on the prowl is a dangerous animal.

Getting professionally educated

Survival

'Kallu Mathai' was one such lone hunter marauding in the darkened corridors of the Medical College.

Before I go any further, allow me to digress, so as to give you an insight into these nicknames that were given to some people and by which they become better known than by their given names. In most instances, no one really knew the origin of these nicknames, and in some cases, they would have had it for so long that no one knew or cared what their real names were anyway. Rewind to Mar Ivanios for a second. If you asked any of the students who their Chemistry Professor was, the answer came with a broad grin, 'Whicheeecan'. Everyone was okay with that and had a good laugh and a lot of stories to share. That is, until someone asked what his real name was. No one had a clue. The reason for the moniker was an oft repeated story though. Every time the Professor taught us anything, say for example, the properties of Oxygen, he would go, 'Oxygen is a gas whicheeecan (which can) dissolve readily in water.' Or if it's about Carbon di oxide, he would go, 'Carbon dioxide is a colourless and non-inflammable gas whicheeecan occur in the Earth's atmosphere as a trace gas.' I don't know if I've got those facts right, but you get the drift, don't you? Once, I counted up to thirty-seven whicheeecan(s) in half an hour of a one-hour class. I lost count after that. If one was attributed a nickname, it stuck for life. There was no escaping it. Imagine someone saying, 'Hey remember that maidanum?' I shudder. I don't think anyone ever knew Whicheeecan's real name or cared.

Coming back to the Medical College, 'Kallu Mathai' was one such name. No one knew the fellow's real name – if it was on account of the enormous amount of toddy he consumed or if there was any other reason for it. Who dared to ask? Like I said earlier, he was a lone hunter. The corridors of the gynaecology wards, which finally opened up near the Ladies Hostel, were his hunting grounds. His lair was one of the smaller rooms on the side.

This route was a shortcut to the hostel and safe, so almost all the freshers took it. We would shuttle along in groups, hoping that Kallu Mathai was not lurking around.

All went well until the weekend I visited the local guardian. The bus was late, so it was past 6 pm when I entered the corridors of the gynaecology wards on my way to the hostel. Twilight! That time when it was neither day or night. The hours when the spirits roamed. My mouth was dry, and my heart was hammering. There was an eerie silence. Bram Stoker's *Dracula* was the last movie I had watched before I left home in Malaya to join the college. Christopher Lee and his blood-stained canines were never far from my dreams. I didn't know who scared me more – Kallu Mathai or Dracula. But my rational mind told me that while Dracula was in Transylvania, Kallu Mathai could be right around the bend. And sure enough, in the darkest corner of the corridor, though I saw no one, I could sense a presence. And then I made out the smouldering end of a cigarette. Terror gripped my heart as I saw a figure move out of the dark and into the fading light. I could now see the cigarette clearly, that it was lightly clasped between the fingers. I watched in horror as the smouldering light made an arch, as he slowing brought up the fag to his mouth and left it dangling between his lips. Then, with his free hands, he flipped the end of his mundu to fold it into half before advancing in my direction. My luck had not failed me (sarcasm here). I'd met my nemesis. *Heck*, I thought. *The heck!* The moment required a stronger cuss word, but sadly, that was the only four-letter word that came to my petrified mind. He approached like he was stalking a prey, eyes narrowed slightly to focus in the fading light, hunched over, ready to pounce. I was frightened, more from the stories about him than of the man himself. When he was about that close, he removed the cigarette dangling between his lips and said in a low growl, 'Angotta molay?' (Where to, child?). And in that split second, that God-given nano second, I let go of all the air I held trapped in my throat. *Molay!* I was so familiar with that endearment. Grandmother always called me that. So, I concluded that Kallu Mathai was okay. He was kind, he liked me. He called me 'molay', didn't he? The fear in me just ebbed away. A warm, fuzzy feeling enveloped me. I smiled at him. Instantly, he drew back, as if scorched by a fire, reminding me of the scene where Dracula saw the cross and faced sunlight. Kallu Mathai was shaken to the core – there was a fear in his eyes that bewildered Moi.

He was visibly rattled. These sorts thrived on the terror they instilled in others. I had unwittingly removed that one hold that he had on his victims. My smile had disarmed him, frightened him. What if word got out that he had not scared the heebee jeebees out of me but that I found him friendly and approachable? His reputation would be in tatters. His silence only encouraged me. So, politely, I told him of the delay in the bus service. In English, Amen to that! He backed away until he came up against the wall and could move no further, and was that panic I saw in his eyes? The cigarette dropped from his fingers, fell to the floor, and burnt out. He stared at me for a second more, then turned around, and, without a backward glance, scurried away down the corridors, leaving me relieved, albeit disappointed. I had wanted to prolong the encounter. I had wanted us to be friends. He had started it by calling me 'molay,' didn't he?

Back at the hostel, I told my friends about the happenstance and how he had called me 'molay' and that he was, in fact, a pleasant fellow. They looked incredulous for a moment, their eyes round like saucers, mouths open. Then, they burst out laughing till they cried or peed or both. They could not get over the fact that I had made a pass at Kallu Mathai and frightened him off. 'Annalum,' they cried in unison. 'Annalum!' (For real!). Once they stopped laughing, they sat me down and taught me the different types of 'molays' in Malayalam. I found out there was 'edi molay,' 'ponnu molay,' 'ka molay,' 'chee molay,' 'anda molay,' and a host of other molays. I was dumbfounded. The ignominy of wondering which category of molay I belonged to in Kallu Mathai's eyes was worth evaluating. God worked in mysterious ways, I realized. But to top it all, I had unwittingly gotten myself a boyfriend, as they started to tease me and pair me off with the most notorious chap on camps. They told me I should develop a taste for toddy and then fell over each other in rapturous glee.

The distance from the Dental School to the Anatomy Lab was a good half hour's walk. The campus was beautiful, with green fields and winding roads lined with Gulmohar trees. There was an open ground where the students played football and cricket during weekends. The only snag was that these long, lonely stretches were the ideal place for the seniors to pick their prey and rag them to pieces. Even though we walked in groups, they would single out the victim and tell the others to scram. By now, having faced the king, 'Kallu Mathai,' and having survived the ordeal, and lived to tell the tale, a rumour did the rounds that I was a tough nut to crack. More appalling was the gossip going around that we, Kallu Mathai and I, were in an understanding and were having a clandestine affair to boot. This was the worst thing that could happen to Moi and made me a target of many 'wanna-be minor ragger kings.' It became imperative that I be conquered. The breaking of Moi become a pet project with the lesser hunters. The thought process went something like this:

If they attacked and subdued me, it would be one up on K Mats, as I had decided to address him in my thoughts, now that we were friends of a kind. After all, we had history! I, on the other hand, thought that if K Mats tucked his tail between his legs on account of my compliance and smile, then that would be my counterattack strategy and weapon of choice when dealing with these mere underlings. So, whenever I was singled out anywhere and everywhere I went, I turned around and deployed my secret weapon – compliance served with a smile. It sent the boys rattling. I lay awake at night, marvelling at my combat technique and the 'compliance served with a smile' missile, with which I would destroy the enemy. I felt I was in a league with Alexander Flemming. Both of us had made our discoveries by accident.

Once, a group surrounded me and enquired why I had buttoned up my coat all the way down. That was what we freshers were expected to do. 'Oouredi button,' (Remove your buttons, girl) they demanded of me, using a rude form for "girl". *Ah good*, I thought. It was a hot, sweltering day, and I was sweating profusely. So, I promptly obeyed. I kept a genial countenance with a half-smile, and showed absolutely no fear. Hadn't I looked the 'king' in the face? They stood around, unsure how to proceed, since I had willingly unbuttoned the coat. Then, one chap shoved his Anatomy book at me. It was the second vol. Cunningham – Thorax and Abdomen. 'Thorakaddi page 54(?)' (Open to page 54, girl). I complied. 'Vaikkadi' (Read, girl). No points for guessing what was to be read – the mammary glands. So predictable that I pitied them, the idiots. I was really more buggered by the 'di' tag than by the diagrammatic representation of the breast. Meh! So, just to get back at them in whatever way I could, I started reading in crisp, proper English, just the way Miss Johnson (the principal at Baldwins) would do. I could mimic like a parrot, you see. After the reading, I looked up at their faces. It was hilarious, and I had to use inhuman force to stop myself from bursting into laughter. *Poor buffoons*, I thought. 'Vittoda! Sathanum rotiya,' someone called out (Let's all scoot. This thing is a Roti). And that was that. Now 'roti' literally means bread, but it was slang to describe someone not totally Malayalee, but rather a kind of a hybrid.

The ladies in the hostel were another force to reckon with. In fact, I think I feared the ladies more than the chaps. The hunting ground, in this case, was the mess hall. Yeh, I have missed quite a few meals, but I had no qualms about that. The food was nothing to write home about. It was the warden that shook my boat. She was a huge, busty, bossy lady. I steered clear of her, but the few times I had gotten up-close and personal with her, I got a bad vibe. Whenever she read me the riot act, I never heard a word she said because all of my attention was focused on two points. I just could not keep my eyes off of her breasts. They were so big and strapped up and looked ready to attack that I swear it was as dangerous as facing an AK-47. Whenever she had to prove a point, she would push her two points into your face. Armed with such artillery she would have no difficulty in strangling you with them. I had often wondered if I dared ask her how she got them to be so statuesque in the hope of improving my own two miserable butter buns. But I was chicken-livered, and I guess I lacked the nerve. For I feared that had I dared to ask, I'd quaver like a leaf while she fired a volley of abuse in thick 'Trivandrum slang' Malayalam. And poor me, I would be struggling to keep my eyes off her assets while wondering where she got her brassieres from. That Morning Store in Palayam? They sold everything under the sun, including large knickers. It was hard not to snigger. Each of us have our different modus operandi for survival. Mine was letting my imagination run wild in any desperate situation. Think me a pervert, but I swear to God, I wasted a lot of time studying the matron and her wondrous assets.

I also think she was of dubious character, because quite a number of gentlemen friends called on her. In the hostel, she had her favourites, usually the seniors. The rest of the girls, she bullied. Us freshers, she ignored. She ruled the mess hall like it was her personal territory and she, the lieutenant colonel. If nothing else, she had the build for it. She would warn us to stick to our quota of food. I sniggered at that. Was she really talking to me, a boarding-school veteran who had survived Matron Ray and Mrs. Goretty, two of the best battle-axes one could ever come across in one lifetime? Anyway, I never gave a tuppence to whatever she said – I used to help myself to a few extra pieces of ettakappams (fried bananas) from right under her nose (we were only allowed 2), and she was none the wiser. But I was never selfish and always shared the booty with my friends. But then, show me a boarder or a hosteler who never took extra food on the sly, and I'll show you a dead goose.

Love was a big deal at the Medical/Dental College. Everyone was either in love, out of love, dying for love, waiting for love (Moi), or in love with the idea of love. Most of the girls were hooked up. In my class, the minute the out-of-state guys set eyes on their girls, they knew they were made for each other. As simple as that.

One got the impression that the Great Medical Institution was like a big cauldron where everyone met and melted and stood the test of time to culminate into this wonderful togetherness. At the risk of sounding conceited, ladies less pleasing to the eyes than Moi seized the opportunities before them and were zinged out of their senses. And then there was the case of a student-nun in the third year who even threw off her habit, jumped the wall, and eloped with a chap and got married. She did a Maria Von Trapp and nothing happened to the world. So, I bid my time. I was going to experience the ultimate zing and get zanged. I could feel it in my bones. But 'le grand amour' eluded me. I was looking at the guys, but the guys looked elsewhere. *Story of my life*, I thought.

As you entered the main grilled doors of the hostel, you came into a very large foyer. A big round table was the centrepiece. Around it, there were six or eight rattan chairs on which the seniors would sit to pick on the juniors, or else just sit and watch the world go by. On the side, in a nook, was the hostel telephone. Hell's bells! If only it could talk!! Girls hung onto the contraption like they would a lover. They cradled it, whispered sweet nothings into it, wept into it, laughed and mooned over it, begged into it, cajoled and smiled into it. Late into the night, once the seniors had left, my friend and I would sit on the rattan chairs for the express purpose of watching this rigmarole between the lovers and the telephone. Pretending to study, but in actual fact, straining our ears to get a word in passing. Sadly, we never even caught a syllable, let alone a word or sentence. So stealthy did they talk. Monosyllabic. 'Mmmm! Ahh! Ooh! Ehh?' It was orgasmic, if anything. Please don't conclude we were gossipmongers or eavesdropping.

We meant no harm but just wanted to break the monotony of late-night studies and get some free lessons on the art of sex through the phone. At the same time, this moonlighting set me thinking. These poor girls seemed trapped like a bee in a honey pot. They were boxed in. They had to explain their comings and goings to their beloved, be at the beck and call of their lovers, comply, and conform, none of which appealed to Moi. *If this is love*, I thought, *I'm better off where I am*. Moreover, there were so many fish in the sea, and I had only just started swimming. To add to that, I realized I had a short attention span where the boys were concerned. Most of all, I did not want to be caged. I needed to spread my wings and fly.

Slowly, things settled down, and I fell into a routine. The novelty that was Moi died down, and the seniors began to leave me alone. Though it was a disappointment, I welcomed the respite from constantly having to be on guard. The serious business of studying took over, though I did not give it much importance. What was it they said? All work and no play would make Jill a dull girl.

The Clinics

Five years of Dental School was like an evening gone. It was here, finally, that I got my 'natukari' (local woman) bearings. Much to Father's relief, the 'Malayaleeness' was rubbing on to Moi. But you know how it is. No matter how hard I tried to blend in, something was always amiss, something always gave me away, and I always managed to stick out like a sore thumb. During the holiday breaks, which I spent with Grandmother, the Kochammas at church (Malayalee Matrons), who were a force to be reckoned with, took one look at me and knew all was not what it seemed with this particular Malayalee girl. Nonetheless, I soldiered on.

At Dental School, much like I did at Baldwins, I made the best friends of my life. They loved me unconditionally. We kept each other safe and out of trouble. I thought, naively, that being a dentist was just about pulling out teeth, and how hard could that be? In my inner wicked self, I even thought I might enjoy the education as it progressed into the practical and clinical stages. I was very aware of that slight sadistic streak, that latent bit of epicaricacy in Moi, though I kept a lid on it. But the joke was on me, as I was in for a rude shock. There were six disciplines and a whole lot of learning to be done before I could actually get my hands on a victim, er… patient, I was to discover. The subjects, number of books, classes, and practicals were forbidding in their intensity. But whatever it entailed, I was glad that we dealt only with the upper orifice, unlike some of our medical counterparts, who were required to look and deal with the lower orifices and privates of men and women. In every situation, we've got to look for the silver lining.

The first day at the Prosthetic Lab was a howler. We had this strange-looking lady professor who had an expressionless face and spoke through her teeth. Whether it was on account of being a dentist or her style of conversation, I don't know. But you could not hear or understand a word she said. In any case, she was miserly with her words, so you had to decipher from her head and hand movements what she was all about. As we stood around her to do our first lab assignment, she stared at me and said, through clenched teeth, 'You block.' I was taken aback. What had I done? Why did she call me a freaking block? Was my stupidity engraved on my face? I recalled Mother's attempts at teaching me algebra ('a+b the whole squared,' she'd demand), her frustration at my blank look, and finally, her labelling me a 'karudha' (donkey). Meanwhile, I'd be thinking, *what did alphabets have to do with mathematics? Are we not dealing with numbers? So, who's the karudha here?*

These were my thoughts when the lecturer looked at me pointedly and said, 'You block.' Was she so brilliant that after one look at me, she'd found me out? It was only towards the end of the two-hour period of lecture that I realised that she wanted me and the rest of us to make a block or cube of 2"x2"x2" out of plaster of Paris. I was utterly relieved to realise that she did not think me a stupid case. Right off the bat, let me tell you, I was not a very ardent student. My roommate, on the other hand, was diligent and hardworking. We complemented each other. She would read out loud while I lay on the bed, closed my eyes, and imbibed the material. I'd let the text wash over me and soak it in as a kind of osmosis. It was an innovative method of learning. In any case, it was better than both of us reading out loud and creating a havoc. She enjoyed studying, while I loathed it. She taught me dentistry; I taught her how to have fun. I hated the mixing and moulding of the plaster of Paris and the silent company of the cadavers in the Anatomy lab. Sometimes, I felt I had bitten off more than I could chew. But seeing as I was neck deep in the program, there was nothing to do but move forward.

Another reason I had to stick to my guns was the fact that Grandmother was so proud of my achievements, and I didn't have the heart to disappoint her. Whenever I went home for the short vacations, she would line up the dhobi, the fieldworkers, the maid, the cow-herd, and a sprinkling of various others for me to do a dental check-up. And here's me not even half way through the first year, let alone the clinics, which would start only in the third year. Our dhobi's wife, a good sixty years old, insisted I check her stomach. I told her point blank that I looked only at teeth, but she said, 'Kuraapam illa molay. Adayalum adelum doctorenu padikugayeliyo. Athu Mathi' (That's OK, darling. In any case, you're studying some form of doctoring. That'll do). So, what do you do? I threw caution to the winds and went into full throttle, playing the dentist/doctor. I played it to the hilt and found myself enjoying it, with Grandmother cheering from the side. Varkey Chetan was another one of my loyal 'patients' roped in by Grandmother. He was the wandering baker of my childhood and had fed me so many butter buns that it was only right for me to return those favours by being his dentist. He had the most atrocious mouth, with paan-stained teeth and a horrifying red tongue. The minute he opened his mouth, a stale fish odour hit me in the face (not yet an era of masks, mind). Being a big, boisterous chap, his laugh was as forceful as the rotten smell, and with each spurt of 'haha,' small sprays of spit and rancid air would bombard my face. I took it like a veteran. Varkey Chetan assured Grandmother that he would spread the word. 'Kochinda kariyam nyan attu (I'll take care of the child's matter) was how he put it. *Well, when you can't beat them, join them,* I suppose. And that is what I did.

When we entered the third year, we had Medicine and Surgery to add to our worries. I was totally perplexed. I just could not get around to being with the sick. I was too bonhomie for the whole illness scenario. You had to have that kind of empathy and commitment. All the same, with a 'never say die' attitude, I trudged along. The friends kept me on the straight and narrow, dragging me along with them. There was this strange networking among the students. If a patient with a particular illness was admitted, they'd spread the word so all the other students could take a look. The end result was that the poor patient would find no peace due to the constant flow of students wanting to do percussions and examinations.

Now, this happened to us. My friends and I were having a meal in the mess hall when word passed down that in ward 3, bed 24 (?), was a patient with a typical murmur. So, we finished our meal in a tearing hurry and trooped off to the wards. When we reached the place, four other students were already by the bedside. An over-anxious, agitated, aggressive patient sat on the bed. We stood around uncertainly. Suddenly, the patient yelled out, 'Nyan evida varumbol oru choma mathram undayerunollu. Aathu koti, koti shayam aaki nee okkaymaati' (When I came here, I just had a cough. But the lot of you knocked and knocked on my chest, and now I have lung disease). I hastily retracted and ran off the same way I'd come and didn't visit the wards for a few days.

My greatest entertainment was teaching the North Indian girls a smattering of Malayalam. A perfect case of the blind leading the blind. For the word 'mathram' (only), I'd teach them 'moothram' (urine), and watch the patients get bothered and embarrassed. Another was 'maasakuli' (menstruation). The word tickled me no end, as the literal meaning was 'a bath in a month.' I taught my Northie friends that the word was 'masakalli' (a monthly game, denoting a sexual inuendo). Oh, it was such fun watching the patients go red in the face. It was hilarious and broke the tediousness of Medicine.

Whenever we finished exams, my friends and I would hit the town. We'd leave the hostel by 10 am and take in the morning show. We didn't care which movie. Then, we'd lunch at Azad, after which we'd rush for the noon show at Ajantha (usually an English movie to pacify Moi), and then the evening show at 5.30 pm. I don't know why we did it, but then again, what else was there to do? There were no eateries or burger joints at that time. No discotheques or cool bars. Nothing. We'd return to the hostel by 10.30 pm (10 pm was the cut off), and warden would be at the grill gates. In her hand would be a huge iron ring on which hung a hundred keys. She would glare at us, and I would try hard not to glare at her breasts. My friends and I had decided earlier on that I would explain why we were late, and so I'd begin in English. It was her weak point so she would immediately put a stop to it. 'Mathi, mathi marubhasha. Kerri po' (Enough of your gibberish. Get in). This, when all the while, some seniors were still out in the garden coo-chi cooing with their beloved. It was amazing how blatantly she bent the rules for them. If I called her a cow, it would be a disgrace to the animal.

When we finally entered the clinics, it was an anti-climactic. All that hype and glamour that we thought would be ours seemed transient. To my horror, I found mouths to be worse than anybody's lower orifice. The joke was on us. Bare hands shoved into a stranger's mouth, with their tongue snaking all over your fingers? Not attractive at all; in fact, it was downright vulgar. It was in the Prosthetic Clinic that I met my Waterloo. Until then, I hung on. But in this clinic, we dealt with missing teeth in a person's oral cavity. We had to make dentures or artificial teeth sets to fit edentulous jaws. It was a long, drawn-out process. But the first step was to take an impression of the patient's mouth. Now, this was a very tricky procedure. There was this material called Alginate, which was in powder form. You mixed this with the correct amount of water into the correct consistency, which you then loaded onto a tray – either an upper jaw tray or a lower jaw tray, depending on the jaw that you wanted to take an impression. I'm of the opinion that students should be drilled on two main points before they try taking an impression. One is that the dental chair should be in an upright position, with the head of the patient slightly tilted forward at all times when attempting to take an impression. The second is that the mixture of alginate and water should be absolutely in the correct consistency and never watery or runny. If the alginate mix is loose or watery, and the chair is reclined when you take an impression, it is only natural that when you insert it into the mouth, the impression material will flow into the throat of the patient, and the patient will invariably gag.

As it happened to poor old Moi. Perhaps I did not pay attention to the lecturer. My mix was watery, and my dental chair reclined for an upper impression. I shoved the tray with the watery mix into the patient's mouth and waited. The loose alginate mix flowed down to his throat, and he gagged, then vomited. My hand was still in his mouth. Now, as I could not remove the tray till the alginate set, the vomit spewed all over my hand. I thought of Varkey Chetan as a whiff of stale fish odour hit my senses. Then, to my utter horror, I gaged and vomited all over him. The clinic came to a standstill. I was painfully aware that all eyes were on us. What a fine pickle to be in. And then an uproar reverberated down the corridors of the dental college.

I hate to tell you what happened in the first Oral Surgery clinic. But tell I must if I'm to be true to myself. My roommate had read out to me thoroughly about the inferior alveolar block, a very necessary injection to be administered before the extraction of the lower molars. She vetted and quizzed me repeatedly on the procedure until I could parrot it in my sleep. She warned me it was a live patient that we would be dealing with, so we had to be extra careful and precise. In fact, we practised at getting the injection point on each other using a pencil as the needle. Both of us felt confident, and we marched off to clinics the next day, secure in the knowledge that we were well-prepared to face the day. As luck would have it, my roommate was paired with me in all practical classes, her name beginning with a K and mine beginning with an L. During the lecturer's explanation of the procedure to follow, we were impatient to get our hands on a live patient.

We were raring to go. Finally, the time arrived. We decided to pick an emaciated person, since we could avoid piercing through too much flesh. First, we moved him to a chair at the corner of the clinic, seeing it was secluded and no one could watch us. My friend told me to go first in spite of the incident at the Prosthetic Lab, or was it because of it? So, she stood to the left of the patient and I to the right. The fellow opened his mouth, and none of the landmarks pointed out in the text book were present. In fact, a lone tooth sat there nonchalantly, on the lower left side of his mouth, asking to be pulled. 'Feel for the ramus of the mandible with your pointer finger, then rotate and inject,' my friend instructed. I complied. But I dared not tell her that honestly, I felt no ramus. I only felt the usual revulsion about putting my hands into another person's mouth, but at the same time, my hand was shaking, and my heart was pounding under the coat. But all went well. She nodded and smiled, and I smiled back. It was not that bad; I was getting the hang of it. 'Now, inject and aspirate a bit to see if you hit a blood vessel,' she whispered. I did. 'No sign of blood in the cartridge,' I whispered. 'Good,' she hissed. 'Go for it. Pump in the anaesthetic slowly.' I felt like a veteran already. I carefully pumped in the juice.

Suddenly, my friend went frantic. She was making all kinds of faces and gesturing with her hands and rolling her eyes, all the while trying not to draw attention to ourselves. I feared she was having some sort of epileptic attack, though the more I watched her, I felt it was closer to the Kathakali dance form. Was the clinical atmosphere too much for her? Was she more of an academician than a clinician? I felt sorry for her. But she kept pointing at the patient's left shoulder. When I leaned over and took a look at the fellow's left shoulder, to the place she was pointing, I saw it was wet. Blimy! It was the solution that was dripping from the tip of the needle that jutted out ever-so-slightly from his cheek. The patient remained calm and relaxed in the hands of two efficient dentists. We gathered our instruments and silently slithered out of the room. My friend was in hysterics, while I was shaken to the core. *Would the chap die?* I wondered. *Would I ever make a go of this business?*

What did I know? There was certainly a lot to learn. If I did not end up killing anyone first.

Budding dentists

For Love

Having completed the course at Dental School, I was doing a house surgency stint while waiting for my degree papers and preparing to go back to Malaysia to take up a job. I had accomplished most of the goals Father had set for me. But without a doubt, the greatest was that I had survived the years away from home and was finally going back to them as an accomplished Dentist. He was so proud of me that he could talk of nothing else, which sometimes became embarrassing. Mother, I think, must have heaved a big sigh of relief that I had come out of all those years without her supervision, unscathed. I'm sure she placed more importance on the fact that I spoke the mother tongue fluently (though a trained ear might pick up an oddity here or there), that my hair was well and truly long, and that I draped the sari like a proper Malayalee pennu (girl). That I had learned to curb my wayward tongue and was successful at hiding my interest in the opposite sex at church. Most of all, I'm sure she was relieved that I had proved my aunties wrong by not acquiring a boyfriend, French or otherwise, but had remained pristine and virtuous during all that time. I, on the other hand, felt I had failed myself miserably, for what was all this for if I had not been able to snag a boyfriend? I had achieved everything except falling in love. It goes without saying the final item was nowhere in the parents' agenda, but it loomed largely in mine. It was a thorn in my side. Why did 'ze amour' elude Moi?

'And I would do anything for love. I'd run right into Hell and back,' thus sang Meat Loaf.

So much has been made of this great passion throughout the ages that one cannot help but be enthralled and drawn into the vortex of emotions it set ablaze. Songs. Verses. Movies. Musicals. Books. All waxing eloquent about its ecstasy and its pathos.

- People died for love (Romeo and Juliet).

- A thousand ships sank for love (Helen of Troy).

- A king abdicated his throne for love (Edward and Willis Simpson).

- A king built a monument for love (Shah Jehan and Mumtaz Mahal).

- A queen was beheaded in the name of love (Henry V111 and Anne Boleyn).

- Noble prizes were won for the love of science (Pierre Curie and Marie Curie).

- Massacres were made in the name of love for religion/ideology/power (All the wars fought).

All in the name of Love. So, what was this great emotion that I was yet to feel? This maddening, exciting, blinding, tender, heartbreaking, all-consuming emotion – love? This zing? I think it was Ralph Waldo Emerson who said, 'All the world loves a lover.' It sounded appropriate. The more I was denied it, the more I craved. '*Is there not a single person, dear God, who could be dumb enough to love me?*' I asked the Lord in prayer. I just wanted to experience what all the hoo-ha was about. Jeez, I didn't even believe in it half the time, and yet, I was sucked into its alluring magic, and the more all the lovers around me extolled on the subject, the more bereft I felt. I'll be the first to admit I'm no great authority on the subject, but then, who was? I had never been in love, nor had anyone fallen in love with me. I wondered if love had simply passed me by. God forbid that be the case. But how could I believe otherwise when I had lived for more than five years in a professional college teeming with so many prospective fellows and was yet unattached? In fact, my greatest disappointed was that I had not been able to brag in the dining hall about having a boyfriend. That worried and depressed me more than the whole romantic thing. I was more peeved at the idea that no one thought me worthy enough to be girlfriend material than the notion that I'd never experienced the emotion. That's the correct thing to admit to. And it's not as if I did not try. Heaven knows, I am as normal a person as the next full-blooded creature. So, it's the absolute truth when I say that I had tried sincerely to fall in love, but to no avail. In fact, I'd tried to cast my net whenever and wherever possible, but love stayed elusive. I'd made a close study of the classmates who were in love, observed their mannerisms, unspoken messages, coveted looks, and secret smiles and made mental notes to execute them should an occasion arise. But like they say about cooking a rabbit soup, I first had to catch a rabbit. Therein lay the problem. It was as if love had a thing against me and kept teasing me, giving me hope only to flit away in the last minute.

I started off in the love business rather well. The Parents adored me. That was love of a different kind, but love nevertheless. My every wish was their command. I was kissed and cuddled no end. An only child till age nine, I sometimes suffered from an abundance of it. Though there were the occasional hiccups, such as when Mother taught me mathematics and my mind wandered. But by and large, it was an endearing relationship, in spite of her unhealthy penchant for my left ear – those were moments when I thought she hated me. But Father was okay and consistent in his love.

Then Sibling came along, and I was totally in love. A devoted slave. I didn't care that the parents' love got divided. I was solely focused on my love for her. This was the longest, most stable love affair of my life; it lasted 50 years without blemish, until her untimely demise.

When I went to school, I met Shoukat Ali. I hadn't the faintest idea why I wanted to share my sandwich with him, and that too a sardine-cheese sandwich with a dash of Marmite and cucumbers. Orange juice too. Was I bonkers? It was unreasonable behaviour for Moi. I did not know what name to give this feeling other than acknowledge that I felt a zing in the pit of my stomach. Thankfully, he stoutly refused my offer and sat with May Ling. And I had the sandwich to myself. I sat alone and feasted on my snack as I watched my classmates laugh and talk and share their food. That was the first time I came across the bittersweet pangs of l'amour. The rejection of love and the relief of not having to share the sandwich. *Love was a double-edged sword,* I decided.

The next attempt at finding love was while at the boarding school. Sundays were breeding grounds for love affairs. The church building was in the shape of a big cross sign, so it allowed much eye-to-eye contact between the Baldwin Boys and the Baldwin Girls. Mary made eyes at Almeida, and Shanti made eyes at Kalil. I made eyes at them making eyes. My friend

Geeta was a knockout beauty, and she got a lot of chocolates and letters. She let me read all the letters and eat all the chocolates. Even if I was not in the love game, I reaped all its great benefits. *Sometimes, we have to learn to be content with the breadcrumbs that fall from the table*, I told myself. *Patience, everything comes to those who wait.*

Moving into the college campus was a big leap, and one I'd hoped would offer better opportunities. So, with love as the specific purpose and education as a secondary one, I had applied to Mar Ivanios, a co-ed college. We were a class of 110 Biology students. On the first day itself, I'd made a detailed study of my male classmates. Sadly, most of the boys were puny and gauche and only interested in themselves and their tiffin boxes. Worst of all, they were shyer than the girls and had no style at all. Not one boy had a pompadour hairstyle like Elvis or a turned-up collar like Cliff Richard. And as for a Beatle style, don't even think about it. They lacked panache. The second language French Class offered better scope. There were 35 of us, and I was the only girl. What more could I ask for? There would be no competition to begin with. But I think the boys were intimidated by my size. I was a big girl – robust really – and most of the boys thought it safer to stay away. Moreover, the language barriers and general outlook were incongruous and jarring. And I think the sari put them off. It was also a pity I had never developed my eye-to-eye messaging skills due to the bad experiences at church during my tenure in the boarding school in Bangalore.

By the time I joined Dental School, I was desperate. The more I was denied a taste of this great passion, the more I needed to sate my hunger. Within a month of starting the course, my classmates had all paired up, and I was left with the Class Joker. Desperate I might be, but I still had standards to maintain and decided I would not stoop that low. My roommate persuaded me to believe that it was my upper lip hair growth that was the culprit that put the boys off. I pointed out that she had a clean upper lip and no boyfriend, to which she counterargued that she did not want one, and that she was not hunting and desperate. I thought I detected disdain in her voice, but I let it ride. *Who cared what she thought? I had to stay single-minded and focus on my goal.* Then I told her that Rem, who was having a 'twidledoo' with one of the seniors, and was making a success of things, had a moustache that could shame mine. But my friend was having none of that. She said she had a plan.

So, we went to the ladies' store at Statue once again. In case you forgot, that was where I'd got my hair bun from as a fresher. We got ourselves two bottles of Annie French, a reliable hair removing cream available at that time. It smelt like fresh cow dung, so imagine the agony of having to apply it to your upper lip, right below your nostrils and smelling it for 5 minutes minimum. But in for a penny, in for a pound. I read the instructions, which said, 'Apply ointment to desired areas using spatula and leave for 5 minutes. In case of thick growth, 7 minutes. Remove cream using gauze and warm water.' In my enthusiasm, I applied a generous amount of the cream and decided to wait 10 minutes to make a thorough job of it. *Or maybe 15, to be on the safe side*, I thought. Then, to my horror, I realized I had no warm water or gauze. The ladies' hostel at the Medical College was not a student-friendly place and offered no nurses' station or sick room or any such amenities that are so essential at a place that housed so many vulnerable girls. I sat around in my room for 5–6 minutes, after which I began to feel a burning sensation on my upper lip. I waited for another 3 minutes, by which time my eyes were welling up due to the burning pain. Having no warm water or gauze, I used my dry towel to rub across my lips. I squealed in pain as I removed the offending cream along with the top layer of my upper lip skin. When I looked into my hand mirror, I saw the raw pink flesh where previously, the skin had protected it. The pain was bloody bleeding excruciating. It took two days for the pain to abate, but a dangerous-looking dark brown shell appeared where the skin had been ripped off. In another two days, it had horrendously developed into a thick, black scab. I stared in dismay into the mirror as the whole effect presented an atrocious sight that looked suspiciously like a giant centipede had crawled up and lay snugly across my upper lip. I broke down and cried. The things we do for love! And yet how unfortunate the outcome. Needless to say, I had a lot of explaining to do in the following few weeks. I struggled with the situation until the scab fell off and the skin blended with the surrounding skin.

In the meantime, even the last remaining Joker decided to keep his distance from me.

SELAMAT KEMBALI

On Being a Dentist

The plane circled over the Penang International Airport at Bayang Lepas. The air hostess announced that we would be landing in a short while. I had not slept a wink during the four-hour flight nor the previous couple of days. My mind was in a turmoil. My friends from Dental School had come to see me off at Trivandrum Airport. It was a heart-breaking farewell. There were no cell phones and all that came with it at that time, and letters were so one-sided and slow. It was a time when if you left, you left, and only memories remained. Every time I closed my eyes, I saw my life as I knew it till then. I was leaving all that I had grown to love and cherish and had become familiar with, to once again foray into the unknown. The only difference was that I was an adult now. Little things remained in the recesses of the mind. How I was introduced to mussels by a friend's father, escapades at class excursions, watching classmates who were lovers argue with each other, decoding the lovelorn looks of the less fortunate, and raiding the pantry in the hostel for anything to eat. How, totally penniless, we entered the Sea Lord's Restaurant at Cochin pretending as if for a meal, when in reality, we just wanted to use the loo. Mercilessly sparring with seniors and getting away with it, and on and on. In a strange twist of events, it felt like I was leaving home.

Then, the sudden thud of the wheels of the plane hitting ground brought me back to the present. The doctor had arrived! A new phase in my life was about to begin. I was awkward and gauche when I first left for Baldwin's. I was now twenty-four and I had come full circle. I had to chalk out a life and earn a living, and I was in a hurry to do both. I searched for the sunglasses. Twin purpose. One to shade the eyes from the harsh tropical afternoon sun; second, and more importantly, this bird was stepping out in style, à la Jackie O.

I had made it a point to label my boxes with 'DR. LENNIE GEORGE' in bold letters. It was imperative to announce that there was a doctor on board. I looked covertly, first left and then right, to see if anyone had read it – if anyone had realised, they were in the presence of an achiever. The parents were ecstatic, and if no one else did, they, at least, read the label twice over. That evening, after dinner, Father read through my Degree Certificate with wonder, and I saw a glint in his eye. He called Mother over to him, and together, they handed me a small jewel box. When I opened it, in the velvet folds lay a pair of diamond studs and a small diamond pendant. I have worn them ever since. They have become my good luck charms.

Since my departure many years ago, the Malay Peninsular had become Malaysia in 1963. It consisted of Malaya, Sabah, Sarawak, and Singapore. My first assignment as a dentist was in Raub in the state of Pahang, very far from where the parents were stationed. Mother went on about how sad it was that I was posted so far away, while I tried hard to hide my glee. I had been free of parental shackles for so long, I feared that if we were to start them now, both parties would be disappointed. After a few days of rest and restitution, I packed my bag and baggage and, along with the parents, drove East to the largest state in Malaysia, Pahang. My posting was in a dental clinic on Fraser's Hill, a small hill station in the district of Raub. We covered over 500 km and drove for close to 7 hours. Fraser's Hill, or Bukit Fraser, as it's known in Malay, was a hill resort built by the British to escape the tropical heat. The final part of the journey was exhilarating, as we had to manoeuvre close to a dozen hairpin bends and wind up a hill. We arrived in the late afternoon, and even then, in spite of the evening sun, it was foggy and chilly. I fell in love with the place – the serenity and quietness. The quintessential Britishness of it reminded me of Richmond Town and Baldwin Girls, Bangalore. It had an old-world charm. Strangely, it gave me the comfort of coming back to familiar surroundings and things. The place was bursting with wild flowers, and small white picket fences lined the roads. There was an air of mystery and expectancy, totally enigmatic. I even fancied I saw a lissom ethereal figure, feet hardly touching the ground, float about in the mist. Fraser's Hill was getting to Moi.

The next morning, we found the 'Kementerian Kesihatan Pergigian' (Ministry of Dental Health), a small charming clinic nestled in the shade of a large group of flowering trees. I met my boss, Dr. Lenora Cheng. She was a slight, dainty, soft-spoken Chinese lady. Unmarried, she lived alone with her maid in a large, rambling government accommodation. I guess two or three comments of mine must have put her at ease because they made her laugh. By the end of the day, she convinced the parents that I need not look for lodging elsewhere but could live with her and even share meals. That was a time when sexual orientation and other such matters were not discussed, or should I say, not known to the parents, or else they would have declined the offer. Thus, all was settled. They left, and I moved in with Dr. Lenora. She was very nice but very private. Being Christian, she went to church a lot, read the bible, prayed, and fasted. I was disgustingly apprehensive if she would ask me to join in. I had a love-hate relationship with my God, and we believed in giving each other space and respect. Most of all, I did not fear my God. The nights were slow, the TV had reruns of Peyton Place, and as much as I was in love with Ryan O'Neal, he was beginning to irritate. Mia Farrow, I hated.

Two months passed without incident, then the parents informed me they were coming down to visit. I spoke to Dr. Lenora, and she was so kind and assured me they could stay with us. In fact, she said she would make something special for lunch that day. I was a bit apprehensive about that, since I knew Mother was a fastidious eater. Neither could I turn down my boss's considerate offer. So, the matter was settled in Lenora's favour. The day after the parents arrived, the good doctor got up before 5 am and left for the market. I wondered at her enthusiasm. *You can't get more Christian than that*, I thought. When she returned, I helped her with the bags and enquired why she had left for the market at such an unearthly hour. She told me she had wanted to get special bits from the butcher's as they would be sold out quickly. My ears pricked up, and I felt a panic. Three things came to mind:

She was my boss and had gone out of her way to welcome my parents.

Mother did not eat pork, and the Chinese never had a meal without pork.

My Mother had a way of saying things rather bluntly.

I was in an altogether precarious position. Here was a time bomb I had to defuse. I nonchalantly asked her what the special bits were, expecting her to say pork ribs or something equally innocuous. I almost dropped the bags as she licked her lips and said, 'You know, the usual. Pig's tongue, pig's ears, pig's foot, pig's tail. All the delicacies. I was lucky enough to manage a 4-inch piece of stomach too,' she ended, almost choking on her saliva. *What? Bloody what? And Almighty what?* And as if that were not enough, she confided in a whisper with a girlish giggle, 'And oh! While at it, I went all out and got us two hen heads and feet.' I looked at her, and for the first time, she looked so ghoulish and macabre to me. I did not breathe a word of this to the parents. I could not breathe, period! I was between the devil and the deep sea. I decided to let lunch take its course. I would rough it out. I might get a transfer from Raub, or worse, lose my job. I stretched out my neck – *Now let the axe fall*, I thought in despair.

We sat down for the meal. The boss smiled as she explained it was chicken-bits gruel soup, and the main dish was pork special bits, vegetables, and rice. *Mother of God, any minute now!* I had warned the parents that the boss prayed before meals, so just follow her cue. Lenora closed her eyes and began with 'Let's say grace.' Mother seized the moment to slyly scoop into her bowl. As she lifted the spoon, a big, well-shaped claw of a hen's leg, complete with nails and scales, rose up from the thick creamy gruel. It really was a scene from *The Addam's Family*. She turned pale and sat there petrified, her eyeballs popping out and rolled upward. She stopped breathing. Ridiculously, all I could think of was that if Mother's eyeballs popped out and rolled any further, they'd fall into the gruel, and then we'd have 'Mother's eyeball hen's claw' soup. I was so spaced out, I wanted to laugh. Father, on seeing this, immediately scooped into his. The grotesque head of a rooster surfaced. The comb was dull red, the eyes half closed, but one had to admire the beak. It was a nice, strong canary yellow. Father, who had until then boasted that he ate anything that did not bite back (tirichu kadikatha andum tinum), looked as pale as death. *Serves him right*, I thought and for a moment I was glad, thinking he'll never be able to boast again about his eating prowess. As for me, my mouth was dry and parched and I wished I was a thousand miles away in Siberia or where ever. When Lenora opened her eyes, I said with a croak that Mother was having one of her spells and needed to rest. As if giving credence to my words, Mother had started to groan in a low, yelping voice, and then her teeth started gnashing and the eyeballs rolled around uncontrollably. As I helped her leave the table, I sternly told Father in Malayalam, 'Mindi poyehkella. Avideh eruneh thinneh. Anda joli kariyam aneh' (Not a word. Stay put and eat. My job depends on it). Till the day she died, Mother would say, 'Aa chinathi aandh jendhuena kitiyalum tinum. Agana avada veetil samadanatil oragum? Nee sushicho. Aanum ravilae alla baghom ondoanu nokiko' (That Chinese woman will eat any creature she gets. How can you sleep in peace at her home? You be careful. Check if all your body parts are intact each morning). As for Father, his boast was now at its peak. Atrocious and unrelenting. He was a man who had tasted a rooster's comb and given a crack at a rooster's beak. I wondered if slowly, he'd add a pig's head for more shock value. The Malayalee Achayans at church, to whom he regaled these stories, were both appalled to the core and fascinated and wondered at such a brave man. I think they were proud to be associated with him. And as for the Kochammas at church, there was no doubt they envied Mother having a daring, dashing husband. However, Mother kept telling Father, 'Don't you dare come anywhere near me, for you are an unclean man.'

But this was the least of my worries. For, unknown to the parents, there was another dire habit that I had picked up from Dr. Lenora. We enjoyed a cigarette late in the evenings after dinner. She had introduced me to it tentatively, allowing me a puff once in a while. And I was beginning to more than like it. *The men have it right*, I thought, *there is something to be said about a fag after a meal.* No doubt, with each fag came the realization that I was venturing into areas of taboo and also cultivating a routine. It also brought home the fact that should the parents get even a whiff of what was going on, they'd drop dead, and I'd be accused of parricide. And then what? As it was, I had already made them taste some strange gourmet meal consisting of pigs' bits and roosters' heads.

After six months in Raub, I got posted at Kuantan, the capital of Pahang State. This time, it was a fully functioning Dental Hospital with a lot of doctors and a busy schedule. Our boss was again Chinese, but he was an older gentleman who was morose and abrupt. He was married to a very young lady, also a doctor, who worked with us. I think they were trying to impress each other. He wanted to show her how important he was, and she wanted to show us she was married to the boss. Between the two of them, we got hell. My friends were three gentleman doctors and a lady doctor. The lady doctor was of an Indian/Chinese ethnicity. What kind of a mix or fix that was, I never knew. But I envied her that she got the best from both cultures, as compared to my dry, dull, single-culture, lacklustre, and uninspiring Malayalee genes. Once, she invited me home for lunch. She told me her mother had prepared fish. I was surviving mostly on bread and jam and cereal, so I jumped at the chance for a proper meal. Now, here, let me educate you on a fruit called durian. It's deceptive in that it looks like our lovable jackfruit. Don't be fooled. It's the most obnoxious fruit on earth. There are those who love it and then those who hate it. There is no in-between. It has the most repellent smell, a kind of putrid flesh odour. The worst part is, if you consumed the blinking thing and went to the loo or peed, the whole house would smell of durian. How about that? That's how bad it is. I always thought it was a good weapon to use against someone you had a grouse against. Just pee in their toilet after feasting on the fruit, (with sincere apologies to durian lovers the world over).

Anyway, I went to my friend's place for lunch, hoping the Indian side of the family would have made the fish curry. Whenever Mother called me, she would remind me not to eat from any Chinese homes and add, 'God knows what creatures you have already eaten.' So, when I told Mother about lunch at the friend's place, and when she questioned about their ethnicity, I just mentioned her Indian roots. At lunch, when I was served rice and vegetables, I relaxed. Then her mother brought in the fish curry, and as she scooped a generous amount with the ladle, I was overcome by that putrid flesh smell. It hit my nostrils like ammonia, and I was stupefied. They had freaking added durian into the fish curry! I watched my friend have two helpings of the curry, and I envied her sense of indulgence as she tackled such a strange dish. This one time, I just could not take it. I just could not pretend and be polite. So, I told her I was allergic to durian and listened to her pity me to death for having to skip the delicious curry.

During all this time, I was earnestly on the lookout for some serious zing. *The time is ripe*, I thought. But unless I was willing to accept a Malay or Chinese suitor and go through life consuming unexpected spurious delectables, I had no choice at all. And I had a nagging feeling Mother would protest vehemently to any Chinese to-do. There would be no mollifying her on that score after the Dr. Lenora episode. She might even disown me forever. On the brighter side, in four months, I had saved enough, and the next time the parents came to visit, Father helped me buy a second-hand Mini Cooper. Maroon and sporty. The fruit of my labour. It was freedom with a capital F. Mother was unimpressed and kept telling me to get a stove and do some cooking and eat decent, safe food. That was all she cared about. Just as I completed one year in Kuantan, Mother developed some medical issues, and I decided to put in for a transfer.

It was time for the wild child to return to the nest.

Dr. Lenora and moi

Me with my staff and the mobile clinic

A Pack of Marlboro Decides

Mother found a packet of Marlboro in my handbag, and that was the beginning of the end of my sojourn with them and my working in Malaysia as an independent professional.

My transfer from Kuantan to Alor Setar, Kedah had come through almost six months back. The Indo-Chinese friend had acquired a few days' leave and offered to drive down with me, but I did not want to impose and did the journey alone. The Mini Cooper did not have a built-in music system or air conditioning. So, I just blasted the small tape recorder I had, rolled down the windows, and let the air in. Neil Diamond accompanied me, and Smokie too. It was a drive I'll never forget for as long as I breathe. On the road, not a care in the world, just the sky above and the wind in my hair. Me, myself, Moi. Short stops along the roadside canteens, gorging on 'koithio,' 'mee-goraing,' and 'satay,' and lighting up a cigarette afterwards. I'd puff in the smoke and let it out through the nose. I had become an expert. It felt good – no, it felt great. I was young, independent, and where possibilities were concerned, the sky was the limit. Lennie was on the loose and running wild.

I joined the Dental Clinic in Alor Star. My boss was again a Chinese man, which made me wonder if dentistry was race-oriented. Again, we were four junior doctors – two Indian ladies, a Malay chap, and a Chinese. One day, I was working on my patient when the Malay doctor approached me and stood around. He was a tall fellow, 6 ft. (maybe more), rugged, but pleasant-looking. He seemed nervous and agitated. As he kept standing by my chair without speaking, I began to get uneasy. Was he about to profess undying love for Moi? I still had to achieve success in that area and so was constantly on the lookout. Did I feel anything for him? What did the Malays eat? Would Mother accept? She had a grouse against belacan or balachong, an Asian condiment made from fermented and compressed fish or shrimp. I can only describe the aroma of said condiment as very strong, though Anna, the wife of the British naturalist, Henry Ogg Forbes, accused her cook of trying to poison her because of the foul-smelling ingredient he had added to her dish. So, I concluded Mother would not take it kindly should I develop a relationship with the doctor. Without a doubt, I would have to decline his love, I decided. I had found out to my utter amazement and disbelief that though the parents were the most irritating two people I had ever encountered in my life, my love for them surpassed all else, and I would go to any lengths to please them and gain their approval. How convoluted was that?

The doctor waited patiently until I'd finished with my patient, then requested that I take over a case of his. No declaration of undying love, then. So much for that hope. Now, taking on another doctor's patient was not ethical, and both of us could get into some serious trouble, so I tried to get out of it. But he was so desperate and begged me to help him. I did not understand any of it, and though I wanted to oblige, I did not want to get into the bad books of the boss either. God knows, my track record was not illustrious in that department, and I've been in too many tight spots during my life to expect anything else. But my heart softened, as it looked like the chap seemed desperate and on the verge of tears. Out of the corner of my eye, I saw my nurse gesturing to me and waving her arms. I knew there was more to the story. So, I told the doctor to give me a minute and went over to my nurse, who was in the registration room. Beyond this room was the patient reception. As I got near, she grabbed my arm and said, 'Look, that is the doctor's patient that he wants you to take over.' And I saw a person, also about 6 ft. tall, but what took me by surprise was that he was a unique-looking individual who stood out from the other patients in an attention-grabbing way. This was about forty-five years ago and we were not familiar with sexual orientation, gender identity, transgender, and all the rest of it. The person was physically very well-developed and feminine. The femininity was accentuated under the tight red t-shirt that the person was wearing. The patient's whole demeanour was exaggerated. The jeans were so tight it was difficult to tell if said he was on the outside trying to get in, or on the inside trying to get out. The way the legs were first crossed, then uncrossed, and then recrossed, Sharon Stone-style, was thought-provoking but not half as attractive.

The nurse said to me, 'Watch, doctor,' and then called out the name. The person kind of unfurled his large frame from the chair and swayed over to where we were standing. There was a reek of cheap perfume, and long-painted nails were on exhibition. Saints alive, a set of fake eyelashes too were visible. After the studied gyration up to the registry, the patient coyly enquired, 'Kenapa awak panggil saya? Saya sudah beritahu awak yang saya hendak Dr. Shafi belanja saya. Tolong chepat.' (Why did you call me? I have told you I want Dr. Shafi to treat me. Please hurry). I watched the person in fascination and absorbed the whole scenario while trying to read the body language.

The nurse looked at me as if she had said it all.

'What? What?' I asked, bewildered.

'Well, she's in transition,' The nurse replied.

'Say what? Who? She? He?'

'Oh doctor, don't act so dumb. She's in mid-transition. Are you blind? Don't you see her breasts?'

'I see the breasts, and I'm envious of them because they are larger than mine, but what are we dealing with here? He, she, or what?'

Very patiently, like she was talking to an imbecile, the nurse explained that this was a married man and father of three who had decided he was a female trapped in a man's body. He was in the process of getting out of his male skin. What concerned us though, was that he thought he was madly in love with Dr. Shafi, and much to the good doctor's consternation, wanted to be treated only by him. I was to be the villain. There was nothing to do but comply and help my teammate. His concerns were grave. This, when I thought I had seen everything.

It was very strange, but I slowly realised that there was nothing really wrong with Mother that needed me to have taken a transfer from Pahang and move home. It had been a ploy. She seemed as fit as a fiddle and behaved like she had won a battle. I might be slow, but I'm not stupid, and it dawned on me that I'd been had. The old folks had done a number on me. But in a wild way, I was glad. I rather loved the fuss they made and the overzealous efforts to please. Sibling and I called them Henry and Henrietta Kissinger on account of the fact that they would drop a kiss on our heads or cheeks whenever possible. I guess they were making up for lost time, and it was very endearing. One weekend, we were all sitting down to breakfast when Mother calmly announced that it was time I got married. I agreed. In any case, Mother had proved to be a formidable adversary at every turn, so it was safer to go along with her. But we had to address the elephant in the room. To whom was I to be married? There were no suitable candidates on the horizon, and I had not contributed in any helpful way. And Mother would never consider anyone outside of our community and never a Chinese. Yet, Mother made the perfunctory remark and was kind enough to enquire if I had anyone in mind. But I felt the undercurrent of the unsaid rule that whoever he was, he better be a 'Nalla Suriyani Christiyani Malayalee cheruken' (a nice Syrian Christian Malayalee boy). Just for a second, as I watched her defiant face, I thought I'd throw caution to the winds and state, '*There was this Chinese boy……*,' but I bit my tongue and held my peace. I remembered how I had made lifelong enemies of my aunties over my suggestion of a French connection years ago. Much water had flown under the bridge since then, and the lunch at Dr. Lenora's had been an epic episode. So, I thought twice about unburdening my heart or making any cheeky retort. By now, I had formed a sort of friendship (?) with a guy, or so I thought. Not Chinese, of course, for obvious reasons, food being the main. I could not put my finger on the exact ethnicity of the person, which was important and a big deal for the parents, but the fact that he could be Indian gave me hope. In any case, how do you say to a chap you've just met, 'Hey, by the way, are you Sri Lankan, Bangladeshi, Tamilian, or a "nalla Suriyani Christiyani Malayalee cheruken"?' And the last breed was a very rare variety. By that, you can guess how much choice I had or how much leeway the parents were offering. I was to stay and work within 'the good Malayalee boy' framework.

Now, this supposed affair of mine was unlike any affair normal people had. This chap and I, we would look at each other. I'd look, he'd look. Then we would go our separate ways. And we'd look again the next time we met. This went on for a couple of days until I began to wonder what we were looking at or for how long we would look until we were in love. *The heck, I thought, it isn't easy, this love thing. Freaking pharmacology, with all those absurd names, was peanuts compared to this.* So, when Mother asked the question of Moi, if I had anyone in mind, I was in a quandary as to how to answer. Was I in love or not? Was he? Were we? I wondered if I should ask the chap outright. Be straightforward about it. Something like this: '*Hello, how are you today? Where are you posted? By the way, are you in love with me?'* Or should I say, *'I'm in love with you'*? But was I? Heavens! What a tricky business. Finally, I decided to confide in a fellow lady doctor. She had a roaring love life, so she should know.

Without beating around the bush, I asked her point blank, 'Do you think the bloke is in love with me?'

She was taken aback and asked, 'Why do you say that?'

'Because he keeps looking at me,' I said.

'Well, that's what he's telling everyone who will listen, that you keep looking at him, and he's wondering why.'

But she really knocked me for a sixer when she said, 'Moreover, he's engaged to your nurse. Eh, the Chinese girl.'

The heck!! No wonder my nurse had been cold towards Moi for these past few weeks. Good thing I had not confronted him. The ignominy of it all. I had to face the fact that I was not cut out for this game of love that seemed to come so easily to everyone but Moi. Well, that answered my question, all right. I went home straight away and told Mother my answer. It was time to search for the man.

The first candidate was a nice fellow. The meeting was casual – just us at the cool bar. He had silky hair that he kept flicking to the side by running his fingers through them. It had a mesmerizing effect. Pleasant face, well-dressed, clean fingernails (very important). He was a medical chap and of course a 'nalla Suriyani Christiyani Malayalee cheruken.' Mother had chosen well. We spoke a bit about inconsequential stuff, stood up, said goodbye, and went our ways. Had I seen Game of Thrones or known of Peter Dinklage then, the outcome of the meeting could have been different. I would have been kindly inclined towards the prospect. For my suitor, so perfect in every way, was only as tall as me. I was in no mood to compromise or willing to listen to reason. I was fixated on a six-footer. Mother was livid. She could not understand what height had to do in a marriage. Father was not tall, but she had done well in life, hadn't she? She had two kids in spite of Father's height, or lack thereof or wharever. So, what was I going on about? Frankly, I was nervous about getting hitched and begging for some time. Mother was pushing it. Father was neutral.

And then she found the Marlboro pack in my handbag. From there on, everything went downhill. Mother stopped talking to me. Father ignored me. I felt cornered and suffocated. God! A fag or two just then would have calmed my nerves, but with all the tension hanging in the air, I curbed my need. The parents were acting like I had broken every commandment in the Bible. Bleeding hell, having a fag was not even one of the sins mentioned in the ten commandments. And all this commotion over a stupid pack of cigarettes?

They decided to send me back to India. But I was not eight. This time I objected. I had a job. I could survive. Then Mother went into one of her fasting prayers. And Father walked around like doomsday was approaching. I knew it was a losing battle. I loved them too much to make them suffer, and I understood they were doing this because they loved me. All is fair in love and war, eh? I did the decent thing and surrendered. The first thing we did to kick-start the mission to marry me off was get a formal picture taken. I slicked back my short hair into a bun at the salon, brought out my favourite orange chiffon sari with the dark maroon border, and went to the studio and took a picture. Mother said my wristwatch was inappropriate – too 'ooh' for a lady. It was a big, man's-type watch with a heavy, broad, velvet strap. Notice, she didn't even have a word for it. But I stuck to my guns, thinking I had to win somewhere. Next, I packed my bags and once again returned to India, this time with marriage on my mind.

Thus, Malaysia's loss become India's gain. *Cherchez l'homme.' Search for the Man*, I thought with grim defiance.

The Mini Cooper

In serious pursuit of a suitor

GHAR VAPASI

The Suitors

A marriage committee was formed for the express purpose of getting me hitched. The Sibling and I christened it 'Operation Goose Chase' (OGC). It consisted of my paternal Uncle Thomas, who assumed the status of President. His main chore was tracking down a prospect and finding out if he was suitable. The two aunties acted as functionaries who took over all other aspects concerning Moi, like dressing, behaviour, hairstyle, and other pertinent matters. Under their expert guidance, I fixed the hair bun and sari to look like a 'nalla Malayalee pennu' (good malayali girl). I tried my darndest to walk the walk and talk the talk. I was accused of laughing a lot, so I curbed that. I joked and spoke nineteen to the dozen, so I shut that down. I had an opinion, which had to stop. So, what have you got left? Not Lennie for sure. Still, if that was the role required of me, I decided to play it to the hilt. Yet sometimes, unbeknownst to me, the genie would pop out of the bottle for some air. And the entire extended family who were marginally included in the OGC would swoop down screeching and perplexed, and the genie would retreat into the bottle.

In the meantime, I had applied for jobs and was called to the NSS Medical Mission Hospital in Pandalam. They required me to set up a Dental Clinic. I accepted, took the project to heart, and did my best. I was given a nurse, Sarojini Amma, who was to assist me in the undertaking. She was a pukka Nair lady of about forty years, from an aristocratic and traditional family. She knew everything there was to know about how a Malayalee girl had to behave. She saw me as frivolous and uncouth and a far cry from the 'adakam othukam ulla pennugal' (prim and proper girl), and so took it upon herself to mould me into marriageable material as required by Malayalee standards. Whenever there was a lull in patients, she would educate me on the proper behaviour one should adopt as a wife, daughter-in-law, and everything else required in the making of good wifely material. Since the genie was tightly corked in the bottle, I had no difficulty in agreeing to all she said superficially. But inside my head, I rebelled at everything; she had no idea she was actually dealing with two of us. But that was the only way I could remain rational. There was the one I portrayed on the outside, and the actual me inside. It was great amusement for me to rebuke every statement she made concerning compliance of a bride or wife to her husband, while vocally agreeing wholeheartedly with the nurse. So, we'd go like this:

'Doctoreh' (Malayalam style). And I'd think to myself, *Oh! O! Another lecture.'* But I really loved her and did not want to hurt her, so I'd listen.

'Doctoreh, namell bhariyamar ananu yeappolum orthonum' (Doctor, we should always remember that we are wives). Even if I wasn't yet a wife, she had already included me in this moralistic crowd as if bestowing on me some sort of award. I'd nod my head and agree on the outside. But I'd think in my head, *The heck, why should I keep remembering this mundane fact about being a wife to X, Y or Z the whole time? What am I supposed to do with this knowledge? Moreover, I'd give the husband, whoever he is, such a headache he'd never forget that he had got himself a wife.'* And then she'd go on about the 'natuns' (sisters-in-law) and how I should be good to them. And in my mind, I'd be thinking, *Right! I'll be decent if they are. But if they're nasty, I'll give them hell. I know a thing or two about ragging.'* Her classic line and where I really tried hard not to laugh was when she explained about the mother-in-law. 'Sondham amayapol nokanum,' (Consider her like your own mother), she'd say in the most straitlaced tone of voice, her face deadpan. The height of it! This last bit tickled my gizzard so much that I'd let the genie pop out, or else I would have suffocated to death. So, I'd say, more to shock her than anything else, 'Sistereh, sondham amma allello. Pina ageneya?' (She is not the real mother; then how do we do that?). She'd look aghast and gasp, 'Aiyo, bharthvinda ama namuda ama tannaya' (Goodness! The husband's mother is really our mother). That thought was as alien to me as it was natural to her. I'd just look at her and shake my head thinking how poles apart we were. But she was so conditioned, I'd be an idiot to argue. She only knew her point of view and was closed to any other way of thinking. So, I let her ramble away to high glory.

OGC met one weekend, and Uncle Thomas, who had absolute control over everything, decided the time was right to set the wheels in motion.

The selection process, of which I only had a vague idea, was complex. There was a person called 'dhellaal,' or marriage broker. He was mighty important and acted as liaison between the boy's party and the girl's party. I can never forget my dhellaal. He had a peculiar walk, like a stork moving on its thin legs. A worn-out umbrella hooked onto his shirt collar and hanging at the black was his trademark. His eyes were perpetually darting from left to right as if searching for his next victim. He had three books, one in which he kept a list of ordinary suckers and another in which he kept a list of rich suckers. When these two books failed to impress, ta-da!! He brought out a third one, the little red book that he kept hidden in a cloth satchel that swung from his left shoulder. That was THE BOOK. In it, he had the names of the crème de la crème of suitors. Their ages, educational qualifications, height, weight(?), family background, and perchance, their financial standing. I'm not sure, but I guess he would have listed how much land, haystacks, field workers, cows, goats, hens(?), eggs(?) et al. How a dhellaal worked was very strategic. I think it was a time-tested method, carefully designed and laid out by the crafty buzzard. He would throw you a morsel from his book for ordinary suckers and watch you bite. He would gauge how hungry you were. How desperate. And accordingly upgrade the books.

The first chap that the dhellaal brought was straight from the red book, by-passing the other two books. I guess he understood the urgency concerning my marriage and that the parents were willing to pay anything. That made him cut to the chase. An engineer from some place or other. Uncle summoned me to the ancestral home during the weekend. The aunties were present. Together, they formed a challenging assembly. My only ally was Grandmother, but she did not have much clout when face by a full battalion. Everyone spoke over my head, as they usually did, as if it was about anyone other than me. I needed a stronger accomplice. So, I called for Sibling to join me. She was studying English at Women's College, Trivandrum, and though so much younger than me, had grown up to be a force to be reckoned with. Her mesmerizing charm, for she was a beautiful creature, hid a steely resolve, and an indomitable urge to fight for the underbitch, Moi. To tell the truth, she actually just enjoyed a good fight, especially if it was against a sanctimonious group, or one like the OGC – full of spurious righteousness. She loved to say and do outrageous things to shock. I'm afraid I encouraged her, like a good elder sister should. Sibling's arrival did not please the committee, as they knew it gave me an advantage.

The stage was set. The boy's party arrived at about 4 pm. I was so full of dread, fearing my life would be over. Sibling reassured me and told me that nothing I didn't want would take place. She also told me that she was going to stand guard on the veranda to get the first look at the boy so she could warn me on what to expect. She was gone for maybe ten minutes before she came rushing back. She was a little breathless as she flopped on the bed. Then we looked at each other. I was anxious, but her face gave away nothing. A second later, she burst out laughing. I wondered if the chap was so ridiculous that Sibling had gone crazy just by looking at him. When she caught her breath, she gasped, 'Relax Ini. Relax. That's not a suitor. That's a clown who's escaped from the circus.'.

And we both started laughing as she described him. The aunts came into the room, saw us laughing, and became hysterical. They stated, 'Eedah kalli tamasha alla' (This is no joking matter). But to their utter dismay and consternation and to my ridiculous glee, Sibling just could not let go and asked them, 'So which zoo did you get this one from?'

After the perfunctory meeting with the boy's party, the dhellaal suggested that the boy and girl talk for a bit to get to know each other. Just imagine ten minutes of mumbling for a lifetime of togetherness. But the best part of the day was just around the corner – who knew? The chap and I moved to the veranda. Sibling moved with us. We sat down, and she sat with us. He asked some random questions, and she answered. I just smiled, but I was roaring with laughter on the inside. Suddenly, the aunties appeared, and they were agitated at finding Sibling with us. They tried to get her to leave, and when she would not budge, they called Uncle. He too did not know what else to do other than ask her to leave, which she stoutly refused. The aftermath of this sorry meeting was both liberating as well as disastrous. Liberating because the proposal was called off, disastrous because we were reprimanded from every side. Even Grandmother disapproved. It was decided that any further meetings would take place at the clinic in Pandalam, in the absence of Sibling.

And that was how the next suitor presented himself at the clinic. My Nair nurse was all business. She fussed over me and advised and cajoled and coaxed. The Uncle had come earlier in the day to warn me to behave. I don't remember too much about this meeting other than the fact that the fellow was a decent enough chap who wore a thick gold watch on his right hand and carried a briefcase, probably filled with money. Or a secret weapon a la James Bond. If only! I did not know what reason I could give for turning down the gentleman or how I could go on refusing any others. What did I want in a man? What was I looking for? I'll tell you this – even I didn't know. But my refusal of this second proposal, or third if you count the one back in Malaysia, was the straw that broke the camel's back. Uncle was livid. The chap was the son of a renowned priest. He had an excellent job in Muscat. How dare I? Who did I think I was? I phoned Sibling and asked her if I should relent. She asked me if I found the chap pleasing. I asked her if she was crazy. She said she was not crazy but I would be if I relented to please Uncle. Then she said with a laugh, 'Hey Ini, what do you call a guy from Muscat?'

'I dunno,' I said glumly, 'What?'

'A Musketeer,' she said screeching with laughter. I too laughed despite the gravity of my situation. And suddenly I felt better.

After I replaced the phone, I dragged my way back to the clinic. I thought of all the phases of my life. The bewilderment of leaving home at the tender age of twelve, the desolate, abandoned feelings as I lay in the sick room at the boarding school, the audacity to shave the 'Downs,' the fear of death at the onset of the menstrual cycle, the cruel taunts of 'maidanum' at college, the ragging at the Dental College, the unconventional lunches with Dr. Lenora, the fags I enjoyed, the hundreds of arguments with the parents, and so many other things. But everything seemed trifle to the humungous weight of the Sword of Damocles that dangled over my head at this point. The heaviness of the responsibility that hung upon me and demanded of me to make a correct choice in so short a time. The horror of identifying a partner to share the rest of my life with.

I did not know if I had it in me to do justice to this life-changing task or if I was wise enough to navigate the path and reach a correct decision.

The official photo to launch a thousand suitors

A Marriage Proposal

A week after I rejected the last proposal, Mother landed in India. She was not laughing. Things were serious. The fun and games were over. She gave Sibling the shelling of her life for being intrusive in matters that did not concern her. Mother was conniving enough to know that in chastising Sibling, she could put the fear of God into me. Mother was crafty in more ways than one. She demanded I look at myself in the mirror. I did and saw a girl in her late twenties, well-built, of wheatish complexion, totally avant-garde, on the threshold, waiting. But waiting for what and for whom eluded Moi. This crucial question was answered that day. Mother declared she was changing the dhellaal and acquiring a more efficient one for the express purpose of finalizing a suitor and getting me a husband.

The mood was heavy. I was told more than once by all the family that I was on the wrong side of twenty and acting like a brat. Mother asked me what was wrong with the Muscat chap that I should refuse. Unfortunately, I recalled Sibling's Musketeer joke and sniggered; even while trying to suppress the rising mirth, then in spite of myself, I giggled. Big, big mistake. She shredded me to bits, then warned me terrible steps would be taken if I did not cooperate. I wondered if she would cut me up, cook me, and serve me to the OGC committee members for dinner. She looked like she would. Here I was, acting the 'nalla Malayalee pennu,' given up a good job in Malaysia, given up fags, given up my very personality. What more could they ask of a girl? How much more cooperation? I was thunderously bewildered. In fact, I told Mother if the Muscat chap was all that great, I would agree. Fortunately for me, we came to understand that he had found a girl and was in the process of proceeding with his marriage. I tell you, I was mighty relieved. I guess I could understand Mother's dilemma. Wherever we went, the main topic of conversation was my unmarried status. The Church was the most judgemental of all places. One would imagine the old baboons' disguised as matrons came to church for prayer and penance. But no, they had mischief on their minds. They would corner Mother and pelt her with questions, one after the other, showing outward sympathy but secretly enjoying Mother's discomfiture. Why wasn't I married? Their daughters were younger than me and pregnant to boot. Others had children of their own. Mother would get into a huff later, after such conversations, and tell me I was spoilt and selfish. Secretly, I think she believed folks thought she was not doing the right thing by Moi, and it bothered her no end. I felt the first stirrings of guilt and remorse and decided to co-operate with all of my heart.

Now the hunt was on in all seriousness. The hounds were on the loose. The bugles called. We were after a suitable boy. I was not asked an opinion about anything, least of all if I wanted to marry. I was ignored, which was a funny situation, as all this concerned Moi. A number of new dhellaals or marriage-mongers (I coined this word from fishmonger, and I hope it would catch on) visited Mother. Strangely, all these guys looked much like the first dhellaal, and it got me thinking that perhaps one has to acquire a certain kind of look in order to qualify and succeed in this dhellaal business. Think two peas in a pod. Tall, thin, stooped over, with the leg of an umbrella hanging precariously over their hand or shirt collar. A cloth satchel swung over one shoulder. A thick, bound, well-worn book under their arm. Invariably, they had two types of moustaches covering the upper-lip. Either a large, black style which covered most of the upper lip, so you never knew if they were smiling, sneering, or just maintaining a neutral upper lip, or a pencil thin centipede style, in which case you were exposed to their betel-stained teeth and gums. Both were ghastly. They would come in turns to visit mother and read out a list of the suitable boys available in their roster.

'Ah, here is a boy,' they would say, with the right amount of surprise, as if coming across this information only just then. 'A doctor, fair, tall, and speaks very good English. He comes from fine stock too.' *Were they talking livestock?* I wondered. 'Now here is another, with lots of land and three huge haystacks. That translates to cows and that, in turn, to dung for the fields. An excellent proposal if you have agriculture on mind,' they would slog on. This was the first time I realized the value of cow dung relating to anything other than as a fertilizer. It amazed me when I heard of how cow dung could be used as a means of enticement to settle a marriage arrangement.

All these bits of information were given with such smugness that you would not be wrong to think that these fellows were actually proud of their 'boys in the book.' 'Look at this,' they would persist, 'Working in America. Very accomplished, church-going, and from an aristocratic family.' I don't know of any "Suriyani Christiyani" parent who can say no to that.

I remember one marriage-monger in particular. He kept the best for the last. With a magician's flare for whisking out a rabbit from the hat, he brought out the little red book from his inner pocket. 'Here, I keep the best,' he said with a smirk. He thumbed through the pages and read out, 'Aristocratic, tall, wheatish complexioned. Engineer working in Madras, 32 years, excellent family, landed.' He looked up and beamed. I could see the smile beneath the thick moustache. He was biding his time to render the master stroke. We waited with bated breath. Triumphantly, he said, eyes gleaming, 'indoor plumbing and sanitation'!

That, people, sealed my fate!

One Saturday in July of 1978, Mother came to the clinic. It was raining cats and dogs. She folded her umbrella and wiped her wet face with the pallav of her sari. She looked tired and defeated, and my heart broke within me. I told nurse to get a coffee from the canteen. When we were alone, I cupped her face in my hands and kissed her. She searched my face and looked at me beseechingly. The furrows on her forehead told me of her frustrations and concern. *She is such a 'worry-monger,'* I thought, *and I have given her plenty of reasons to have many sleepless nights.* Fish monger, marriage monger, and now worry monger. I was getting into the habit of "mongerizing" everything. *Was I losing my bearings*, I wondered.

I smiled. 'What is it, Mother?' I asked tenderly.

Slowly, she answered, 'A boy will come today. During your lunch hour. Be nice.'

Automatically, I said, 'Of course.'

She gave me a silly, whimsical grin. That did it. I wanted to please her more than anything in the world. I would have died for her at that moment. If this chap was worth the half of anything, I decided I would agree. Nurse came in with the coffee. After the drink, Mother looked more like herself.

More collected. So, I thought to discuss the specifications I had put to her concerning any suitor. My aim was to tease her.

I ventured.

'This boy, Mother, is he a six-footer?'

'No.'

'Silky-straight hair?'

'No.'

'Does he wear a gold watch on the right hand like a ruffian?'

'The watch is not gold. And you can get him to tie it on the left hand.'

'Hummm. Good looking?'

No answer.

'Perfect,' I said with a sigh.

Things were at a dead end. An impasse. The driver came. She got up to go.

'He is robust and healthy. And you. You will never change,' she said impulsively.

Then she left. Even today, I wonder what she meant by that. With my back to the wall, and no one to turn to, I decided to talk to God. He, at least, would listen in silence and not argue. So, I asked in desperation, 'What are You playing at, Dear Father in Heaven? Haven't You wreaked enough havoc on an unsuspecting young girl all these years? The marriages I see around me are like boxing matches between two people who tolerate each other and find no way to escape. You've created so many victims already. Will You never be satisfied? And I know how You entice those trapped in these marriage messes to recruit the vulnerable like Moi. Or else why is Uncle Thomas and the whole of OGC involved and full of unholy glee at the prospect of tying me down? I'll bet they want me to suffer like they all do. And using Mother as bait was below the belt, Lord. I never expected that of You. I wish you would pick on someone Your own size and with Your power and leave poor me alone. And while I'm at it, dear Father, let me tell you, sometimes, Your silence irritates. Amen.'

The 'Amen' was a sarcastic rejoinder, but I guess it was lost on the Lord.

Then I braced myself and waited for the lunch break, like the condemned wait for the noose.

Enter the Dragon

There was every sign that the noose was tightening – that much was obvious to Moi. I decided to make a quick call to the Sibling at Women's College, Trivandrum. I told her that Mother had visited and that a chap was coming to take a dekko. I also told her of my desire to cave in; enough was enough. She told me to stay strong and not be bullied by Mother. Easier said than done. A little before noon, I told Nurse to wind up and clean the place. Then I told her to stand by the door so she had a clear view right up to the hospital gate. Just like Sibling did, I wanted her to give me a heads-up. We idled for a while, then suddenly, she perked up.

'Doctoreh, randu pear bikeala varununda' (Doctor, there are two guys coming on a bike).

(The following conversation was in Malayalam, but I will write it in English. Those readers who can translate it to Malayalam for authenticity and effect may do so).

'How do they look?' I asked.

'I cannot see clearly; the sun is in their faces,' she replied.

'Can you see them now?' I asked after a pause.

'Yes.'

'So?' I questioned, eager to get a morsel of information.

'Doctoreh, everything is not about beauty,' she said complacently. God forbid, I thought I'd get up and box her ears.

'Answer my question,' I said with controlled patience.

'The chap riding the bike is ordinary,' she conceded.

'And?' I waited, hoping against hope.

'The pillion rider is very healthy looking,' she said with a sigh.

'What? What does that mean?' I asked. I was at my wits' end. What had health got to do with anything?

'Men need to be healthy. That is a man's beauty,' she said with finality.

There was no moving her after that. So, I let it go. Both of us waited, and presently, we heard footsteps and a tap on the door. Nurse was like a hen that had just laid an egg, all flutter and fluster. I tried to steel my nerves. The first chap to enter was decidedly ordinary, with a huge, extraordinarily white-toothed grin plastered on his face. A dentist's dream. I will not go into too much description for obvious reasons. He was clearly not my type. It was an out and out 'no,' however you looked at it. Even if it should kill Mother. Close behind was the pillion rider, decidedly healthy. That's what struck you first. His buoyant health. He had a half grin, sort of a quirk, and by comparison, I stress here, by comparison to the friend, almost handsome. Well, that is, if you like the rough, rugged, macho type. A man's man. I prayed to God that if this be the suitor, then let the festivities begin. I was done with this Naive American War Dance. The first entrant kept the wide, white-toothed smile fixed in place at all times. *Is it something to do with my being a dentist?* I wondered. *And don't his jaw muscles hurt, for Pete's sake?* Seriously, it was a stretched, ear-to-ear grin. Very carefully, he pulled up a chair and sat down. Nice and quiet.

The other chap was more relaxed. Before he insolently drew up a chair with his feet(!) and sat down, he turned to Nurse and suggested,

'Sistereh, nilkendah. Oru kaserah konduvannu irikku' (Sister, don't stand around. Get a chair and sit down).

I saw Nurse melt before my eyes with that one stroke. The traditional 'Nair Stree' (Nair woman) jumped out of the window. In its place stood a hand-wringing, blushing girl.

'Oh, vanda sarreh. Ninolam,' said Nurse, blushing against her will (Oh! No sir. I'll stand).

I saw his smile widen and watched in horror at Nurse almost going into an atrial fibrillation. This blatant seduction of my moralistic nurse both excited and frightened me. Chivalry in this part of the world was new to me. And daylight seduction?? Out of my league. His posture was ramrod straight, no slacking. Military like. Arms straight out, resting on his knees. The fingers were long and strong. He had a good, thick moustache (I liked my guys clean-shaven) and the smallest pair of eyes I had ever seen. But I tell you, they watched and saw every detail. We spoke in a mixture of English and Malayalam. Later, I found out that Uncle was outside the clinic and had told them I was comfortable with English. The bike rider began.

'My name is Thomas. I'm a Physics professor at the college.'

'*So, is he the chap*, I wondered. No sign to indicate anything.

'This is my friend Abraham,' Thomas introduced his friend.

'Nyan Malayalathil samsarikam. Anikku adanu comfortable,' Abraham said with a hint of amusement in his voice (I will converse in Malayalam. I am comfortable with that).

This was said with that same quirk on the lips as if to take the sting out of the words. *Okay, wise guy, so what's your Malayalam word for 'comfortable'?* I questioned in my head. I remembered my promise to Mother and kept the wise-cracks to myself. Still not an iota of a sign as to who was who. I looked to Nurse for support, but she, of course, was busy looking elsewhere. After about 10 minutes of twiddle-twaddle, Thomas got up and said he would look around the hospital. Ta-da! It was not as if he was going to buy the hospital now was he, that he wanted to take a look around. Immediately, I understood he was a sort of 'pseudo dhellaal,' and he was leaving to enable us to have our 20-minute chat.

Later, I was to know that these two friends had made a pact. If the girl was not worth the effort, Thomas would continue to sit, and then both would leave after a decent interval. But if the girl was okay, then Thomas would leave to look around the hospital, thereby signalling his approval and giving Abraham some private time. How strategically planned was that? Right, everything was set. Nurse, discreetly though reluctantly, went to the canteen to get some bites and coffee. Finally, we were alone, appraising each other. Reminded me of a cock fight. Of course, I was in the dark about what he saw in me. But I saw a cocky, self-confident, care-a-damn attitude in the chap before me. Healthy, of course, handsome even, in a rugged, roguish, impudent kind of way. The watch on the right hand added to the aura. I didn't know what to make of it. This was new to me. This aggressive machismo. We had no brothers, Sibling and I. I wished Sibling was with me.

'Clinic kolammello,' he said, looking around (The clinic looks good). In a bid to break the ice, I suppose.

'Ya. Nyan anna set up chaithadhu,' I replied, a tad proudly (Yes. I set it up).

'Malayalam ariyamello, Uncle paranyadhu ootum samsarikathilla ana,' he said pleasantly. (You know Malayalam. Uncle said you could not speak the language at all).

'Samsarikam, vaikanum aruthanum ariyathilla,' I clarified (I can speak. I can't read or write).

A pause. The following conversation is etched in my mind for all time.

'Aanoda andhangilum chothikan undo,' he questioned leaning back in the chair (Do you have anything to ask of me?).

I searched the whole of my head, but could not come up with anything pertinent, so I asked him about the first thing that I enjoyed doing – reading.

'Vaikarundo?' I asked (Do you read?).

'Oh! Pinna,' he replied with a smile (Oh! Sure).

That quirk was now more pronounced. I should have been warned. Later, I was to find out he never touched a book for leisure reading. He was more outdoorsy.

'Aanda book ana ishtam?' I probed in all sincerity (What sort of books do you like)?

'"Kochu pustakam." Ketutundoo?' He asked, watching me closely (The small book. Have you heard of it?).

The quirk was now a wide grin as if suppressing a laugh. The eyes betrayed a mischievous glint. Oh! How the lamb was led to the slaughter.

Not wanting to appear ignorant, maybe even wanting to show off a bit, I put my foot in the mouth.

'Ketutunda, vachitilla. Malayalathielleh?' (I have heard about it. Never read. Isn't it in Malayalam?).

This time, he threw back his head and laughed with total abandon. No decorum. No constraints. Where he was or what this meeting was all about hardly bothered him. It was infectious. I didn't for the life of me know what he was laughing about. But I just joined in, not his wild laugh, but a half laugh. Nurse and Thomas came in about then.

'Kolamello. Randu perum thamasha adikugayano. Nyagalkuda cheramo?' Thomas asked, looking surprised (That's good. You guys are enjoying a joke. Can we join in?).

'Pinnanna? Lennie kochu pustakatina kurichu ketutunda. Vaichutilla,' he offered magnanimously (Why not? Seems Lennie knows about the small book. But has not read it).

Renewed laughter from Abraham as he said this. Thomas looked decidedly uncomfortable. Nurse was horrified. I knew I had been had. Abraham sat as cool as a cucumber. After they left, Nurse told me in a panic, fumbling over her words, that 'kochu pustakam' was slang for a pack of cards. In some ambiguous circles, it was also the name given to the 'naughty blue book.' I wondered how far down my mouth I had put my foot. I felt it come out of my arse. As soon as Abraham and Thomas left the clinic, Uncle cornered them. Nurse had already followed them outside to gather news and bring it to me. She was acting so out of character, I was concerned. Gone was her 'Nalla Nair Stree' avatar.

'Did you like the girl?' Uncle asked Abraham anxiously.

'Let Lennie give her opinion first,' he replied, without giving away anything.

'That's ok. She will do as I tell her,' Uncle said off-handedly.

'No. Don't force her. She has to give her answer free of pressure,' Abraham said adamantly.

Nurse came tearing back with this bit. Uncle followed her into the clinic.

'Lennie, what is your opinion?' Uncle asked. I detected a cautionary sign in his voice as if to warn me about giving a negative answer. I weighed the pros and cons. The balance tilted slightly to the pros. Even if I was peeved about the blue book, the fact that he had told uncle that I was not to be forced into an answer tipped the balance in his favour. I heaved a sigh, and with a thundering heart, gave my answer.

'If you think it's good, I'm OK with it,' I said, trying to sound brave.

Uncle jumped out of the clinic like he had been bitten in his butt. Nurse followed like her butt was on fire. She lurked about to get the news. I didn't know what it was about getting me hitched that made monkeys out of these people.

'Lennie has agreed,' Uncle beamed.

'Good. Then I am also in agreement,' Abraham said with a grin.

'But don't you have to discuss this with your parents?' Uncle asked, astonished.

'Why? What's the need? I'm the one marrying her. Not them,' Abraham retorted.

'About the dowry…' Uncle's voice trailed away.

'What you give your girl is your business. Not mine. I don't need to know,' Abraham cut him short.

'But that is a big issue to be discussed by elders,' Uncle said, flabbergasted.

'My parents will stand by my decision. There is nothing to worry,' Abraham said as he prepared to leave.

Nurse came running back to the clinic, took both my hands and sobbed into them. I was aghast. *Did he say no*? And more worrying, what had happened to my pragmatic and stoic Nair nurse?

'Aanda? Aanda Sistereh? Vanda aanu paranjyo?' (What? What is it sister? Did he refuse?) I enquired, the bile rising in my throat. If he dared to reject me, the joke would be on Moi for having refused so many.

'Eella. Eella aanda doctoreh. Eendoru purushan. Daivam konda tannada,' said Sister, almost reverently (No. No, my dear doctor. What a man. God has given him to you).

And then she told me all. I ran to the phone booth. I called Sibling. I regurgitated the events.

'I thought this was just a dekko. You're spoken for now?' she asked incredulously.

'Even I thought so. But Mother and Uncle…' I began, but she cut me off.

'Say no more. I'm coming down. Let us start a plan to get you out of this hapless, hopeless, mess,' she said in an ominous, determined voice.

But when the Heavens conspire, the moment is right.

The one that bagged the cat

A Marriage is Fixed

There was no pacifying the Sibling. She called me back the same Saturday evening. 'Ini, one spends more time buying a duck in the market,' she argued. 'What do you know of this chap? His family? His brothers and sisters? Is he an only child? He'll be a selfish bugger then! Buck up your gizzards! This weekend is over. I'll come down next Saturday, and we'll figure out something. Stay positive.'

I mulled over Sibling's observation. It was true. Father scrutinized the fish he bought at the market for more time than Abraham and I had spent talking. I knew practically nothing about this fellow, except that he read the 'kochu pustakam.' Even that I doubted; I was sure he was having a laugh at my expense. Anyway, what was I going to do with the knowledge of reading a 'kochu pusthakam,' whatever that was? I was in a sticky puddle – that much was clear. The next day, Sunday, was crucial. A meeting was called at the ancestral home. All the members of the OGC were present. In addition, there were Mother, Grandfather, Grandmother, various minor family extensions, and of course, Moi. Sibling was conspicuous by her absence. Uncle called the meeting to order. He began in a solemn voice, like a priest intoning a ritualistic reading of the Psalm.

'We are gathered here today to discuss and finalize the arrangements of Lennie's marriage. The boy, Abraham, is an Engineer and belongs to the Komattu Family of Maromon,' he said with such aplomb that I thought he had birthed the chap himself and was responsible for all of his achievements. He continued, 'The father is a retired Headmaster and the mother, a home maker. They have ten children.' He paused for effect, stroked his moustache, and looked around.

I snapped awake. *Wait, what? Ten? Really? Was that even possible? Could anyone have ten children? How would one remember all of their names, ages, and birthdays?* Even the Von Trapps only boasted seven. I searched Uncle's face to see if he was joking. He was actually beaming and bursting with pride, his attitude declaring, 'Look what I have found!' His face radiated a glow akin to what Christopher Columbus would have had when he sighted the New World for the first time. I looked at Mother. Her face gave nothing away, but I got the feeling she approved of Uncle's announcement. *Oh, wait till Sibling hears this!* I was dying to run for the telephone, even if there was only one of those contraptions in the village, and it was situated in the post office. Using it was like telling the whole world your business. Uncle went on, 'Abraham, fondly called Raju at home, is the 9th rank holder in his family! He works with Siemens in Madras.' Rank holder? Did he actually say that? Was that an achievement, being the ninth born in a family of ten? There were only two in my family, Moi and Sibling. I was already feeling inferior. My parents suddenly became such underachievers in my mind. *I am already at a disadvantage even before entering this marriage*, I thought. Then Uncle took out a list he had prepared and went on to read out the name, age, qualifications, and so on of the eldest of the children, and worked his way right down to the youngest. They were all educated, with a number of doctors, engineers, and teachers, and one brother even in the army, serving the country. I could not follow or keep up with the who's who of this illustrious family. The only thing that registered in my head and shook my jillie-billies to the core was the fact that the eldest son was older than my own father. What a conundrum. I was suddenly dying to laugh.

I went back to the clinic on Monday, and the week stretched out threateningly in front of me. The challenges I had to face were innumerable, the first being a really daunting task Uncle had set for me. He had passed on the list of the names of the nine siblings of the boy, as well as the names of their spouses and children, and I was to make a study of it. I had passed all of the dental exams. Now this was the Marriage Entrance exam. Would I have to do a multiple-choice question paper? And that was not all. As they were scattered all over the world, I was to brush up on my geography and make a study of Kuwait, Muscat, England, Canada, Singapore, and Chennai. Nurse was blissfully unaware of my inner turmoil and kept advising me on all the things essential for the making of a good wife. She also ruminated on the visit made by the two friends when they first came to see me, and she could not say enough to extol the virtues of Abraham. She could not get over the fact that he had invited her to pull up a chair and sit down with them. 'Shoo,' she kept saying, 'Shoo onu alojeechea' (Just think of it).

It was in the midst of all this, two days later, on Wednesday, that a new dhellaal appeared on the horizon. He came straight to the clinic with another proposal, that of a doctor, working somewhere or the other. Like the proverbial dying person, I clutched at this straw. Nurse was outraged. She reminded me that I was betrothed. Was I? Nothing was official in my eyes, except that OGC had held a meeting. I ran to the booth and called Mother. Now, here's the thing. The only phone in our village was at the post office, and I have told you how that worked. Our house was just across the road, so we used the phone like our own. The phone rang, and the postmaster came on the line. I identified myself and asked if I could speak to Mother. He said of course I could, but he did not let me go that easily.

'So, your marriage is fixed, I hear. Lucky boy. We hear he is a very healthy chap.'

I detected a leer in the tone. And what was this business with the man's health?

'Mmmm,' I said, giving away nothing.

'Anyway, all of us at the post office congratulate you and informing you of our happiness.'

Why were they happy at my misery, for God's sake?

'Can I speak to Mother?' I asked, ignoring his bonhomie.

'Sure, sure. Why not? Anything for our bride,' said the postmaster, with a raucous laugh.

I heard him ask the errand boy to run over and call Mother, and in the same breath, he announced to all and sundry that it was the bride calling. 'Namudeh kaliyaneh pennu' was how he put it. Ye Gods, since when was I the village property? At 11 am, I knew the post office would be packed to capacity. After a moment, the postmaster informed me that Mother was not at home and added as an afterthought that Mother had a telegram from Father saying he would be arriving in two days. And that the engagement was fixed for Saturday. Well! It seemed like the postmaster knew more about Moi and mine than I did. I understood the village grapevine was in full throttle. Since there was no way of contacting Mother over the phone, I thought I'd go home after clinics and talk to her. But an even bigger surprise awaited me at the clinic when I returned from the phone booth at the office. A beaming Nurse informed me that Abraham had made a cursory visit and was waiting inside. He was alone – no friend this time. He informed me that he had some relatives close by and had come to visit them and inform them of the impending nuptials. But I think he had just come to check on me. It was a good thing too. Immediately, I saw an advantage to his visit and decided, first, to ask a favour from him, and second, to tell him something that had been plaguing my mind.

So, straight out, first I asked him for a lift home. I knew it was nasty to use him to get home to discuss another proposal. But what's a sinking damsel to do? Nurse was horrified when I asked for the lift. I expect she thought me too forward; it was not the way a blushing bride would behave, and for once, she was at a loss for words. I think she was also too scandalized and frozen to make an objection at my suggestion and Abraham's ready acceptance of the matter.

Next, I broached the subject of my hair in an undertone. I kept it low, trying to keep it out of the Nurse's ears, since even she was unaware of my false hair bun. At first it did not register with Abraham, so I had to speak louder and tell him about my very short pixie haircut. Nurse heard this and made a choking sound and slid behind the door.

That quirk appeared, and he said, 'That's ok. Have you noticed; my hair is also short, but I'm not apologising. I won't ask you to grow yours if you don't ask me to grow mine.'

I grinned in relief, picked up my bag, and left to thumb the ride home. I did not check to see if Nurse had aroused herself from her stupor behind the door. In any case, I was a bit peeved with her, seeing that she was biased, and the pointer on her loyalty meter was flipping to the opposite side. During the ride home, I wondered if I was doing the right thing trying to get out of this conundrum and into another. The chap who sat in the car, softly whistling some obscure tune and taking me home, seemed a decent sort. He had even taken the truth about my hair with nonchalance.

The ride was worth it, even if only to see the astonishment on everyone's faces when we got out of the car. The boy and girl together? Before marriage? Did we know each other from before? Did we have an understanding? What were we doing together? Or more to the point, did we do anything together? The questions were fast and furious. Abraham did not stay to answer, but he grinned as he gave a parting shot and a knowing look, 'Lennie allam parayum' (Lennie will explain all).

I guess my reputation was shredded to bits by this subtle innuendo. I was to find out later in life that the appearance of the trademark quirk was a warning that he was going to do something outrageous or say something brash. I spoke to Mother about the dhellaal and the new proposal, and she almost plunged the carving knife into Moi. I got the message. Wasted journey. But Mother had an even more shocking piece of news to give me. I could sense she was nervous. She made two cups of coffee, and we sat down. She took a few sips, perhaps to steady her nerves. Then Mother told me she had had a visitor from Abraham's village who had informed her that the groom-to-be was a real wild child. He lived on the river Pamba in a 'vallum' (small boat), fished, swam, and hunted.

'So? He's outdoorsy. What's so bad about that? Maybe I'll have to live on a vallum too,' I said, more to spite Mother than anything else. He was her find.

'You don't mind?' Mother asked in shock.

'Not if he's not already married. No,' I said.

'It's OK then? The whole family is well educated and well placed. Regular church goers too,' said Mother, more to assure herself than me.

'I think I'll be OK. You don't worry,' I said flippantly.

My life was moving faster than the speed of light. One rainy Saturday morning, Mother had come to the clinic, and by afternoon, I was spoken for. It was decided that the following Saturday would be the formal engagement, and the marriage was fixed for the third Saturday, 5th August of 1978. Three weeks in which the greatest change in my life was to take place.

I had a thousand questions. Which young girl didn't? There was no Google to search and find out things for yourself. I had no formal sex education in the correct sense of the word. Or even a talk about such matters with any person who knew something about the subject. In fact, I don't think anyone thought there was a need for it. You were expected to discover things for yourself and improvise as you went along. Of course, we had our girlie chats and discussions at school and college, but there was nothing definitive. We knew what went where, that sort of thing. But most thoughts, questions, and doubts were kept under wraps. It would be death to your dignity if someone had even an inkling that you thought those thoughts! You could be branded a promiscuous wanton, and then what's your status? Everyone was so busy being moralistic. You never spoke to mothers about carnal doubts. Eeeks! As for married cousins, they would tease that you were in a hurry to know things, then never told you anything. And sadly, I had no idea how to get hold of the little blue book. But more than all this, I just needed a mentor who was nonjudgemental, kind, and understanding to mentally prepare for my transition from carefree girl to dutiful wife. What to expect when we enter a new family and how to treat it as our own. To help me understand and accept the family dynamics of my new home, which would most definitely be different from mine. To explain the steps required to stay sane and calm under the new regime. Just someone to listen to my anxieties and placate my fears.

Finally, Sibling gave me an idea, even if this was not her area of expertise. 'Ini, you have two options. One is to ask Abraham about all your doubts. Anyway, isn't that the Mephistopheles you're selling your soul to? Or two, ask Nurse. Being married and all, she'll definitely know what's what.' Then she laughed her head off.

'Dear God,' I beseeched of the Almighty one last time, 'I'm all alone in this adventure, help me navigate through the labyrinth. Show me the way.'

Sometimes, it's so easy to hate Sibling. I knew she was angry with me for caving in to the proposal, for not waiting for her to give her judgement on the matter. Between Mother and Sibling, I was becoming persona non grata, as both wanted me to comply with their ideas, and I wanted to please both.

Father arrived soon after, and before I could say 'hell's bells,' it was Saturday, and everyone had gathered for the engagement. Usually, only the elder men folk came for the finalizing, not the groom. But as the car drew up, Abraham stepped out. True to form, he had thrown traditions out the window. They did not matter to him, as he did things as he pleased. We were watching through the window. It was Father's first glimpse of the son-in-law-to-be. I heard him draw in his breath and say, 'What a healthy young man!'

Could too much health destroy a marriage, I wondered.

The Ten

A Husband is Acquired

The wedding was a modest affair by today's standards. No videos, drones, MCs, marriage organizers, or online streaming. Only black and white photos to record the event. There were no beauty salons either, to do your hair and makeup. It was unheard of. In any case, good girls did not use lipstick or mascara or go to beauty salons. And here I was, addicted to all. As usual, Sibling came to the rescue.

'Ini,' she said, 'Ini, it's your freaking wedding. Do what you want. Paint your face green and to hell with everyone.' It was good to have a reckless person as an consultant. Anyway, that settled it, and so, together, we organized my hair and makeup. It was presentable if nothing else. Mummers about the lipstick and mascara were inevitable. But the big uproar was about my earrings. Two ridiculous white stones and not dangling gold, the elders scoffed. I refused to raise to the bait and stuck to my guns. I was not going to waste my breath explaining what solitaires were to a group of cranky Chedathies. Besides, they were precious gifts from the parents. When we were ready to leave for the venue, Father called me aside. We went to his room and closed the door. He took me by the shoulders and said, 'Darling child, I have brought you up as I would a son. I have given you an education and the freedom to think and act. I want you to live to be worthy of those. You should stand your ground if you think you're right and never hang your head for any reason. You are an equal to anyone. Promise me.' I promised him, and I have never failed him.

There was just a lone photographer scouting around when we arrived at the spectacularly beautiful old church in Abraham's village. Nurse arrived in her glad rags – a red and green Kanchipuram sari – and a load of jasmine flowers in her hair. She told anyone who was willing to listen how she had manoeuvred for the whole thing to come together. She also kept an eye on me like she expected me to abscond in the middle of the ceremony and as if she had a moral duty to prevent it. But I was resigned to my fate and went with the flow. The bishop, in all his finery, officiated the rituals, which were long and laborious. He chanted in Hebrew or Syrian to a congregation of Malayalees, and I wondered what anyone understood. His tone of voice sounded bored and jaded to me, and I wished he would put some enthusiasm into it, if only to brighten a young bride's day and give her hope. Suddenly, there was some activity around us, and I realized it was time for the 'minnu kettu.' This is considered more a cultural ceremony than a Christian ritual. Five or seven threads were removed from the 'mandrakodi' or ceremonial sari, waxed together, and the 'minnu' or blessed locket, worn by every married Syrian Christian woman, was looped onto it. Once this part of the ceremony is completed, your goose is as good as cooked. The whole shebang was over, and it was followed by a scrumptious meal, as if to make amends for wasting everyone's time.

I watched Sibling have a gala time catching up with cousins, and I'll bet I was the butt of their jokes. After the meal, immediate family members were to gather at the boy's home for a formality called 'kacha kodupu,' where a ceremonial sari was given to the bride's mother by the groom, and she reciprocated by putting a gold chain on the boy's neck. So, Abraham and I, now officially man and wife, trooped into the bridal car along with a relative and the driver to go to his house. Suddenly, Abraham asked the driver to stop the car and called out to Chinna Chetathi, 'Chetathiye poru, caril keriko' (Sister. Come on, get in the car). On the side, he explained to me that since the woman was a widow, she was considered bad luck, and no one would give her a ride. All the while, his relative in the front seat was vehemently protesting the invitation offered to the Chetathi. 'Adha oru dhushagunum aanu,' he cried frantically (It's a bad omen).

'Oh! Oru pavathina sahaichal mudiyunagil aangu mudiyata. Keru Chetathi,' said Abraham defiantly (If helping a poor soul will perish me, then let it be so. Get in, sister). When she still stood by hesitantly, much to everyone's amazement and Chetathi's discomfiture, she was hustled into the car by the groom himself. Chetathi folded herself into herself, as everyone glared at her accusingly. She must have been somewhere in her sixties and kept smiling in gratitude at Abraham. She had a pair of ill-fitting dentures which kept slipping off her jaws when she smiled, making her look absolutely comical. That being so, I was relieved to think that the last thing anyone could do was accuse my young groom of being attracted to Chetathi. In the end, I sat squashed between Chetathi and Abraham, sweating it out in my wedding finery. Neither could I move, as Chetathi was sitting comfortably on my 'mandrakodi pallav' (wedding sari), making a mess of it, nor could I breathe as I had requested the windows be raised to keep my hair in place. I did not want my faux hair bun flying off in the breeze. That would really get my knickers in a twist. Airconditioned cars were not even a notion back then.

The 'kacha kodupu' ceremony was a big, boisterous affair with lots of jokes and leg-pulling. Abraham introduced me to a thousand people, none of whom registered in my brain. I just wanted the whole thing to be over and get into some comfortable clothes and get a moment of peace and quiet. I was also beginning to have a pain in my jaws from constantly having to feign laughter. And balancing on a pair of stilettoes the whole afternoon had done no favours for the comfort of my feet. It had a pleated design for straps that looked absolutely gorgeous, but in reality, they cut into my skin and made me wince every time I moved my feet. The Husband wore the big gold chain that Mother had put around his neck with pride, unaware perhaps, of the message that he was henceforth chained to me for life. And Mother was hanging onto the beautiful sari he had given her as if she had never owned one before. To me, it seemed like they were the only two people who benefitted from this whole episode.

As was the custom and since the marriage took place at the groom's place, the first three days after the wedding were to be spent at the bride's home. I think this was a rule orchestrated by the elders of our sect, out of the kindness of their old hearts, for the comfort of innocent brides. These girls who were roped into marriages for which they had no preparations or sufficient knowledge, never objected to any situation, however uncomfortable or unjust it may be. Like good Malayalee girls, the brides would deal with their uncertainties and discomfiture in their own inexperienced way or learn to ignore it. Rather than struggle in a strange home, perhaps, the old grouches who formed the religious committee before the beginning of time, could have laid down this rule of spending the first few days after marriage in familiar surroundings. In which case, I decided that the great patriarchal leaders who ruled the families with total control were kinder and more humane than I gave them credit for, although no one thought to revise the rules or ask the opinions of the group to whom it pertained. So, as done from time immemorable, I went home to familiar surroundings, probably to get over the embarrassment and unease of my first sexual experiences. To help me settle down and get used to what was expected of my wifely duties and maybe ask for advice from an elder sister or even Mother. This freedom or bravery to do so, I would never find in my new husband's home. Whether I will get any help from Mother was an altogether different matter. And I had no elder sister.

Anyway, right after the 'kacha kodupa' and tea, the bridal entourage left for my home. Everyone was plum pleased. The girl was hooked, booked, and cooked. Mission accomplished.

The 'first night' in the life of any girl brought up in the traditional way was one of great embarrassment, not so much for her as for the family and cousins and everyone else. Don't ask me why. Forty-five years later, I'm still trying to solve the puzzle. I noticed the household walked around on eggshells and avoided eye contact. They pretended to busy themselves doing this, that, or the other, but actually did nothing but sit around waiting for the bride and groom to enter the bridal chambers. Would they then place their ears to the door and try to decrypt what went on inside? I haven't the faintest idea. Everything was moving with military precision, and the Parents could not have been happier. Only Sibling seemed subdued. After dinner, I prepared for sleep and went to the Parents' room to look for a blanket. I heard a sniffle behind the door and found Sibling crying silently. My strong, brave, critical, cynical, darling guardian angel. I hugged her, and we held each other tight.

'I don't want to lose you, Ini,' she said between sobs.

'Never Ini, never,' I said. 'Why do you think that? You'll always stay first in my heart for ever. That's a promise. No matter who comes or goes, you will come first for me. Weren't you the first in my life?' I consoled.

She quieted down, then grinned, 'Watch out for Mephistopheles. He does not play by the rules.' Something told me she had warmed up to him. She loved breakaways – those who didn't toe the line – herself being the best example. Mother, a woman who believed in tradition and conformity, was always grumbling that she could not understand how she got two daughters who enjoyed the shock factor. She blamed Father.

'Yeh, yeh, Mephistopheles reports to Lucifer, and you know who that is,' I added, laughing. We smiled and hugged, and I was glad she was back on track. I went to the bedroom with a resolve. There was nothing special about the room in spite of it having become a bridal chamber. Except that a man with a quirk lounged on the bed. I said in a stern, matter-of-fact voice, 'Get one thing clear. The most important thing in my life is my sister. You should treat her right. You should treat her like you would your sisters.'

The quirk widened, 'I have five sisters; I'll make it six.'

'No,' I said. 'This is important to me. I want your word.'

He looked at me, the smile gone. He took in how serious I was. He stood up and said, 'Call her.' From what little I had come to know of him during the few days we interacted, I knew he was brash and impulsive. So, I was nonplussed and a little scared about his demand. But the quirk appeared again as he cajoled, 'Go on. Call her.'

We were both aghast and a little terrified as I persuaded her to come to the room. Abraham sat us both down on the bed while he pulled up a chair and sat facing us. He watched us like a cat would a mouse, his tiny eyes almost a slit. Then he took both of Sibling's hands in his and said, 'When I married your sister, at that moment, I became your brother. You have not lost your sister but gained a brother. I will never try to take your place in her life. I will make my own place.' With that, Sibling became his devoted follower and advocate, and he earned my respect.

After Sibling left, he said to me, 'Pedipichallo' (You terrified me). I knew he was laughing at me, but I let it slide.

'Come on. Sit down. Relax. Let's discuss how our life is to be. I'm going to call you Lee. Do you mind?' he asked.

'No. As long as it's not Bruce Lee that you mean,' I said getting back my own brand of humour and overcoming my nervousness.

'You sure act tough like him,' Abraham said with a smile.

'I'm going to call you Raju. Do you mind?' I asked, referring to his pet-name.

'Oh! No. Raju is fine. That's my name,' he retorted.

'Even without an Achayan tag?' I asked, as I knew it was a big deal with Syrian Christian wives to address their husbands with the 'Achayan' tag to show respect and obeisance.

'I don't believe in that,' Raju said flippantly.

'Good. Good. Because anyway, I was not going to use it,' I rejoined.

He laughed at that.

'Your uncle said you were sharp. Looks like it,' Raju observed.

'Someone told Mother you lived on a vallum,' I offered.

'True, when the fancy takes me. I enjoy the open.' A pause, then, 'You know, we are ten children. Ten of us,' Raju said with a glint in his eye.

'Yes,' I replied.

'It is the wish of every parent that the children do better,' Raju said, looking at me from hooded eyes, his quirk appearing.

I was silent. The waters were getting murky.

'I think twelve is a good number for us to aim for, don't you think?' he questioned. I could not make out if he was serious or joking. Besides, wasn't it too early for this line of conversation? I remained silent, a little nervous even. Then I remembered what Father had said. I was an equal, no less, and I would have my say. 'I'll settle for two or three. For the rest of the nine, you'll have to get a new wife,' I replied, throwing caution to the winds. He threw back his head and laughed boisterously, then said, 'It's been a long day. You must be really tired.'

He rolled over, and in a few minutes, I heard him snore. Suddenly I felt like a deflated balloon. Was this what it was all about? Was this all there was to it? I had been warned snidely by many that newlyweds hardly slept the first night. And what about all those relatives outside, with their ear to the door? I smiled into the darkness. Yes, I should have known that this was no run-of-the-mill husband.

The next morning, I got up and went in search of Mother. She kept asking me if I was OK, and I kept wondering what on earth was wrong with her, until the penny dropped. *God!* I thought, *these coded dialogues will be the death of me.* She gave me a cup of coffee and told me to give it to the Husband, in case he was the type that needed coffee as soon as he opened his eyes. Who knew? I went to the room and nearly dropped the cup. The Husband stood on his head, eyes closed, arms folded, ram-rod straight and back to the wall. I didn't know what to make of it or how to tackle an upside-down man. I was just getting used to an up right one, for crying out loud!

I called out for The Parents. *They found him, didn't they? It's their headache to sort him out and figure out what was wrong with him. What's he doing standing on his head, for pity's sake? Wouldn't there be a sudden rush of shit to the brain?* They came running, Sibling included, thinking the worst. We stood around gaping like stupefied monkeys. Raju remained stiff, silent, and dead-like, as if he was an Egyptian mummy, only upside-down. Then Father broke the silence. I heard a faint whisper of pride and amazement resonate with a tinge of regret, of a man who had no sons, mixed with the smugness and incredulity of a man who had just procured one. He turned to us and said with awe, 'Do not disturb him. He is in the "seershuasana" position.'

Sibling and I looked at each other. We were totally at sea. Then she shrugged and said, 'Gosh Ini, this time, you've bitten off more than you can chew. Don't say I didn't tell you, but this time your knickers are positively in a twist.'

Yes, indeed! I was afraid and apprehensive about what else I'd have to see along with the thought that there'll never be a dull moment in my life any more.

Hooked, booked, and cooked

The Riddle That is a Husband

I watched with some trepidation and amusement as the Husband weaved his magic on the Parents, then Sibling, the maids, and the neighbours who came around to gawk at the new bridegroom. Within the three days that he stayed at my home; he had the household eating out of the palm of his hand. In a strange, funny way, I felt a sense of ownership and pride. Here was a man I've never known from Adam. Just three weeks ago he was a stranger and suddenly, here was Moi wanting everyone to approve of him and accept him. What a preposterous, weird way the mind works in. On the third day, the mother-in-law arrived with two of the sisters-in-law. They looked like the Mafia, minus the goggles. Formidable. They were all tall – 5' 8" maybe – to my 5'1". They were equally arresting in their appearances. The three of them stood looking at us while Mother, Sibling, and Moi stood in a row and looked at them. It was a face off. I discovered mother-in-law to be pragmatic and direct in her approach. Instinctively, I knew she tolerated no nonsense. It would be best to be frank when dealing with her. She had the authority of a person who ran a household with draconian rules. After all she kept ten children in line. They had lunch at our place, and then it was time to go. By that time, Mother was in awe of my mother-in-law. I could tell she had begun to consider her the paragon of womanhood, what with having birthed ten children and still calling the shots, while Mother still suffered from the aftereffects of her second and final delivery. As we moved to leave, Mother, who till then was so keen to see me married and moved out of our home, suddenly broke down and cried. I saw Sibling's eyes well up, and for whatever reason, mine did too. What were we? A group of spineless lizards facing the Amazonian gang of girls? Mother-in-law immediately assessed the situation and took matters into her hands. 'Listen,' she spoke directly to Mother, 'I have five sons. I am giving you one. You can keep him as yours.' As simple as that. With that promise, she marched out and got in the car, and we followed. All through the journey, I recalled the one salient point Mother had argued on in favour of this proposal. She had told me a hundred times, 'Lennie, in a house where the mother rules with kindness and fairness, you will be safe. And a boy who grew up seeing this will respect and value you, as his father does his mother.' Her prediction was so accurate. Throughout our life together, the Husband and I were one, and I was that one. I'm not sure who said that, or if I just did.

Early the next morning, at about 4 am, I was awakened in my new home by a shrill, strident voice bellowing out a popular hymn, totally out of tune, using the power and strength of the whole of her lungs. It sounded absolutely like all the utensils in the kitchen were being thrown against each other. 'Wha, wha, wha?' I asked, beady-eyed and confused, sitting up in the bed. I had slept the sleep of the dead after the nightly shenanigans. No one had told me that after a full-fledged dinner of chicken and rice, you were required to do a bout of vigorous exercising before sleep. I never in my wildest dreams imagined that one part of a marriage involved energetic, pulsating, perspiring exercises prior to repose at night. I knew brushing your teeth before bed was acceptable and more sedate, and it was something I was used to. But this nightly workout where you don't know where your hands are, or where your legs are, or what's going where, was ridiculous. You're sweating a bit, you're hurting a lot, everything was a hurry, it's dark, and you have to keep it quiet so no one else knows about the ruckus that was going on. And when was that ecstasy bit that everyone glorified in the books going to happen? You wait and wait and then wham! It's over. Did you miss something, you wonder. And you're left with an afterthought if you needed to say thank you. Or were you to be thanked for being so obliging? What gibberish did they feed you in those storybooks and movies about love? Was this what Helen of Troy gave up King and Kingdom for? Was this most ridiculous, unladylike positioning of the human body really enjoyable? I'd have taken up some gymnastics in school for better participation, had I been warned. 'Keeping up with the Komatts' (Abraham's prestigious house name) was proving to be more competitive than 'Keeping up with the Kardashians,' and together with all the swimming in the Pumba and balancing on the vallum, my senses had numbed to a stupor. So, it was little wonder that I slept like the dead.

'Wha?' Again, I asked groggily of the Husband. Relaxed, with his eyes shut, the Husband told me it was the wake-up call to prayer, which was a must for all under the roof. He told me that being a new bride, I could be excused. Really? Did he think I was going to start off this new chapter like a chicken? Being left out of the real action? It honestly sounded more interesting than the nightly escapades. If nothing, I had to see this to convey the gossip to Sibling. She had told me to give her a point-by-point account of everything. I heard several doors open and people join in the pandemonium, creating a raucous choir. Curiosity might have killed the cat, but this cat was willing to take the risk. This was beyond belief. Sweet Jesus! What a sedate life I had lived till then. This was like being in the discotheque in some exotic city. I crept out, and like everyone else, picked up a rolled mat kept on the side and sat down. Mother-in-law nodded, showing her approval that I had not slept in, but chosen to join the group and so, motioned for me to sit next to her. I obliged. I think that was the first time she was accused of favouritism. Though I had never played chess, this, I think, was checkmate. The Queen was mine. It is well to remember that I was not all that new to this call to prayer episode in a proper Syrian Christian family household. My memory went back to the Big House, ruled by the iron fist of Grandmother and her early morning wake-up and evening calls to prayer, so similar to Mother-in-law. It gave me a sense of belonging.

My take on this new life was as if I had come out of a silent monastery in the mountains of Tibet into the hustle and bustle of an open flea-market in Kozhencherry. During the day, the house was bursting at the seams with vibrant, pulsating life, and Mother-in-law had the pivotal role. She was everywhere, and though she was not a polished, stylish lady, she was the essence of the family. Like the salt of the earth. Like Pearl S. Buck's heroine O-Lan in *The Good Earth*. She had only two sets of 'chattas' (blouse) and 'mundu' (lower garment). When one set was being washed, she wore the other. Her children gifted her with plenty, but she gave them to the needy. When the children protested, she said, 'You gave them to me. It is mine now, and I can do what I like with it.' Once, I caught her behind a huge haystack, her head covered, tears on her cheeks, praying. She was not embarrassed or coy about it. She explained to me that she had ten children. They were all out of her reach, and she could no longer watch over them. So, she had to keep reminding God to put in some extra effort and keep an eye on them. I recalled that moment and the importance of her words years later when the Boy left home to pursue his higher education and follow his dreams. I emulated her example.

Of all the memories that I cherish, the one memory that's so endearing and that makes me smile is this. One day, I called the Husband by name in front of the Father-in-law. The latter feigned horror, and half-jokingly, half-seriously, reminded me to add the Achayan tag. Mother-in-law immediately came to my rescue and said, 'You stay out of their business. What they call each other is between them.' Father-in-law shrugged his shoulders and responded with a sheepish grin, 'As always, you are right.' I realised then that though Mother-in-law was old-fashioned in her dressing and rough in her ways, she was pretty forward in her thinking. I realized there was a lot I could learn from her.

I came from a small, contained, 'How do you do?' kind of family to join this boisterous, brash, 'Oi, coming for a swim and some fishing and a bit of toddy on the side?' kind of family. The impact was jarring. I was always in control of my feelings, but the Husband wore his heart on his sleeve. And the kitchen! That was the place to be. Large and airy, it had three cooking areas where the firewood burnt incessantly. It was the hub and the heart of the house. A minimum of four women worked there with zeal and vigour and a lot of laughing and joking and pranking would take place. The Husband was the centrepiece. I fear his mother gave him a lot of leeway, and found an excuse for his mischief. I watched how he teased 'Kunjali' and 'Kunju' and 'Kiliamma' who toiled and cooked to feed the large multitude of people living under the roof. *Whoever named them?* I wondered. I wrote down the names to pass on to Sibling, knowing full well that she would not believe me. The Husband was hands-on about everything and would help pound the rice, thrash the sheaves of grain, and gather the coconuts. He would sing some stupid, idiotic song with no tune, and the women would laugh, showing their paan-stained teeth and say, 'Aaiyo kunjeh. Njagal chaidolam' (Hey boy, we'll do it). And there were four other brothers to reckon with. To say I was out of my element would be putting it mildly. By the end of August, the Husband, who worked for the HVAC division at Siemens, Madras, had to go back to join duty. We decided to make it a honeymoon kind of thing. We would drive up to Cochin, spend a day, and then take the train to Madras. It sounded perfect. At Cochin, we chanced to meet a Naval Officer buddy of the Husband's whom he had not seen in a long while. The Husband persuaded him to stay the night with us in our room to catch up on stories and reminisce about the old days. All bonhomie like! I was petrified that the hotel staff would think it was a ménage à trois! Times were strange then, in that he did not think to ask me if the arrangement was all right with me, and stranger still that I did not protest. But I'm eternally grateful that I did not make a fuss, for the dear friend met with his end shortly after in a tragic road accident.

The next day, goodbyes were said, and we chugged off to the Metropolis. We were guests to number seven of the famous ten. She was a beautiful, authoritative figure who dwarfed me to insignificance. It was here that I told the Husband that I needed to visit a beauty parlour and get a facial done. Hotel Ashoka offered the service, and I had benefitted from it many times on my trips home to Malaysia. At that time, beauty salons were a rarity in Kerala, and girls who frequented them were considered licentious.

'What's a facial?' The Husband asked suspiciously.

'It's something girls do,' I replied mysteriously.

'I have five sisters, and none of them do it,' the Husband said incredulously.

'So? Maybe they don't want to do it. I want to.'

'Fine, but don't change your face too much, or I won't be able to recognize you,' he said, wanting to please me. I spent about two hours at the parlour, while the Husband slept on one of the gilded sofas in the enormous reception areas. When I returned, he pretended not to know me and kept up the farce for the rest of the day. It was annoying, and when we returned to the sister's place, he told her, 'Lennie did a facial and changed her face, and now this strange woman is with me.' And of course, number seven at once told the rest of the family ramifications scattered all over the world about my facial. It was delicious fodder for quite a while.

We were still in Madras when the Husband got word that his visa to Kuwait had finalized. So, he resigned from his job, and we returned home to Maromon. I resumed my clinics at Pandalam, and he began his preparations for the Middle East.

The month was September, the month of Onam. The 'Vallum Kalli' or Boat Race began right in our backyard. It was the oldest river boat fiesta in Kerala. The Husband brought out his own 'odi vallum.' Boy o boy! Did we rock it!! He took me upstream and then down. We kept close to the banks so as not to disrupt the mighty 'Chundan Vallams' or the Snake Boats. I felt I was perpetually on a high, in a euphoric state, like I had smoked a joint. When the Mother-in-law finally caught us, she almost had a heart attack. She gave the Husband such a dressing down, saying my parents had only two kids and that she was accountable for my safety. She pulled me ashore, and the Husband backed off, laughing and saying, 'Ok then, keep her off the boat and put her in your glass cupboard.' I can't tell you how disappointed I was to be pulled out of all the fun. But being in the Mother-in-law's good books was important, so I obliged, albeit sadly. The Parents and Sibling came over to see the boat race. Fifty-two snake boats from all over. Men dressed in crisp white mundus and turbans. The Chundan Vallams moved in pairs to the rhythm of a full-throated 'vanchipattu' (Boat Song). Everything ended so grandly, and the finale was the 'Valla Sadhya' or Boat Feast. Food was served in plenty. Such splendour at my doorstep brought me great pride and happiness. Such was the pageantry of Onam celebrations.

In the last week of October, about two and a half months after our wedding, we went to Trivandrum to spend a few days with Sibling before the Husband left for Kuwait. One evening, we took Sibling to the Sree Kumar Theatres at Thambanoor to see the movie *The Exorcist*. Sibling and Moi held our breath as Regan MacNeil slowly transformed from a sweet girl to the ugly ghoul. We gripped the edges of our seats and dug our fingernails into each other every time Damien Karras so much as blinked. Suddenly, we heard a sonorous, throttling kind of an eerie sound much nearer to us. We gawked at each other while Damien Karras' mother lit up large on the movie screen and made a 360 degree turn with her head. Petrified, Sibling convulsed. I turned to the Husband for reassurance and realised he was fast asleep and it was his ragged snoring that was making the hideous noise.

When Sibling revived, she managed to say, 'Blippers! Ini, I don't care what you say, but they are really a scary, noisy, boisterous lot, your new family.'

I felt an urgent need to protect my new relations from my own family. What was wrong with me? Was I beginning to change sides?

Two days later, the Husband left for Kuwait, and suddenly, there was no more fun in anything.

The Telephone Conversation

After I had just been married and was in the first flush of bridal ecstasy, I faced a heart-breaking situation. After two months of bliss, the Husband left for foreign shores to make our fortune. We were going to be rich and live happily ever after. During the time apart, we found solace in letters, which were sent to and fro with as much regularity as the call to Angeles at a convent. As is the case with all marriages, before long, we had our first difference of opinion. But it was difficult to put up a long-distance fight through letters, however regular they were. The disputes lost their momentum, and the verve to argue a point fizzled out. These things needed a continuity, and in any case, letters were so one-sided. It was just then, like an answer to a prayer, that the post office in my village upgraded the telephone to include overseas conveniences.

I remember the first time the telephone was installed in the community, some three or four years earlier, catering to only local calls. For days, it was the talk of the village. A machine that talked? No one believed it. All and sundry hung around to take a look at the new gadget. No one had quite known how to set up the instrument, since the instructions where in English and very technical. The postmaster finally requested the help of a retired English teacher who lived in the village. Together, they unravelled the puzzle that was the telephone and succeeded in installing it. That done, the postmaster called the crowd to attention to educate them. All who cared to listen were told that the telephone could also be called a 'phone,' for convenience, of course. That it had its own number called 'the telephone number' (obviously) and that the significance of this number was that it was similar to how each of us were known by our individual names. The details of how to dial another number (which would be the telephone number of that phone), particulars about the ring tone, dial tone, busy tone, and all other matters pertaining to the phone were meticulously explained by the postmaster in an ostentatious voice. We were told that anytime the phone rang, we were to lift the receiver and call into it the word 'hello' in a normal tone of voice. 'Aiyoo, eeniyum English padikkanno,' the ladies giggled (Jeez, will we have to learn English now?). The questions in between were fast and furious, and as much as the postmaster tried to quench everybody's quest for knowledge, he had his limitations.

Finally after successfully installing the telephone, the stage was set, and it was time to try out the first call. This call was to be made to the neighbouring post office, not because our postmaster had an affinity for the neighbouring postmaster, but simply because no one else had a telephone. Anyway, the peon at our post office had cycled over the previous day and had already acquired their number. There was an air of expectancy, as no one quite knew what to expect. Our postmaster adjusted his reading glasses and read out the telephone number slowly and loudly as he dialled it out. He held the receiver a little away from his ear, out of fear, in case it exploded or burst into flames or some such I think, and waited. There was a crackling and buzzing, and then we heard a ring tone. After a couple of rings, someone must have picked up the phone at the other end, for suddenly, the black box came alive. Someone called out, and we heard a faint but distinct 'hello?' The postmaster looked doubtful as to how to continue, a few of the people in front stepped back in alarm, and one lady who had come in for some stamps screamed and ran out.

Anyway, such was the time when the darling and I had our first tiff. We had 'backed and forthed' our argument in many letters, but there was no resolution to the matter. So, the installation of the telephone with long distance facilities at the post office was a Godsent. I thought we could sort out our differences in a more personal and congenial manner. Accordingly, I wrote and informed him of the telephone number and suggested he call on a certain day at a certain time. It was arranged that I would wait for the call at the post office. It was an operator-assisted person-to-person call.

For those of you unfamiliar with the nuances of this type of call, I can explain. Three people were involved. There would be the Husband or 'the caller,' Moi or 'the recipient,' and the operator, who would connect the two of us. It went without saying that the postmaster would attend the call first, as only he was authorized to do so, and if the call was for me, then he would give it to me. The telephonic connections at the village were not the easiest to avail on the best of days, and if it should rain, then the whole exercise would have a snowball's chance in hell. Anyway, since I was resigned to the fact that luck had no place in my life, it did not surprise me that it rained with a vengeance on the appointed day. Still, one should not belittle the powers of youth and love. I braved the elements to reach the post office much ahead of the scheduled time. Surprisingly, in spite of the heavy winds and rain, there was a healthy crowd buzzing around. I did not think much of it at that time, though it did cross my mind that no one was buying stamps or posting anything or sending a money order or whatever else one did at a post office. However, I was too preoccupied with my own affairs to bother too much about the crowd or what they were doing. I was battling with the strange emotions that constricted my breathing and did strange things to my composure as I thought of the impending conversation with the Husband. That was, until Mrs. Simon tapped me on the shoulder.

'Your Mother told us about the call you are to receive from your husband about now,' she informed with a bright smile.

Suddenly, I knew why the post office was packed to the nth in spite of the rain. Mentally, I decided to kill Mother the minute I got home. I did not care if it would be the first case of matricide in the whole of the village or state. Or country, for that matter. But I would get her for this. Out of the corner of my eye, I watched in horror as everyone waited with bated breath, as they would at a circus. I connected with their feelings. I have sat at circus ring-sides and waited with uncontrolled excitement for the big bears and tigers to appear. Those waits had been both exhilarating and anguishing. Exhilarating at the thought of what was coming, anguishing at the delay. That was the predicament I read on the faces of the people at the post office. They were exasperated by the delay but unable to tear themselves away. In the midst of all these muddled emotions, the telephone rang. Harsh and loud. Everyone froze and looked blank. Then they looked at each other. No one knew what to do. Some moved to the door to keep safe. Others stared at the instrument. I did not know if it was for Moi.

I looked at the postmaster.

He looked at the telephone.

Fortunately, after three rings, the cantankerous noise subsided, and the postmaster seemed relieved to have escaped from the enigma of having to answer it. An argument ensued. The crux of the matter was what we should do should the phone ring again. Everyone had an opinion. I played no part in any of this, as I was too busy contemplating Mother's murder. I had to devise a plan and carry it out at the earliest, preferably that night itself. She had this peculiar way of needling me to death and then slowly weaning herself back into my affections. This time, I was in no mood to compromise. In fact, the argument with the Husband had become a thing of the past. I had forgotten my points of debate, and my anger at him had diluted a thousand times compared to what I felt towards Mother. I presumed the general discussion about who would answer the phone the next time it rang concluded with the postmaster negating all other proposals and officially taking charge. Just then, the phone rang again. This time, he had a strategy and grabbed the phone. Personally, I felt there was no need for such aggression.

'Hello,' he bellowed unnecessarily into it.

Then he listened for a bit and yelled over the noise of the wind and the rain, 'Yes, yes, she is here.'

Frantically, he started waving his hands and legs in my direction, and a number of the on-lookers followed suit, waving and gesticulating along with him. The whole thing looked like some sort of awkward flamingo dance. Even before I could move, Mrs. Simon shoved me forward. I staggered and would have fallen and knocked out my teeth had it not been for a bench on the side that broke my fall. By now, I was even more determined in my resolve to kill Mother, and I included Mrs. Simon too. I was getting demented. I took the receiver from the postmaster, and as I did so, I spied Mother coming in from the rain. She was wet to the bone and looked tired. But I had not believed for a moment that something as small as the elements of Nature would keep her away from where the action was. In fact, I had been wondering all along why she had not yet appeared. True to form, she materialized at the right time.

'Please, God,' I prayed, 'give me the patience to reach home before I carry out the master plan. Let me not kill her in front of the village, thereby giving them another entertainment to gloat over.'

Mother folded the umbrella and looked around. The gathering was impressive. The first long-distance call to the village, and made to a member of her family. She would be the envy of the women-folk, and this would be the topic of conversation for a very long time. I tried in vain to concentrate on the chore at hand.

'Hello?' I called into the receiver.

'Hello. Hello. Hello,' some moron went on at the other end, unmindful of the fact that I was answering. It was a raspy, irksome voice. Not attractive at all.

'Hello. Hello,' I called again.

'Long distance call for Lenin,' the voice informed. No one said Lennie. It was always Lenin of Russia. Mother had to answer for that too. Today was the day she would answer for all her sins, I grimly decided. She could have named me a plain Sarama or Chinnamma and made it convenient for all.

'That's me,' I called out into the phone.

'Ah! So, you are Lenin. Nice name. Nice voice too,' the operator said.

'What? Who are you?' I asked, bewildered.

'I'm me, of course!' came the answer, with a guffaw.

'And who are you?' I asked, starting a headache.

'I'm the operator,' said the voice, sounding offended.

I noticed the crowd stare in disbelief. I could read their minds. They were wondering who was calling me if not the Husband. I could see their imagination run amok. I would be made out to be an adulteress, home-wrecker, spy, anything by the end of the day. Mother stepped forward, and I knew that any minute now, she would grab the receiver.

'Ah I see, you are the operator,' I called out loudly for everyone's benefit. Mother fell back, relieved. The crowd nodded at each other, with approval.

'At your service, molay. Hang on while I connect you to your husband.'

I hated his familiarity, but what could I do? Did he really say molay, or did I imagine it? Immediately, I thought of Kallu Mathai. Which molay did he mean? The audacity of the man was unnerving. There was a short silence. Then I heard some dittos and dashes and a humming. All the while, I dreaded the thought of the public conversation I was going to have.

Suddenly, the phone line came alive. 'Hello! Lee. Darling,' said the beloved voice.

I'll tell you, all that pent up anger just melted away. I was so choked up with love. I missed him so much. I no longer felt the distance; it was as if he was right there beside me. My eyes welled up with happy tears.

'Hello,' I said shyly, softly, not wanting to share even a word with the crowd. I was so aware of the pin-drop silence in the room. The quiet was so thick you could cut it with a knife. I felt every ear strain in my direction in the hope of catching a single word. The rest, they would just conjure up. Welcome to the village of Ayroor.

'Speak up, or he will not be able to hear you,' advised the operator.

That took the wind out of me. What was he doing sitting in on us? It took away any intimacy I had hoped to share with the Husband. The coziness that had enveloped the two of us for a split second just cracked up.

'Lee darling, how are you? Do you miss me?' the Husband enquired.

I answered 'fine' to the first question and 'yes' to the second, mindful of the fact that the operator was listening to every word. I guess I sounded cold and distant, when actually, I was on fire with pent up passion. I wanted so much to tell him that. But how do you do that with about thirty-five people in the audience? And an operator in the middle? Then, as if to make the curse complete, the line disconnected. The Husband and I could hear the operator, but neither of us could hear each other. In his desperation, the Husband told the operator everything he wanted to tell me and told him to pass it on. I hung on to the receiver while the operator repeated to me, in a harsh, bored, discordant tone of voice, all that the Husband would have told me in his cultured, baritone, bedroom tone of voice.

The following conversation ensued:

'Ishtamaneh atherah,' the operator said. (Says he loves ya)

'Humm,' I murmured.

'Valateh missuchaiyunnu atherah.' (Says he misses ya)

'Humm,' I said, without making eye contact with anyone in the room.

'Valatheh agrehikunnu atherah.' This time, there was the hint of a sneer in that infuriating voice. (Says he needs ya)

'Humm,' I said with a sob in my voice. I felt so exposed.

'Hey Lee, your husband says I should put some feelings into my voice. What do you think? Anyway, have you got nothing to say to him?' the operator asked.

I stayed silent to that remark, red in my face. Lee? Did the oaf really call me Lee? I felt so repulsed at having to convey my tender feelings to the Husband through this moron. The thought of the involvement of a third party was abhorrent. To whisper those sweet nothings to my beloved through this morose brute seemed blasphemous to my marriage and to my loyalty. Yet, what other option was there? I decided to play it neutral.

'Say I am sorry,' I said, remembering the argument we had in the last letter.

'What about?' The operator enquired with unbridled audacity.

'Just say it. He will know what about,' I snapped, so irritated by this ruckus. 'He will know what I mean.'

'Hey, don't go being like that. I'm the good guy here. Trying to be helpful and all that. One would think you would be grateful. I need not be doing this, you know,' said the operator, pretending to be hurt. Then he laughed as he passed on the message.

After a minute, the operator said, 'He asked you to be happy and not to worry. Not to take these tiffs seriously.' Then, in a conversational tone, he continued, 'Having a tiff, are you? Separation and loneliness do that to people.'

I stayed silent, not wanting to encourage him on the subject. Unmindful, he went on, 'We men like to tease our young brides so that they get all righteous and indignant and angry. Then we fellows follow it up by begging for forgiveness, and tell them how much we love them. All at once, they cry and repent and are so full of remorse and ready to do anything for the husbands.'

I was mortified at the suggestive innuendo in the conversation.

'Hey! You still there? Say something. Your man wants to know why you are silent,' the operator asked me.

'Tell him his mother came to visit,' I said, choosing a safe topic.

'Really? Did she? Piece of advice. Watch out for these mothers-in-law. Nasty piece of work if you don't treat them right.' Then I heard him convey the message.

I sighed in frustration. The situation was so out of control and useless. I had no say in the way the conversation moved. The futility of my predicament was scream-worthy. I held the receiver tight and closed my eyes in silent agony. Misunderstanding my silence, the operator enquired with concern in his voice, 'Molay, are you crying? Don't! Please! For me. God, I could kick your husband for doing this to you.' By now, I was openly sobbing. I did not care who heard me or saw me or what they thought of me. I really could not fathom at which point the operator's relationship had turned intimate with me. I cried hysterically into the telephone at the sheer helplessness I felt at the lost opportunity to say sweet nothings to my beloved and my inability to choke the life out of the operator. How many murders could I commit in a day?

'Listen molay......' the operator began again, but I cut him off. I slammed the receiver down and turned to face the shocked crowd with unseeing eyes, blinded by tears. They stared right back at me, angry that I had robbed them of their full share of 'thamasha' (gossip). I ran out of the post office, unmindful of the rain. But not before I heard Mother apologetically explain to everyone present. 'It is the separation that gets her so unnerved. See how she loves and misses her husband. Poor thing. Although she is crying, I know for a fact that she is so happy and satisfied to have talked to him and heard his voice. We must arrange another telephone conversation for her in the near future.'

Echoes of the shouts of agreement from the crowd rang in my ears as the cold rain and wind hit my face. But I was thankful to Nature. She wept with me. The rain on my face cooled my anger and washed my tears. When the unreasonable emotions gradually settled, I knew with complete certainty that matricide was no solution. Mother was capable of needling me from beyond the grave.

Even today, every time I answer the phone, I invariably think of the post office, the postmaster, the operator, and of course, Mother.

MARHABA AL KUWAIT

Motherhood

The changes were subtle. A bit of unease, a little fat on the waist. Nothing alarming. I took to a bit of toe-touching in a bid to get the stomach flat again. And I found my old skipping rope and did a bout of skipping to get in shape. And then, a strange behavioural pattern started to emerge in Moi. I watched myself, and I was aghast at my findings.

The Husband was settling down in Kuwait, and I was waiting to join him at the earliest. I was still working at NSS Medical Mission, Pandalam, and dear old Nurse was still my right-hand person. During our lunch breaks, we would relive the events that led up to my wedding, with Nurse always going goo-goo ga-ga over Abraham inviting her to draw up a chair and sit down. I would have my meagre sandwich, and Nurse would open her 'pothichor' (a packet containing rice and all that goes with it, packed in banana leaf) and eat it with finger-licking relish. Till then, I had preferred my dry lunch to her mish-mash. But of late, I just could not keep my mind off her food. I kept fantasizing about it. *What did she bring today*, I'd think. *Will there be 'urala kezhaga mezhukuparati' (fried potato), maybe 'cheera thoran' (spinach), or perhaps some 'aviyal' (hodge podge)?* I would blush at the thought that I was so greedy and wondered what was happening to Moi. And of course, by now, I had stepped up my exercise to vigorous, in order to get rid of the tyre forming at the waist. I wondered if just thinking of Nurse's 'pothichor' was making me heavy. How unlucky was that? This went on for a while until one day, in spite of myself, I blurted out to Nurse asking about the contents of her 'pothi.' She stopped halfway through opening her lunch and gave me a look – an incredulous, open-mouthed, astonished look.

'Aana sisteryeh?' I asked. (What is it, Nurse)?

'Kollamello doctoryeh. Patticho? Sar midukkenanello' (Good for you, doctor. I think you have been tricked. Sir is a smart chap).

I swear, I thought she was talking in riddles. I had no inkling what she was on about. She then informed me that it was better not to do a pregnancy test in the hospital where I worked, as it would give reason for talk, but that we should go to Pushpagiri Hospital in Thiruvella. Keep it under wraps. *Now, wait a minute*, I thought to myself, *so, who's pregnant? Not me! I couldn't be! What have I done to get that way, other than a bit of nocturnal exercise?* You people reading this are going to think, 'Heck, as if! One can't be that stupid.' But I tell you, one was, because at that time, one really was! Mechanically, I let Nurse guide me, and she was efficiency personified. I think she totally enjoyed the whole thing. I had no notion or clue as to what to do, so I thought, *'it's better that she shows the way. Lead on, MacDuff'!*

And thus began my life of indignity.

About three days later, after a rough ride in the KSRTC Express, the two of us landed in Thiruvella and made our way to Pushpagiri Hospital, where I obliged with a urine sample. Nurse was so carried away and involved, bless her, that she even argued with me to let her come into the toilet and hold the cup while I took a pee. I had to make her understand that there had to be some sort of privacy in all of this madness. When we got the result, I was silent. Yes, I was pregnant. No, I did not have the faintest idea what to do. I felt like I'd been caught with my hand in the cookie jar. How was I going to explain this? Tell the parents? It was a declaration to my having had sex. The taboo thing. The thing we never spoke about. My throat was dry, and my mind was in overdrive. What was my strategy? Who could I confide in? Then I hit on a brilliant plan. I would present the situation to my comrade in crime. Once we reached Pandalam, I told Nurse to go ahead to the hospital while I made my way to the post office.

There, I sent a telegram to Abraham stating thus: PREGNANT. ADVICE.

I got a return telegram at the earliest. It said: DON'T BLAME ME. I'M HERE.

'Am I married to a clown', I wondered. It goes without saying that it was an absolute relief when this reply was followed by a telephone call from Kuwait to the NSS Hospital Office. The Husband told me that he was thrilled beyond belief. As his job was still not secure, we decided I would go to Malaysia and stay with my parents. So, I left Pandalam and a heartbroken

Nurse, who I think secretly thought she would help with the birth of the child, to return home to the parents. To my sheer surprise, Mother was utterly complacent and calm and confided in me that she had made a 'nercha' or promise to God. She had prayed to be blessed with a grandson before the first anniversary of my wedding. I was aware of the emphasis on 'grandson'. Mother was working in tandem with God to organize my life once again. What chance did I have? And in appreciation, she had even made an appropriate offering of gratitude to Him. I thought that was bribery of the highest order, but there it was!

The months stretched before me, and my only contact with the Husband was through letters. But letters were so one-sided, and if anything, they only helped to create more confusion and misunderstanding. Abraham, being in a new job, could not visit. But you cannot blame me for thinking that he was shirking his responsibilities, leaving me alone to face an event in which he had an equal part. I did not discuss these heartaches with the Parents. In order not to get too bored, I joined a local clinic, which helped me maintain some sense of balance. I will not shy away from admitting that I was really scared and apprehensive as the days passed and brought me nearer to the due date. The little comforts and sweet nothings one yearned for during these delicate times were so absent. They cannot be substituted by Parents. I felt a loneliness that I did not understand. Much later in life, I wondered at the cruel trick that life had played on us. That early period of courtship and the time required for two strangers to come together, to learn to live, love, and trust each other had not been given to us. How then could two people be expected begin a life properly in tandem without the required period of getting to know one another? When I joined him one and half years later, it was as a mother and with the responsibilities of a child? In a strange twist, perhaps it was because we did not think or dwell too much on these things but accepted our lives and responsibilities for what they were, that we made such a fine success of it. Perhaps the Gods themselves acknowledged that it was a malicious trick they played on us and made amends by giving us a wonderful life.

Father was blind to these chaotic thoughts and the unhappiness that weighed heavily on my mind. He was blind to everything except the imminent arrival of his grandson. He was confident of the gender, and there was no swaying him otherwise. He went so far as to buy a wicker basket and arrange a small blue quilt and all the other necessary trappings to carry the baby, as baby carriers were not as yet in vogue. Sibling came down for her summer break. It was such a welcome change. We went for long walks, and she calmed me down and filled up a lot of the big holes I felt in my heart. One day, she warned me, 'Ini, it's such a great responsibility you carry. Father is so single-minded in his desire for a grandson that I fear the magnitude of his disappointment should it be a girl.' I could not give an answer to that. In those days, we had no way of knowing the sex of the unborn. I just hoped God would not play another of his Machiavellian tricks on Moi. He seemed to have a penchant for playing havoc with my life.

In the meantime, at every turn, I was asked to pee or lift the skirts while thousands (maybe a bit exaggerated, but who cares, I've got to keep the pace) peered down there. My legs were hoisted up in stirrups. My privates were no longer privates, they were public (quote borrowed form Sibling). As I lay on the examination table, legs up, staring at the ceiling, while 'I don't know who' was doing 'I don't know what' to me, I suddenly realised the significance of Mother's questions all those years ago when I was a young girl in Kangar and why she asked every time I had a bath, 'Lennie did you wash between your thighs?'

I was due on the 17th of June, but there was no sign of anything happening. Whoever was on the inside decided to stay in. By the 21st of June, Father was at the end of his tether. He declared dramatically, 'Either the little fella comes out, or I get into a in our neighbourhood box.' He could not wait any more. So, we consulted with the gynaecologist in our neighbourhood at Alor Star, and it was decided to induce labour. But Father was not having anything to do with the local hospital. He hand-picked the Gleneagles Medical Centre in Penang for the birth of his Crown Prince and decided we would make the three-hour journey. He did not forget his wicker basket; it sat on the front seat between him and Mother. It was rambutan season, and the fruit was being sold on either side of the road. We bought a hundred-fruit bunch of red, lusciously sweet and fleshy rambutans, and I ate almost half of it. At the end of the journey, we crossed the ferry from the mainland over to Penang and reached our destination by late evening on the same day.

I was wheeled into the labour room by 8 pm. The door shut with a finality behind me. I was on my own. As Sibling predicted, there was no way back, only forward. What irked me most was that everyone in the labour room was happy, chatty, and smiling while they went about the dehumanising business of ignoring the person that was Moi but paying total and undivided interest to the area below my waist. The first thing they did was give me an enema. I was totally mortified when they flushed out all those rambutans the back way without so much as a 'Do you mind?' The shame of it all does not bear remembering. By 9 or 10 pm, a young Chinese doctor, full of cheer and empathy, came to the bedside. We exchanged pleasantries, during which time he came to understand I was a dentist. The inevitable question followed: 'What's a good toothpaste?' I wondered if he was mad. Here I was, legs hanging up in stirrups, my what's what exposed, everything on public display, couple of people standing and looking down there, taking notes, and discussing in undertones, and I had to name a toothpaste? I was so scared, wondering what they were going to do to me, and the doctor wanted a dental consultation? Wasn't there some rule against harassment? And then he came out with another brilliant query. Did I want a boy or a girl? I said in my head, 'Heck, I just want to get the hell out of here.' But I managed to say that it did not matter as it was my first child. In the midst of all this melee, the irony was not lost on me that two people in cahoots put me in this ignominious situation, yet I alone faced the music. I was mighty peeved at Abraham and could have throttled him had he been in the room.

Suddenly, in the midst of all my rambling thoughts and the camaraderie between the hospital staff, I felt, somewhere far away, someone invading my innermost being and a warm flush of fluid flowing out, wetting my thighs and back. And then the pains began, slowly at first and then with a vengeance. By about 9 am on the 22nd of June, I was so delirious with pain I thought I was knocking on the gates of purgatory. The doctor seemed cheerful and made one last effort to get an answer out of me. 'Boy or girl?' he asked. Someone else shouted, 'Push, push.' In all of the mayhem, my deep-seated desire to please Father got the better of Moi, and I admitted to the doctor, 'A boy, a boy!!' And at 9:20 am, I delivered a boy, weighing in at a whooping 9.8 lbs. The bugger almost tore me apart. And this I remember so clearly. The doctor said, 'One boy ordered; one boy delivered.' It was probably a standard joke with him.

The nine-month wait had been an anticlimactic experience. Each day, you watch yourself, wondering what's new. But those six days after the given due date were nerve-wracking. Of course, the excitement and expectations from the parents were at fever pitch and added to my burden. Father was beyond positive it was a boy. Mother just wanted a grandchild. I became the vessel that bore their aspirations. There was none of that 'throwing the blood-drenched baby with umbilical cord intact onto the mother' kind of thing. Anyway, the father of the child was nowhere around to cut the cord. About two hours after the delivery, I was called, along with all the other mothers, to come in to feed the baby. That was my first introduction to the Boy. He was clean and wrapped into a tight bundle. He looked at me, and I looked at him and I cannot explain the surge of emotion I felt. I think it was love at first sight. Sibling later told me that when they were informed, Mother bent her head and gave thanks to the Lord. Father just wept openly with happiness. Two days later, we drove home. In the front seat, in the wicker basket, lay one lucky Boy, while the grandfather chauffeured. We ladies sat in the back and thought about all the stories Father would have to tell his friends about his Prince. We sent a telegram to the Husband, who was safe and sound in Kuwait, away from the madding crowd. After all, he had done his bit, and my parents were eternally grateful to him and praised him to High Glory. When the Boy was six months old and I was confident about handling him myself, we boarded the plane that was to take us to Kuwait. It was time the father and son made their acquaintances.

Abraham, of course, had the last word. All his life, he delighted in shocking others saying, 'Soon after marriage I left for Kuwait. A year later, she followed with a boy. I'm a good sort, so I took them in.'

Who can deny it? It was the truth.

The first of the Three

And Then There Were Three

Once in Kuwait, I realised that managing a home was no easy task. The life at boarding school, the colleges, dental exams, the ragging – everything seemed trifle in comparison. Between handling a big, surly, petulant husband and a small, mewling, puking baby, I was wasted. And then there was the cooking, of which I knew zilch.

I'll admit that when I was told it was time to get married, I complied more to please the parents than anything else. How they had come to that conclusion, that it was the right time for me to settle down, still baffles me. Perhaps it was my age. As a result, a suitable boy was dug up from somewhere, and before you could say 'Abracadabra,' my life took those predictable turns, much like Mother's did, and her mother before her. I guess I was a fast worker, and as a result, the developments that followed should not have surprised anyone, least of all Moi. And yet, I was a little dumbstruck that I could get married, be pregnant, and become a mother myself at lightning speed. I had not been like the usual pregnant ladies – tired, lethargic, and vomiting. In fact, I had a voracious appetite and ate like a horse. I guess that message must have passed on to the Boy because he turned out to have an insatiable need to eat from Day 1. It's a wonder he did not eat through my uterine walls.

From the start, I was in a hurry to introduce him to all aspects of life. I wanted him to experience everything, taste everything, know everything. Oh gosh, was I impatient. I'd never heard of good parenting or read any books on the subject. And jeez, there was no Google at that time. If there was something to go by, it was Mother's brand of Mothering, which wasn't much. But I was equipped. I had my knowledge and my common sense. *What more does any mother need,* I asked myself. I pictured a big strapping youth. Educated, smart, kind. And so, I began my work to achieve that goal. I started him on baby cereal and egg yolk from the fourth month. Mother told me it was too much, *but hey, I'm the mother here,* I told her from inside my head. To his credit, the Boy was like an amoeba. He would just gobble up anything in his way. I made him listen to the Jazz and the Blues, while Mother kept saying I'd spoil his ears. *He will play the trumpet*, I decided. I read James Herriot out loud in the hope that he'd develop some humour (In later years, I feared I overdid the humour bit). I played songs by Neil Diamond over and over again on my cassette player, hoping he'd grow up to strum a guitar and sing like Neil in that adorable raspy voice. It shocked me out of my wits when, in later years, he became a heavy metal follower and covered the walls of his room with posters of Van Halen and Meatloaf. I fed him Marmite, but sadly, he stoutly refused it, and it remains my only failure to this day. But I got the fright of my life when, at six months, I offered him a bite of my Mars Bar. The little tyke bent down and took the biggest bite he could, and the sticky piece got stuck in his throat. The Husband was at work, and I was alone at home. The Boy made some gurgling sounds, his eyes rolled, and he appeared to be choking. The gooey piece of chocolate refused to go down, and the Boy had no idea how to spit it out. That was a moment in hell. I was at my wits end and so nervous that I needed to run to the toilet to relieve myself. While I sat on the toilet seat, I kept the Boy on my knee. In a brainwave, I stuck two of my fingers into his mouth and down his throat. Suffice to say, it ended well. I decided to put a hold on chocolates and also to slow down on my project, though I cannot say I was always successful. Being a first-time mother was a challenge. There were no previous experiences from which I could take references, and the parents were so far away that they could not offer any help or advice. Telephone calls were rare. Our Pakistani (or were they Iranians? Afghanis maybe) neighbours were not all that friendly, and in any case, language was a barrier. They had children by the dozen, and I wondered how the lady coped. So, when a Kochamma from church suggested that I start the boy on rice at six months, I was eager, as my aim was to get him to be big and strong at the earliest. But I guess I was too naive to realise that there would be many a slip between the cup and the lip before that could happen.

One time, the Husband and I were invited to dinner at his boss's place. I wanted to make an impression, so I spent the day planning which sari I would wear and which accessories should go with it. I had in mind a new sari in silver grey with black mango motif print and a dazzling pallav. A pair of black stilettos could give me the required height. I had it all planned, and by late evening, I had bathed, fed, and dressed the Boy and got myself organized. There were no baby car seats at that point in time, so I kept the Boy on my lap whenever we went out. The Husband started the car, and we were about to leave when suddenly, a big burb escaped from the Boy, along with a bit of the cereal and milk I had fed him earlier. I tapped him on his back to make him comfortable. He turned around and looked at me with his big black eyes, and then he smiled. I was so in awe of this little creature that was mine and overcome with motherly love that I bent down to kiss his upturned face. And at that moment, a torrent of vomit hit me in the face and flowed down my sari and into the car's seat. I was too dumbstruck to react. When I finally did, we rushed back to the apartment, and while the Husband bathed the Boy, I got out of my soiled clothes and washed myself. As there was no time to waste and since we did not want to be late for the party, I got into a pair of blue jeans and a top, and after having soaked the sari in some soap and water, we made it to the party in time. Upon returning late into the night, I checked my sari and found that the black colour of the motifs had run, blurring the pattern and turning the sari into a hideous, dull, slate grey. My first lesson – always expect the unexpected.

Pretty soon, Elder and Younger – the two daughters – followed. Suddenly, the kids became a majority. All through the first few years of our married life, the Husband and I kept going through the drudgery and routine of our jobs and the hassles and tribulations of child bearing and rearing, not to mention housekeeping, with one thing in mind. We'd take a cruise on the Mediterranean to reward ourselves. That was the proverbial carrot before us two donkeys. It goes without saying that we had planned the event for when the children stopped their feeding-bottles, were able to walk on their own, and were properly toilet-trained. And of course, after we had earned enough for a total of five tickets. Without a doubt, it would have been idyllic for the two of us to get away alone, but the littles rapscallions had so ingrained themselves in our hearts that we could not think of going anywhere without them.

It was not easy hanging on to our sanity when three children aged six, four, and one decided to take over our lives and the running of our house. The minute a tiny mass of a person is able to move from point A to point B, your life as you know it is over. Things get misplaced and toppled over, and if you are not careful about closing the bathroom door, they will enter and drop their toys into the toilet, or worse still, splash about in it. I could never understand why they loved to play with the pots and pans rather than with the toys we bought them, or why they slept during the day and stayed awake at night. They had a knack for vomiting just as soon as you had them dressed in their Sunday best and a peculiar affinity to pushing the chairs around. They never ate from the plate, but the minute the food was toppled over, they licked the floor with remarkable gusto, vigour, and appetite. Bath times were a riot, and bathing three children could test the patience of the Holy Mary. That I got wet, wet, and wet after each episode of bath was a forgone conclusion, but that I had to mop the entire apartment after each affair, as a routine chore, was becoming a torment. To sum it up, I was forever cleaning either the mouth or the butt of one of the three. In later years, when my Boss proved to be particularly tiring, I just thought of him as another child in the bathtub who needed a stare down, and surprisingly, I was able to handle the situation and get him, the Boss that is, under control.

But through all this, when the Husband saw my harried and exhausted person, he would put his finger to his lips, shake his head, and remind me of the gift we had promised ourselves – the Mediterranean Cruise. At such times, I would just shake my head in mute agreement – not because I did not want to scream, but because I was too tired to convey my frustration in a more fervent manner. Once, we just happened to mention our mind-boggling day-to-day schedule to a friend and his new wife. Just out of a sheer need to share the experience with someone. Just to check if there were any fellow sufferers-cum-survivors out there somewhere. It was without any intention of discussing our superhuman efforts or any idea to brag or wallow in self-pity. Just to get it off our chests to a good mate. But the fellow just looked at us incredulously, and with a tinge of cynicism just enough to make us feel guilty, enquired if we had not heard of India's slogan proclaiming, 'Hum dho, hamara dho' (We two, our two)? And he did not stop there. He added for good measure, that in spite of India giving us permission to have two children, any sane, educated, cultured person would have limited their production to one, and that too, with definite planning and calculations. He went on to explain that a fellow would know he had slipped up if he had two, and that he had blundered if he had three. 'Where have you been?' he asked with renewed disbelief. And on the side, he advised us in a cynical tone of voice that there were methods to go about the carnal business without actually reaping its benefits. I was horrified and greatly offended by his suggestions, but the Husband looked nonchalant and the quirk appeared. 'Look here,' he countered, 'we were not complaining, and each of our children is important and unique. Do you know that I myself am the ninth rank holder in a brood of ten?' (Ah! That infamous line that I've had to listen to, time and again, until out of sheer frustration, I once pointed out that I was the first in my family of two). Anyway, his grin became cheeky as he continued with a laugh, 'We are in Kuwait, where the average Kuwaiti has five children. Do you want them to think us Indian men incapable and our ladies incompetent?' He went on to explain that if his father could survive with his brood of ten, then he saw no reason why we could not, as we only had a paltry three. We left soon after, but not before I heard his friend's cryptic parting shot suggesting that the Husband was in competition with his father! That thought had never occurred to me until then. I shelved the information to ponder on it at a later, more convenient time.

We were brilliant, the Husband and I, in how we managed our full-time professional lives with total élan and balanced them magnificently with the demands made on us by our young family. No one will believe me when I say that we spent most of the first ten years of our lives without a fight – not one! And without the need for any family planning on the production front either. There was just no time for either. It was not that we were so totally, blindly, overtly in love with each other that we were impervious to each other's faults. Neither were we saints that were always ready to forgive and forget. There was no special formula that we followed that would explain this strange situation of neutrality. But there were three reasons, and as I said, they were aged six, four, and one. We had our difference of opinions, petty quarrels, and sexual needs, but each time one cropped up, we would shelve it for a more convenient time to sort it out. And the fact of the matter was that such a convenient time never arose, or if by some twisted fluke of fate we did get a moment to ourselves, we just did not have the inclination or the energy. In any case, by then, we would have forgotten the point of argument, or the flames of desire would have died down. Anyone who has been married will know that a good argument depends on how sharp your memory is about the details of the squabble and how well you debate your point of view. You have to have your wits about you and fight each point with clinical precision, or else the other party would get away with it and leave you wondering for days if you could not have used a different point of approach and strategy and won the case. In our situation, the demands made by the children left us with no time or oomph to summon up the will to argue or have a good solid fight, let alone seduction. To bring it all out, thrash it to shreds, and hang it out there. So, we would shelve each fight or desire for a more convenient time, and that time, thankfully, never came.

Of the two of us, I was the more impatient one. The one who got angry easily and was ready to punish the children at the drop of a hat. Probably because I spent the entire day with them without a break, and the demands on me were constant and exhausting. The Husband always calmed me down, reasoning that they were behaving as children do, and we had to be patient and kind. Easy-going. I tried but was not always successful. One day, I was particularly harassed trying to make the Boy drink his milk. He was distracted, rolling his toy truck over the sofa armrest and everywhere else, and I was giving him a good shouting when the Husband relieved me of the chore, saying I lacked tolerance. I handed over the glass of milk to the father and said, 'Be my guest, O Great and Patient One, and thank you.' Then I went to the kitchen to cool down. I could hear some cajoling and coaxing to begin with, and then, about ten minutes later, a disgruntled Husband stormed into the kitchen, demanding a cloth wipe. I followed him back to the living-room where the Boy stood drenched in milk from head to toe. 'I'll give him a bath, and don't you dare say a word,' the Husband barked before I could open my mouth.

I don't know if half of what we did was right or wrong, but as Frank Sinatra said, 'We did it our way.' And the outcome is proof enough that whichever way you do it, if done with love and genuineness, the result is brilliant, and the reward, ten-fold.

The rapscallions at ages 7, 6, and 3

Biting Off More Than I Can Chew

An ordinary working day for us would begin at 5 am. Like clockwork, the baby would be up and bawling. That was my cue, and I'd dutifully roll off the bed and mechanically, like a wound-up toy, sleepwalk to the kitchen. First feed of the day to attend to. Meantime, mechanically, the Husband would pounce out from under the covers and try his utmost to hush the baby, or we would have two more sleepy heads to placate and attend to. We did not want a catastrophe even before the birds were up. Moreover, if we started the day badly, we had discovered that that would set the pattern for the rest of the diurnal. We would rather die than let that happen. Bedraggled and sleepy, I would be lucky if I did not pour hot water on my hands, but the flip side was, should that happen, it would wake me up proper and set me straight on the task at hand. In a haze, I would try to recollect how many times I had got up that night. Usually, the Boy needed to go to the bathroom once, and that would be followed by a request for a glass of water. If he had the slightest inkling that I would be co-operative, he would readily start a story about 'Tom and Jerry' in between the drink, and I would have to put on my no-nonsense face to get him back to bed.

Childr en have this special knack of knowing what you want them to do and then doing the exact opposite. They know how to make your life miserable without even trying. The little girl would have two nightmares, a visit to the loo, and if she had any clue that her brother had had a drink of water, she would demand the same. So, in all, I would have an average of three wake-up calls each night. Each time I got out of bed, I did so, encouraged by the thought of the holiday I would take from this entire chore one day in the near future, as promised by the Husband. 'The Cruise,' I'd whisper to myself. 'The Cruise.' Like some unfortunate resident doctors on their rotations, the Husband and I alternated our call to nocturnal duty. I would take Monday, Wednesday, and Friday nights, while he suffered on

Tuesday, Thursday, and Saturday nights. Sunday nights we left to chance. After all, we needed some excitement and enthusiasm in our lives, and the unpredictability of who would have to get up on a Sunday night added mystery and intrigue to our marriage.

In this melee, I had reason for a private victory. Our sex life was as good as dead. I always remembered the parting shot the Husband's friend had made after the unfortunate discussion about children. It had set me wondering if the Husband was indeed on a mission to better the father-in-law's record of ten. I had always looked at the mother-in-law with awe-inspiring reverence. I came from a family with a less ambitious father – we were a miserly two! Now, I watched the Husband from a different point of view. Maybe, subconsciously, somewhere in the secret recesses of an adoring son's mind lurked a desire to emulate his father or even better the old man. And what if this desire to do better, though latent, was dangerously potent? This new revelation was playing havoc with my mind. So, when our time and energy were drained by the demands of the children, I was secretly glad of the adverse effect it had on our intimate relationship. I believed it was divine intervention and heaved a sigh of relief. I looked upon this natural turn of events with approval, viewed my acquittal from wifely duties with candour, and welcomed the situation with immense relief. For once, God was working for Moi and not against Moi. However much I loved the children, I was beginning to feel like a martyr with every nappy I changed and every feeding bottle I washed. I was sure there were times when the Husband felt the same. But at each harried point, we reminded each other of the vacation that awaited us, which would give us the strength to hang on. I would often hum 'Santa Lucia' in an effort to make it more tangible.

'Now 'neath the silver moon, ocean is glowing,

O'er the calm billows, soft winds are blowing,

Here balmy breezes blow, pure joys invite us,

And as we gently row, all things delight us.'

Since we were working full time, we had to have a plan of action for executing even the simplest day-to-day chore. Take, for example, the case of a clean feeling bottle. Baby needed about six feeds per day on average. Then there were the bottles for fruit juices, drinking water, and semi-solid foods like Cerelac or Farex, which, due to the pressing demands on our time, we bottle-fed. And of course, we always kept two spare bottles, just in case. So, we needed at least a dozen washed, cleaned, and sterilized bottles to begin our day. A daunting prospect, for twelve clean bottles in the morning become twelve dirty bottles at night, and then comes the awful question of who will wash them, sterilize them, and dry them. We never argued the point. Waste of time, energy, and effort. We just extended our night duty roster to include the bottle washing too. As I mentioned earlier, I worked the graveyard shift on Mondays, Wednesdays, and Fridays, with the bottle washing thrown in, and he took the other days. Sundays were, of course, left to chance. But even when we thought we had each move planned to clockwork precision, there were the odd incidents that scared us out of our wits.

Like the incident with the locked door. I remember the day clearly. The Husband had gone to work, and I was holding fort. The Boy had just celebrated his fifth birthday, and we had bought him a bicycle. An over-indulgent aunt had given him a red toy car big enough for him to drive in. Since his birthday, he was at all times firmly fixed in either the car or on the bicycle, manoeuvring it in our tiny flat, running it over his sisters' fingers, or banging it into furniture. His skills improved, and soon, he was negotiating the vehicles between the sofas, under the dining table, between the chairs, and a particularly difficult spot between the refrigerator and the washing machine. Imagine me in a tiny kitchen with the baby on the countertop, the 3-year-old hanging onto my apron strings, bawling, and the Boy seated in his car, wedged between the fridge and the washing machine, making engine noises to get it out of the spot. And as there was not enough space, I'd be standing on one leg. But the real challenge that got me agitated was when he would try to reverse either of the vehicles between his sisters. I feared he would end up running the wheel over their fingers or toes, and once a screaming session started, there was no stopping the girls. They'd try to outdo each other. But even then, some part of me hung on to my sanity, and I told myself to think of the blue of the Mediterranean and cool myself.

Until one day, everything went berserk, and I turned into a banshee. It was the day he finally ran a wheel over Younger's foot, and she in turn shrieked like she could wake up the dead. Seeing Younger in such a state got Elder bawling –even if just to keep her sister company, I guess. I was already in the process of trying to soothe the inconsolable 4-year-old who had caught her finger between the bathroom door. After that fiasco, I sent the Boy outdoors to play on his bicycle, hoping it would tire him enough for him to want to come in later and watch some TV silently on the sofa or fall asleep. There were ghastly rumours doing the rounds that children were sedated at the various daycare facilities available in the neighbourhood. Much as it was a terrifying prospect, I was beginning to empathise and understand the point of view of the agencies. These cute little cuddly people could be monsters when they choose to be. Anyway, the Boy was out for about half an hour, during which time, calm was restored in the flat. Younger was pacified and put to sleep, and Elder had gathered an assortment of my cooking vessels and was busy cooking in the parlour. After I kept the rice to boil on the stove and had a hot cup of coffee, I thought it was time to bring the prodigal son home. I stepped out the door, leaving it ajar. Our apartment was on the second floor, so I had to lean over the banister and call out to the Boy. I did not see him immediately, so I moved a little to my right and went down a step or two. That was when I heard the smooth click of the front door. The sound did not register at first, but a second later, fear gripped my heart. Perhaps it was the caffeine that did not freak me out immediately, for by then, I had guessed what had happened. I turned and looked at the closed door. Then the click registered. Elder had locked the door from the inside. Of course, she did not know the significance but had just imitated an action she had watched me do every time I closed the door. Now, she had turned the key. I felt a flutter in my underbelly, then a pain, as if I was going into labour. My tongue turned dry, and in an instant, my heart began to pound against my chest. Even as I became aware of these physical changes, I stood rooted to the spot, unable to move. Then, somehow, I willed myself to keep calm, moved up to the door, and in a quiet voice, called to Elder. I did not want to alarm her. I coaxed her to slowly turn back the key. Anti-clockwise. I knew I was being silly to think she would understand that. I heard her giggle. I thought of Younger asleep on the bed. If she should wake and turn, she would fall off the bed, and the thought paralyzed me. The rice was cooking on the stove. I did not let my thoughts dwell on that. Blinding myself to the turmoil in my head, I called softly to my daughter.

'Turn the key, darling,' I cajoled her, then repeated, 'turn the key.' But how do you explain 'anti-clockwise'? Or 'to the left'? Did a four-year-old know right from left?

What followed was nothing short of a nightmare. I had no means of contacting the Husband, as he was at the worksite. Remember, there was a life before cell phones? I wet my lips and tried again. 'Turn the key, honey,' I kept saying. 'Turn the key,' I repeated hopelessly. And finally, obediently, she managed to turn the key, but only to double lock. 'Breathe,' I told myself. 'Breathe. Be calm, Lennie, think.' Finally, I knocked on my neighbour's door, though I had no idea what he could do. Mercifully, he was at home. He was kind enough to come to the door and coax my daughter in a heavy Arabic accent. I myself could not understand what he was saying, then how could a child of four? It was of no avail, and perhaps it was a stranger's voice that upset her. Or else she sensed that something was wrong, for I heard her sniffle and prepare to cry. That would wake Younger and create a whole new set of problems. Meanwhile, the building security guard came over to enquire what was going on. He started off with a volley of questions in a loud rough voice in rapid Arabic, throwing his hands all over. Stupidly, I watched him, wondering why these Arabs gesticulate a lot when they talk. Hearing this commotion, a few more of the tenants came around. Gradually, the gathering got bigger, and along with it, a wide range of ideas, advice, guidance, recommendations, suggestions, opinions, and warnings followed, none of which helped to open the door.

Then, as if God decided enough was enough, He answered my prayer. I spied the Husband coming up the steps and felt a great relief, knowing that everything would be all right, or at least, now there was someone who would be as concerned as Moi. As soon as he had an understanding of the situation, he came up with the first reasonable solution. He decided to call the fire brigade. Some of the neighbours said he was mad to do so, while others said it was just the thing they had been thinking to do. Within minutes, all hell broke loose. We could hear the siren from miles away, and the sound grew to alarming proportions as it neared. Those who did not know of our calamity were alerted of the same, and soon, people from other buildings came around to join the state of affairs. A lot of explanations and discussions ensued. A lot of whispers and head shakings, and a lot of comings and goings. Finally, the firefighters decided to break into the flat through the balcony's glass door. They used a ladder to lift themselves to the balcony, and once there, they broke it open and entered the flat. In a minute, the front door was open. Younger was awake and crying, but mercifully, she had not fallen off the bed. Elder looked petrified and was too shocked to cry, and the rice on the stove had bubbled over, spilled all over the stove, and looked useless. The Boy was thrilled at seeing the firefighters, and as for myself, I became the best-known face in the neighbourhood.

It took us a while to settle down after that alarming incident. But with time, we soon became complacent again. The children started school, and we got into a system of sorts for the rhythmic conduct of our lives. We paid particular attention to the house key, but soon found that other things could go haywire as well. An incident on a cold winter morning taught us that. Every night, the Husband would set the alarm for 5 am, boasting each time that he did so that it was just a precaution and that he did not need the ring to wake him up. He had this 'built-in awareness,' he was fond of saying. He was, after all, a veteran father of three, he'd brag, though he could have done better on that score, had I been more cooperative, he was fond of pointing out suggestively. He said he set the clock anyway to wake me up, as he thought I slept like the dead. One night, as he checked the clock, to his horror, he found that the glass had cracked, and the clock was lifeless. I seized my chance and said, 'Why do you care, since you have a "built-in system" that beats all systems?' Then, to rub it in, I added sarcastically, 'Surely, we have nothing to worry about since we can test out your system for a change and see how effectively it works.' He looked at me to see if I was mocking him, but I put on my, 'I really mean it' face, and probably, my earnest look and the late hour placated him as he crept into bed. I do not remember how long we slept, but sometime during the course of the night, I guess something set off the 'built-in alarm system.' The Husband jumped up and woke me. It was winter, so we thought nothing of the darkness outside. He went to the children's room and began to wake them up, while I rushed to the kitchen to make the coffee, milk, breakfast, snacks, and juices. In between, I got all the pairs of shoes together and did a quick polish. I organized the uniforms but could not find one of the school ties. I heard odd noises from the bathroom, and I knew he had overloaded the brushes with toothpaste. I called out to reduce the paste, but he was a firm believer in the '2-inch paste' policy. The children gagged on the abundant froth in the mouth, but as the Husband firmly believed the extra paste suffocated the germs, this tussle between him, the children and the germs went on forever. I did not want to get involved, as I was, after all, only the in-house dentist. What did I know? In a while, the kids were all cleaned, fed, clothed, and exhausted. The Husband looked at me triumphantly and remarked snidely that all one needed was a bit of 'built-in awareness,' and things were not so bad. Younger lay nestled on his shoulders, fast asleep, as she was dog-tired by the rigors of getting ready for school. In his right hand, the Husband clutched our rebellious Elder, who protested at every turn of preparation. The Boy carried the water bottles while trying his best to look awake and chirpy. I carried the bags, locked the door, and the lot of us went down to wait for the school bus. But strangely, there were no other children out and about. The sky was exceptionally dark, and the wind was still cold. The Husband wondered if everyone was late. I wondered if we were early. I asked him if he had checked his watch, and that was when he sheepishly glanced at it. It was near about 4 am. We stood for a while to get our bearings. I wondered if it was a good time for an argument. I could win this, hands down. He was smart enough to read my mind, so before I could gather my points, get my ducks in a row, and checkmate, he admitted his mistake. 'Relax,' he suggested, 'think of good things to come, think of the cruise on the Mediterranean. Blue sky, blue sea.' Blue was a good colour, and the thought relaxed Moi. I breathed and allowed the harmony and serenity to take over. Yes, we owe us a vacation. We would have one to make up for everything. Or we could buy a new alarm clock.

'Now 'neath the silver moon, ocean is glowwwwing,' I sang loudly into the dark night so I would not say what was really on my mind and pick a fight.

In spite of our busy schedule, we tried to do everything right by the children. It was not their fault that we worked two shifts and had obnoxious bosses. Nor was it their fault that Santa Claus visited children and brought bags of presents. These rules had existed before we got married and started a family. So, as Christmas approached, the kids wrote letters to Santa, asking for presents. As the Husband and I organized our Christmas party, funnily, it seemed to rekindle our romance. Perhaps, after all, there was something about Christmases, cakes, cards, carols, presents, and Santas that made magic in ordinary lives. We got a close friend of ours to act as Saint Nicholas. He had an over-indulgent paunch, and so we thought he would be the perfect candidate. Everything was fine, though we were taxed to the limit in our efforts to keep the whole thing secret. The children made their wish lists and kept them under their pillows. I retrieved the same and went about the business of getting the items and hiding them at our friend's place. We, meaning I, filled three large garbage bags with toys of every description. Thundercats, fire engines, monopoly sets, a toy walkie-talkie, a superman outfit, a cooking set, Barbie dolls, a toy pram with a rag doll, a handbag, a red nail-polish bottle, a doll that cried and laughed, a water-pistol, and everything else listed. It brought back poignant memories of my own Christmas gifts, especially the red cheongsam with the dragon motif and handbag.

However, on Christmas Eve, the unthinkable happened. Our friend was laid up, and there was no way he could come. It was a crisis. We were in dire need of a Santa Claus. We raked our brains and mulled over the problem, but with no solution in sight. We contacted a few friends, even some without bulging bellies, asking them to step in and help out. But at such short notice, no one was free. There was only one option left. The Husband would have to step in and do the needful. At first, he was horrified and pointed out that he did not have a paunch. I told him that a cushion would fix that and asked if he had any other suggestions. He noticed the glint in my eye and gave in, but once the idea set in, he was excited. We drew up a plan. Now, we had to smuggle the three bags of toys from our friend's place into our house. I took the kids to the zoo while the Husband brought home the bags and hid them under our bed. He got together his disguise and perfected his act. By the time I returned from the zoo, exhausted and ready to die, I was greeted by an excited and overenthusiastic Husband who could not wait to set things in motion. After I had had a bath and a coffee, we held a meeting. We told the children that Santa had replied and he would come on the 24th, late into the night.

On Christmas eve, we asked them to go to bed early, as it was the night Santa Claus would drop in. We suggested they leave a snack or a fruit on the dining table in case he was tired from visiting all the houses and needed some refreshment. The Boy left an orange; Elder, two toffees; and Younger, her leftover sandwich. I packed them off to bed and shut the door, and then we set to work. First, I got out the three garbage bags filled with toys from under the bed and put them outside the apartment. Then, I got the Husband to dress up as Santa. We tied a cushion to his waist to create a paunch, and I helped him into his Santa costume. He wore a Santa mask on his face. Then he went out of the flat and stood in the area outside the apartment and rang the bell. I acted all enthusiastic and excited and rushed into the children's room and told them Santa had come. The Boy said that he heard no reindeers. I ignored the comment. The girls jumped out of their beds eagerly. We gathered in the parlour just as the doorbell rang again. I had tutored the Husband on the 'Ho, Ho, Ho,' but as I opened the door, he came in with a 'Ha, ha, ha,' spoiling the effect. He walked into the room, and it was worth all the effort to see the surprise and wonderment on the children's faces. Then the Husband went totally out of script and did the most ridiculous thing. He caught hold of me and gave me a resounding kiss. Whoever heard of a Santa kissing the mother of the children? At once, the Boy was on the defensive. 'Where's dad?' he turned and asked me, thinking his father should be around, since the Santa was flirting with his mother. 'Focus on the toys,' I said to him, with half a mind to kick Santa where it hurt. By then, the girls had offered Santa their refreshments, and the bags of toys were handed out. I noticed the Boy was reserved. He was peeved and objected to a stranger being so familiar with his mother. Slowly, I noticed that the amazement on the children's faces were becoming replaced by misgivings, and I thought it best to wind up the whole thing. Just then, Elder shouted out, 'Look at the socks he is wearing. It is dad.' I pushed the Husband out of the door and rushed the kids to bed. 'But Mama,' they began. 'Shush,' I said sharply. 'Don't let Santa hear you doubt him or he will not come next year.' With that, I switched off the lights, closed the door, and went to let Santa back into the flat. Thankfully, the next few days were so busy with opening presents and Christmas festivities that an in-depth discussion on Santa never occurred.

Thirty-five years have passed, and a lot of water has flown under the bridge, but now, as we watch them going about their business, independent, assured, undaunted, ready to take on the world, and maybe one day, even play Santa to their own children, we know it was well worth the effort, mistakes and all. Today, we bask in gratitude and humble appreciation, albeit with a tinge of cynicism when they offer us protection and even throw in the occasional word of caution and advice. And we kept the promise we made to ourselves and cruised on the Mediterranean. We took the children along because, all said and done, they had motivated us to achieve that particular goal.

Who let the dogs out?

By the Periyar

Zelzella

I want to be able to say that I owned the clinic in Kuwait and that I ran it with the utmost professionalism and efficiency. But I can't say that, for you see, the truth was that it was not my clinic, per se, nor did I run it as I liked or with the competence required. The clinic belonged to Syed Hassan Zelzella, an 86-year-old Irani-Kuwaiti who was the first dental surgeon in Kuwait. He would tell us often of a time when he carried a pair of crude dental forceps and some other abstruse instruments and made door-to-door calls, offering his expertise. But I think he was well-respected and made good money, for he had two wives and umpteen children and grandchildren. But that did not stop his roving eye, and he was always on the lookout for a third young bride. He had confided his desire to marry again many times to me, but I, being a married woman and stupid, thought nothing of it until my faithful nurse, Ratnabai, warned me that he was making a pass. *Bleepers, what a pickle*, I thought. But it's happening in this world, right? Like in the M&B romance books. Older, rich man; young, beautiful (erm…I like to think so) doctor. But there was one snag. This paragon of manhood, even if I should override his much-married status, age, and number of children, was not in the best of health. He had done a hemi-maxillectomy. That is to say, his left maxilla had been removed due to cancer, and that side of his face sagged. As a result, he drooled and slurred while he shared his heart's longings with Moi. Then again, I'm not vain or hard-hearted and could overlook the asymmetry of the face; it was the language barrier that got me. For he did not speak Arabic but a thickly accented Farsi. As for the running of the clinic, in spite of all the snide, sweet somethings that he'd make, Ol' Man Zelzella had handed over the reins to his trusted Irani-Armenian man, Daud, or David, as he liked to call himself. The two of them formed a monolithic duo that wanted no change or modification in the workings of the clinic. And then there was my faithful friend and nurse, Ratnabai, from Tamil Nadu. If you exclude the errand-boy, the cleaner, and the electrician, the four of us formed the principal pillars of the clinic. Zelzella, the owner and my sponsor; Ratnabai, the nurse cum advisor to me; Daud, the technician and man-in-charge; and of course, Moi.

The clinic, though small, was a busy place, especially on Thursdays, when there would be no room to swing a cat. The majority of our patients were big, strapping Iranian men who were too big for the dental chair. It was a real challenge to extract one of their upper molar teeth. I have been tempted so many times to hang myself from the forceps and use my whole-body weight to get one of their upper teeth out. But thankfully, more often, these narcissistic chaps came to grind down their lateral incisors and give themselves gold caps, which Daud so obligingly did. There were two reasons for this great demand in gold caps. One was that these fellows believed that tiny bits of the precious metal from the gold caps would invariably be consumed, and over time, they would acquire inhuman strength and fortitude. The second was more romantic. Leaving their wives and children, they have come so far away from home to make their fortune. They wanted to return as wealthy men, and what better way to convey that message than with a flash of a gold smile? Moreover, the wives would think their husbands looked handsome with the golden sparkle and would be titillated at the thought that their menfolk would have gained strength and prowess in the required areas for the great reunion and the rekindling of marital bliss. And to think we dentists facilitate this great passion was most satisfying for Moi. I would also do a bit of business to profit the clinic by bargaining and suggesting to the patient that perhaps all the pleasures would be doubled if both the lateral incisors were gold capped instead of one. This way, I brought in more revenue, and all parties were satisfied. In fact, I think Daud must have relayed this message to Old Man Zelzella, and it pleased him so much that he renewed his pursuit of Moi in earnest, much to my consternation and Ratnabai's delight and amusement.

A congenial atmosphere prevailed in the clinic. We each played our part without encroaching into the other person's space. In spite of our differences, or rather because of it, we formed a compatible group with a strange bond and were fiercely protective of each other. On retrospect, it was a good group if you can overlook Zelzella's harmless leering. In fact, Nurse and I even started to enjoy it and looked forward to it. The ol' man arrived daily at about 11 am. And Ratnabai would announce to me in Tamil:

'Daketer unga kanavvar vanthachi' (Doctor, your lover has come).

To which I'd reply, 'Irukatum sister. Inda clinic kedachal nallathu thannà?' (Let it be, Sister. Isn't it a good thing if I should inherit this clinic?)

And we would have a rollicking laugh. Each of us had our own idiosyncrasies, and yet, rather than break us, they bonded us. Perhaps it was because we were all equally simple, good at heart, and able to see humour in any situation. At least, I would like to think so. I've told you about Sayed Hassan Zelzella. Like I said, every day without fail, he'd stagger into the clinic with the help of his walking stick and man Friday. He had his office on the side, but he'd first come to the clinic and push open the surgery door, and to hell with decorum.

Then, he would enquire in a raspy whisper in Irani, 'Chitoraè Doktor? Hallett shumma khubae?' (How are you, Doctor? Is your heath good?)

I would be neck deep in someone's mouth and totally unprepared for any social chit-chat. Even so, I'd raise my hand in acknowledgement and say, 'Balè. Hallett man kheili khubaè' (Yes. I am very fine)

No matter how busy I was, I always made it a point to acknowledge him, as I knew these people set great store on paying close attention to niceties. He would then hobble over to his office to draw up the accounts for the running of his two households.

Let's dissect Daud next. Here was a short, well-set, prim and proper man, modelled à la Poirot. Minus the moustache, of course. Courteous and correct to the core. He had the bluest of blue eyes. Azure. And as if they were not blue enough, he would sometimes wear a cobalt-blue shirt to enhance the colour, perhaps. Lapis lazuli? The result was so piercing one could not look at him without gasping from all that blue. The colouring seemed to have been collected from the abyss of the oceans and poured into his eyes. It was a startling effect.

As Ratnabai never tired of observing, 'Andavar evanuk yan inda neram yellamà koduthu erukaranga?' (Why has God blessed this fellow with all this colour?)

Daud had been educated up to the 4th grade. Later, he apprenticed as a dental technician. His Achille's heel was the English language. He knew some sporadic words, which he'd throw all over in a bid to converse in English. But that was not good enough to get him a Canadian visa. He was trying to migrate to Canada and had already gone for two interviews but had been turned down by the Embassy. So, I picked up the gauntlet, and thus, Project 'Educating Daud to Speak English' took shape, much to Ratnabai's enjoyment.

'Aadhu mattum than ungaluku eneyum thavai,' she laughed. (That's all you need now)

Daud and I made a pact. We would speak only in English, we decided. Of course, I had to step down my English, while he would, no doubt, have to step up. But I gave him full credit for trying. When one is enthusiastic and willing, half the battle is won.

In my lowered English style, I'd say, 'Daud how you, how you?'

'I good. I good. Ya. Ya. Come early today. Ya. Ya. Is traffic. Too much. Too much,' Daud would stammer.

Not to be outdone, I'd add in my new brand of English, 'Ya. Ya. Me too. Me too. Police stupid. What do he? Stand here, stand there. No help. No help.'

'Ah, he lazy. Only money. No work. No work. All police same. I drive car slowly. I come,' Daud would reply.

I don't know why, but we repeated everything twice. Maybe I subconsciously wanted to hammer home the language as quickly as possible. Then, I realised one day to my horror that rather than teaching Daud, I was adopting his mode of conversing. I realized that when the Husband asked me why I repeated everything twice. But there was no backing out now. So, it went on. I also did Daud's banking and corresponded with his bank – The Royal Bank of Canada, if I remember correctly. I mention this to tell you what Ratnabai would jokingly advise me. She would say:

'Annage Docketer. Ungga perè pottu paisavà anapunggu. Evanuku theriya povath illai. Konjum yean perukum podunguo.' (Come on doctor, send the money in your name. He will not come to know of it. While at it, put some in my name too)

We would then laugh so much at the idea that it was enough to keep us on a high for the rest of the day.

Once, when she was teasing me about the banking letter, Daud came to join us and said, 'All happy, all happy. Good, good.'

'Ya. Ya. I saying you English now good. You clever. Learning fast, fast,' Ratnabai said with a straight face, giving nothing away.

She said it so smoothly and on cue that I just lost all composure and cried laughing. Worse still, Daud joined us in the laughter. But when Sister added,

'Aiyo, evan yadhuku seerikurano, Andavarè' (Why is he laughing, dear God), I just gave up and ran to the loo.

Another day, during clinics, I was busy with a patient, and Ratnabai was in attendance, when we heard Daud call out, 'Leg broken, leg broken.'

Ratnabai gasped. 'Ai, ai, yo! Avanodà kallu odanchu pochu pol irukudhu. Poi paringalè. Ambulance kupidunuma?' (He has broken his leg. Go and see. Shall I call the Ambulance?)

'Vanda, vanda. Nan paketum modalè,' I replied. (No, no. Let me look at it first)

We ran to the lab and saw Daud kneeling on the floor. Both of us jumped on him and heaved him up and placed him on the chair. His usual sparkling electric blue eyes turned into midnight blue. For a minute, I think he feared we were going to rape him or worse. He started to get up.

'No, no, Daud. No stand, no stand,' I shouted.

'Why? Why? What do you? What do you?' Daud asked anxiously.

'You sit chair. Sit. Sit,' Ratnabai admonished sternly.

'I look leg. Leg falling down,' Daud said in dismay.

'Ayi, ayi yoo! Evan yennenamo solruran. Yanakku onumà purielleyà. Andavarè!!' Ratnabai said desperately. (Goodness, he is blabbering something or the other. Dear God, I don't understand anything)

'Don't move Daud. I check your leg,' I ordered. Then, in my most professional doctor's avatar, I caught hold of his leg and began to feel it. He jumped out of the chair and out of his skin and stood as far away from us as possible, his back to the wall. He really looked petrified, and that's putting it mildly. Then, his hands shivering, he held up his spectacles as Ratnabai and I stupidly gawked at him; then, the penny slowly dropped.

'My glass leg broken, glass leg. Not my leg.' His eyes beseeched for us to leave the lab.

The patient I had been treating stood at the doorway, glaring at us and demanding to know what in the world was going on.

Turning to me, Ratnabai said, 'Dayavu saidha indha English padutham nirthidunga. Eniyum namma evana angalammo pidikum yandra yaruko thrium? Yesu Appa, nalla valliya katunga.' (For God's sake, stop this English study. Who knows where else we will end up feeling him over. Jesus, show us the right way.) That was her parting shot.

Needless to say, I taught him the English language. He got through his interview and is now a Canadian citizen. Ratnabai is happily retired and settled in her hometown near Nagercoil. She calls me often, and we have a good laugh over so many of our shenanigans. Syed Hassan Zelzella died in the Gulf War. So, I never inherited the clinic. Nor did I get the chance to find out what could have been. C'est la Vie.

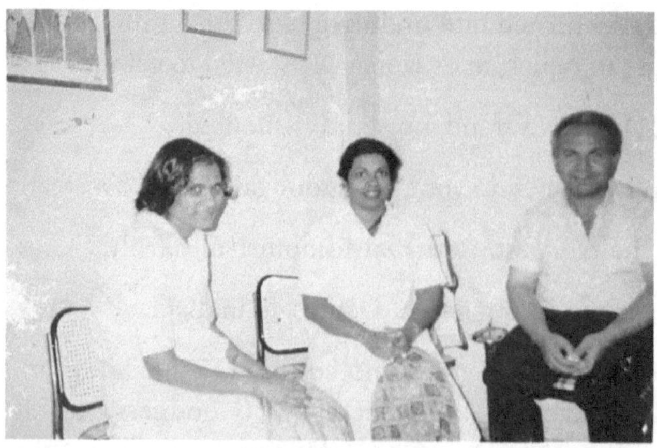

Ratnabai, Daud, and Moi

Getting An Education While Educating

I have always thought I was lucky to get a proper education from good schools. But how do you gauge good? By the size of the campus? The school building? The uniforms? The teachers? The students? A combination of all of the above? Probably. My parents were pleased that they had done their best for me. I was accomplished, or so they thought. I thought so too. Until I got married and the kids came along. To my horror, I found I knew nothing. The realization that I was an ignoramus nincompoop began in Kuwait. The Boy was the first to go to school. In Class 2, he started Arabic. Ya Allah! (Dear God!)

ARABIC

The Arabic teacher sent me a note saying she wanted to see me. So, I trotted along. We had the most interesting conversation. And I got an education.

Teacher (T): 'Zer is a broblem (problem) with your Boy. He doesn't say ze Arabic from ze throat.'

I was at a loss, so I said, 'Beg your pardon?'

The teacher emphasised, 'Ze Arabic, it should come from ze throat.'

I (Totally at sea): 'Could you explain?'

T: 'Zain.' (Ok). 'Ze "kha, kha." He is saying it "ka, ka" from the mouth, not from ze deep throat. Inteh fakham?' (Do you understand?)

I: 'Oh, I see. Yes, yes. I get it. What do you suggest?'

T: 'You have to make him say "kha" not "ka." Make like a retching sound. Ze "kha" come from ze back of ze tongue and ze deep throat, but the "ka" come from the mouth.'

I: 'Retching sound?'

T: 'Yes, yes, Habibi. It should be between ze tongue and ze deep throat. Try it. Ze "kha," from deep in the throat. La taqhlaq.' (Don't worry.)

I: 'Taklak?'

T: 'Ouddhubilla!! (Heavens!). See? You say "Tak, Tak." I say the "taqh, taqh" from behind ze throat. "Taqh, taqh." Fakham?'

I'm blindsided. 'Zain. Lekin ma indee fikra…' (Ok. I have no idea…)

T: 'Ah, see? "Indee." No, no. It is wrong. It's "aiin" not "in." From ze nose and ze throat. It must involve ze nose. Not only ze throat.'

I: 'Malesh. (Sorry). I will try to make him use the guttural sound.'

T: 'Guttural, you say? Zain, thamam.' (Right. Good.)

She turned to go, and I should have left it at that. But me being Moi, I opened the trap and said, 'Lader, min fudlek.' (One moment, please.)

And she came at me hammer and tongs. 'No, no. Not lader. Ladher, "ladh" come from ze throat. You must retch. Adh, adh. Say it.'

I: 'Dh, dh.'

T: 'Not enough. From ze deep throat. Look! Adh. Adh.'

And I gaped into her mouth and saw her uvula flipper. She had a high-arched palate and two class 1 fillings. And by God! A large cavity on the lower left 6. I never dreamt Arabic was so anatomical. Dental, to be precise. Or was I just being a Dentist?

T: 'Now see here. Not fudlek. No, no. The "fhah" from the deep throat. Between teeth and tongue. Yallah!!' (Go on.)

After a good half an hour of retching and grating my nasopharyngeal region, I escaped with the Boy. At home, the Husband asked me why I was late. I told him it was because his son was not guttural enough. He was shocked. He thought it had something to do with the little fellow's Crown Jewels. We engaged an Arabic teacher to tutor the Boy, and guess what? I had to sit with them so that I could pick up the finer sounds produced between tongue and deep throat and the nose and throat. I had to get it correct should the Boy go wrong. The Husband, of course, had his own brand of Arabic-Hindi-Malayalam mix that he used at the engineering site on the unsuspecting workers. I did not want the Boy to be contaminated with that mix. So, I kept vigilant by educating myself along with the Boy. Besides, I wanted to be ready if that Arabic teacher ever called me again.

And thus, I started my education.

KARATE

The children were enrolled. I'd take the empty seat beside the Dojo and listen attentively. I imbibed each lesson. The posture maintained while bowing to the opponent. The short shout 'Kiai'; the stances (Tachikata); the punches (Tsuki); and the kicks (Geri).

When we were at home, I'd get the kids to practice. I'd say the carpet area was the Dojo.

I: 'Posture.'

Elder: 'I want to see the cartoons.'

Younger: 'I want a sandwich.'

I: 'Not now. After half hour of karate practice.'

E: 'I want to learn dance.'

I (shouting): 'Senza!'

Both jump to it.

I: 'Choku Zuki.' But heck, I'm wondering what it was. I had forgotten.

Boy: 'No, mama. We have to say 'Onegaishimasu first.'

I: 'What?'

They stayed silent. And I didn't have a freaking idea what the word was. I didn't know how to say it or what it meant.

I: 'Ok, say it.'

B (grinning): 'What?'

Bleeding heck, how do you weasel out of that fix? Were all mothers suffering like I was? Was I overcommitted? The fathers seemed to be having it easy. One week of the various postures, stances, kicks, and punches, and I was a good-for-nothing mass of flesh.

SWIMMING

I enrolled the three for swimming, as this was my Waterloo. The one thing that defeated me. I could not swim to save myself from a sinking ship. So, I was adamant to rectify that shortcoming in the children. I paid close attention to every instruction. I figured I could pick up some swimming tips for myself on the side. The instructor was merciless. 'Hold your noses and dunk under the water,' was his first order. Next, the kids had to hold onto the edge of the pool and flap their legs. *Right,* I thought, *both those exercises can be practiced in the bath tub.* Only, they would have to go in one at a time. So, the following evening, I filled the tub to the brim and got the three into the bathroom. The effort involved in getting the three boisterous kids to the bathroom was tremendous and a story in itself. I almost aborted the mission. But I prevailed. When one is a mother, one has to be tenacious. Then, I told the Boy to do the dunk.

He gave me a grin and said, 'Quack, quack.'

And all three of them laughed.

'What's that?' I demanded.

'I thought you said "duck," Mother,' the boy said, grinning, while the girls sniggered.

I: 'Okay. No cartoons today.'

That was my 'card up the sleeve.' Always a winner. I knew it was a bit below the belt, but the Opposition was cunning. As expected, the laughter died down to the sound of suppressed groans.

B: 'OK. But you show us first.'

I was appalled. Blimey! I had never held my head underwater, ever. There was never any need to up until then. Yet there was no backing down here. The Opposition might be small, but as a Union, they were strong. I knelt by the tub and put my face into the water. Immediately, I choked and sputtered and raised my head. I coughed and gaged and retched. *This is the best way to learn Arabic*, I thought.

PIANO

The teacher was a man and an Indian and a bit of a dandy, but otherwise all right. However, he did have the habit of knocking on the knuckles of the children when they got a musical note wrong or played indifferently. Many times, I was tempted to remind him that they were children and it was important to keep them interested in the lesson rather than hate it. Fearing I might interfere, I did not creep around much trying to get an education from him. Moreover, I was quite proficient in that area and was confident I could make them practice using what knowledge I had. And yet, I hung around because no matter how much you know, there is always something you can learn from another. But as time passed, I was beginning to realise the teacher was starting to need protection from the children. The union was getting stronger and his knuckle-cracking strategy was beginning to rile them up.

Chilli powder was one of the weapons they deployed on an unsuspecting enemy. I was witness to this. As this atrocity happened to the Husband, we were not sued or reported to the police or anything as drastic as that. Although the three were not suave and lacked panache in the execution of the methodology and strategy of their attacks, the results were devastating. And ruthless. It was over Mathematics lessons with their father that the unfortunate incident unfurled and came to a head. I am a blockhead when it came to numbers and so the Husband took over the arduous task of familiarizing the three with facts and figures. He was forever pointing out to me that Mathematics, which was his main subject at college, required a brain, unlike science. The insinuation was clear. But when three children are being taught by an adult child who is unbending and lacks the required knack to cajole them into obeying him, the whole combination could be volatile.

As it turned out to be. After one particularly snarling, scolding, crying, uncooperative Maths session, the two parties were out to draw blood. As usual, I had to remind the Husband that he was older, supposed to be wiser, and above all, a father. He withdrew. But it was different with the Union. They stood their ground and wanted their revenge. They laid out their plans in cunning detail and neither of us grown-ups were the wiser.

The Husband took an afternoon nap every day, and he was serious about his snoring. He would inhale the air with a whirling sound and let it out like deflating a big balloon. His large nostrils would quiver, and many times, the children would stand around and watch in wonder at this comical and fascinating exercise.

'If you stand too close, I might just inhale you into my system,' he had warned them once. I guess they kept that in mind. So, to get back at the Husband for humiliating them, the next time he took a nap, they held a spoonful of chilli powder to his nose. I swear to God, I guess the Union never imagined how dreadful the consequences could be. The Husband lay dazed and dead for almost one hour during which time all hell broke loose.

So, when I caught Elder smuggle a small bottle of chilli powder along with her music books, I knew there was mischief afoot. But I guess the music teacher had a lucky escape. Saddam struck, and we found ourselves rudderless, having lost everything. We were without jobs, money, or a home. Three young children to care for, and with no notion on how to go about it. Times were hard, and difficult decisions needed to be made. The future seemed austere and bleak. But we had our youth and our desire to survive. And we were alive. That should suffice.

We shifted base to India and faced a new curriculum where Hindi and Malayalam featured prominently. Both of which were alien to me.

Singing lessons at home

Karate practice

AFTER THE WAR

Getting An Education While Educating

We were actually on vacation in India when Saddam invaded Kuwait. We had exhausted every penny we had in a grand tour of Delhi, Agra, Mysore, and Chennai. We were to leave for Kuwait on the 2nd of August 1990. Sadaam put a stop to it by entering the kingdom before us, on the 1st. Stranded in India and with our jobs gone, our future looked very miserable and uncertain. But whatever the calamity, one thing was certain. The education of the minions was not to be compromised. They would have to get on with it. The show must go on. And so, we enrolled them in a reputed school in Trivandrum. The Boy in class 6, Elder in 4, and Younger in 1. It was a daunting task to get the children acclimatised to the rules and regulations of the new school. They were at a stage when they had started to question the options offered and the choices we made. They wanted a say in everything concerning them. But the worst was when I realized that they had to be introduced to two new subjects, Hindi and Malayalam, both alien to Moi. However hard I had tried, I could not cut the mustard where Arabic was concerned. I wondered how much better I would do with these two challenges. But what else was a mother to do but try. Malayalam was a tongue twister.

'Nookkkada namudà margà kidakkunna markkada nee onu mari keeda shada' (It's something to do with somebody asking a snake that lay across his way to move aside.)

That was not for the faint-hearted. It took me more than 13 days to get it right. Once I got it, I used it liberally when I wanted the kids to move from point A to point B. I kind of rolled it over my tongue. I felt an achievement at having mastered it. I guess I was in a fool's paradise to think I'd master the language in no time.

After the first day at school, I called the three to get an update. Younger was miffed and really upset.

I: 'What's the matter? What happened?'

Y: 'The teacher called me a bad word.'

I: 'Oh? That's not nice. What did she call you?'

Y (Cupping her hand over her mouth and in a loud whisper): 'Edi. She called me "edi" three times.'

Serious gasps from the other two.

I: 'Sometimes, it can also mean "girl,"' I said to pacify her.

Y: 'That is "penneh". Edi is a bad, rude word Mama. And she used a loud, angry voice.'

I: 'Maybe it can mean a naughty girl,' I reassured her.

Y: 'I don't like it.'

But a couple of days later, the horrifying result of my lackadaisical answer hit home. The Boy was disgusted that his teacher would send him out of class for calling one of the girls 'edi.'

I (Horrified): 'Why would you do that?'

B: 'She was irritating me. I told the teacher that I meant it like, "naughty girl."'

So, I then had to retract and rectify. I said, 'Fine. No one uses "edi." It's a rude form of girl.'

Y (complacently): 'See, Mama. I told you.'

B: 'Gosh Momma. You better get educated in the different nuances of the Malayalam words. Or else we'll be drinking all kinds of soup.'

I turned to the Elder.

'And you? How was it for you?'

E: 'Mama, do you know I'm learning this language called Hindi? You have to draw lines all the time. It's really strange.'

I turned to the Boy. He simply raised his hands and flopped on to the divan.

B: 'I surrender to all the misery and misinformation that I'm being exposed to. I confess I fear I will grow up to be a very complicated, confused individual. I might even become schizophrenic.'

MALAYALAM

I found a Malayalam tutor who was supposed to be patient and thorough. He was a man of small stature, but he had an impressive moustache. I guess one made up for the other. He was a good teacher, but he was no match for the union. Sadly, tuitions were at 4 pm, when I had my evening clinics. So, I was not there to referee, and the Tuition Master was under the mercy of the three. After a few days of classes, I asked the tutor how things were going.

The teacher asked me with concern in his voice, 'Eedh andha ee kutti thunda il ninum karkichu samsarikunnadu?' (Why does this boy retch and speak from the throat?)

I looked at the Boy, and he explained, 'That's because I'm still in Arabic mode.'

And he kept up the Arabic charade at all times, much to the helplessness of the poor man.

T: 'Kashtam. Edhu Malayalam ellà? Adhinu thundaudà avisham eella' (Such a pity. This is Malayalam. You don't need your throat for that.)

To the girls, the tutor would go, 'Ka ekha ga egha ngya.'

And the girls would go, 'Ka, ka, ga, ga, nya.'

In the end, to get the situation under control, I had to change the time of tuitions so I too could attend.

HINDI

The teacher was very stern and uncompromising. She insisted on speaking only in Hindi at all times. That in itself was so taxing. Who the hell knew what she was saying? I didn't, let alone the kids. At first, the Boy refused to sit with her. He complained he did not understand a word she said since she spoke in Hindi all the time.

I stood my ground, and he finally gave in.

She began: 'Ka, ekha, ga, egha ngya.'

And the children chorused: 'Ka, ka, ga, ga, nya.'

As she spoke only in Hindi, the children refused to obey any of her commands. I suspected they knew what she meant, but just to needle her, they told her they had to understand her in order to obey her. And then there was the big question. They wondered if 'ka, ka, ga, ga, nya' belonged to both Malayalam and Hindi, and if so, how were they to know which 'ka, ka, ga, ga, nya' the teacher was referring to at any given point in time. For a split second there, the little rascals had me confused. Then the Boy came up with the obvious explanation: 'Hey girls, it's easy. If the Malayalam dude is teaching, it's the Malayalam Ka, ka. But if it's the Hindi witch, then it's the Hindi Ka, ka.'

When we stumbled on 'nokada nammudà' in the Malayalam class, I burnt the midnight oil to get it right. I prayed I'd never come across another daunting lesson as hard as that tongue twister. But when the Hindi teacher told me the Boy was not getting his 'hedu, hedu, madu, bhooda kalom sè vakyom ko pura karro' correct, I wept. She was appalled by my reaction and thought I was having some sort of breakdown. Little did she know that I was on the verge. I was further disappointed when one evening, I cornered Younger and asked her to repeat the 'ka ekah.' She asked me in all sincerity if she should do the Malayalam or Hindi 'ka ekah.' But without losing heart, we toiled on, and pretty soon, after the initial hiccups, it all panned out to some sort of smooth sailing.

BHARATANATYAM

What true-blooded Malayalee mother worth her salt will refrain from teaching her girls Bharatanatyam? Besides, the girls went on about how all their friends were enrolled for the same and how they danced on the stage at school. Though I did not have the faintest idea about this dance form or the music involved, I agreed. We were Indians, after all. Even if I was already neck deep in the Malayalam and Hindi lessons, I figured I could make time for a bit of the arts. Now, I knew that my girls were a tricky, sneaky lot. And the two together meant double trouble. So, I would have to keep vigilant, hang around, and roll my eyes to keep them in line. Moreover, like I did with karate in Kuwait, I had to learn and understand the art form myself so I'd be able to coach the girls at home. So, in spite of my disastrous attempts at karate and swimming in Kuwait, which had caused me to have some genuine doubts about my abilities, I decided to take a chance. I squashed any thought of my weaknesses as soon as its ugly head reared up, and I promised myself I would do better this time.

But to my misfortune, the dance teacher did not encourage the parents to stay in the dance class, though she was not averse to our watching from the windows. I was desperate to know what went on inside, so I was thankful for that little morsel of opportunity she threw at Moi. In any case, I could not be put off that easily. I turned over a flower pot, stood on it, and peeped in through the window. There were about twelve students. My two stood in the front row. I noticed they were frequently given a smack on their legs for some wrong step or the other. Straight off, I knew they were hopeless. No rhythm. Perhaps they didn't understand the music or the 'Tham thi Tham, thegada thai thi thai.' *All I need to do is set them on the path*, was how I saw it. So, I got a book and pen, and while balancing on the overturned flower pot, I noted the different postures diagrammatically. I was myself doing a 'tham thi tham' of my own on the flower pot, so to speak. Once we got home, I found a small wooden stick, turned over a vessel, hit on it, and went, 'tham thi tham thegada thai….' The girls stood staring at me as if I had gone stark raving mad, and the Boy came running thinking it was the gong for supper. Seeing our practice, the big flat-footed oaf joined in, and it became something like a laughing Yoga session. He called out to me:

'Jeez Mother, don't be a stick in the mud. Join in and letsss partyyyyyyyyyyy.'

TENNIS

This was the death of Moi. I enrolled the Boy at the Trivandrum Tennis Club (TTC) in Kowdiar. He was at an age when he refused to move his body. There was no moving the mass from here to there unless it was to La Delicia, which was opposite the TTC and sold such delectable items like curry puffs and meat rolls. The Tennis coach would say 'warm up,' and all the kids would have to run around the court four times. Everyone would be gone a full minute before the Boy started. I'd be itching to kick his backside. There were days when I ran with him – well, sort of a brisk walk – just to motivate the immovable. I'd even promise a stop at his favourite pastry shop. But unfortunately, after each game, we'd have such a fight, and as a punishment, I would forgo the delectables at La Delicia. And guess who was the sadder?

At home, between the "Tham thi Tam" of the Bharatanatyam and the back hand, fore hand, and volley of the Tennis, I think I developed my calf muscles and biceps to an alarming degree. That was the only positive outcome.

CAR NATIC MUSIC

This phase was beyond ridiculous. No matter how involved I was, I never got to the grassroots of the behavioural pattern of the vocal cords. I got a private teacher to come in for lessons, so the girls could have a better understanding of the classical music. Perhaps it would in turn help them with the Bharatanatyam lessons. Both girls howled 'sa re ga ma pa' as best as they knew how, but somehow, the teacher was never pleased. After a few lessons, our Alsatians, Maxie and Roger, joined in. Actually, they howled more musically than the music students. The Boy warned me that he too was tempted to partake in the cacophony of sounds. At this point, I had to make a major decision. For the greater good of all concerned – our neighbours in particular – I decided to end the lessons. We tried for four or five months, and they were as good as the day they began, if not worse.

Some evenings during weekends, the children would all group together in the backyard, playing games or teasing each other. The dogs would be running around in circles barking and running after the children. Even the maid would finish the work in a hurry to join in the fun. But the most comical was watching the kids, all three of them, do a Bharatanatyam dance, singing 'nokada namudà margà kidakkunna markkada nee onu mari keeda shada,' in Carnatic Music style, with the dogs howling in the background. Then the maid would accompany them on an overturned steel cooking vessel, banging on it with a wooden ladle as loudly as possible. There are not enough words to describe the scenario, and at such times, I would join in the dance and complete the madness, much to the enjoyment and delight of the children. *Live the moment and create a memory.*

It was hilarious. What can you do but laugh till your guts spill over. And love the twerps.

Fancy dress at school

Tackling the Union

'You know, the only saving grace in all of this is that everyone is burdened with a mother. Well, as long as you are blessed with an umbilicus.'

Those were pearls of wisdom flowing effortlessly out of the Boy. I looked at him incredulously. He sat beside me in the little red Maruti I used to ferry the children to and from school. He had on the ridiculous sunglasses his father had discarded. He had pulled back the seat and lay casually cradled in it. His sisters alternated in carrying his water bottle. It was not a 'guy thing' to hang a water bottle around the neck. He had coaxed them into thinking he was doing them a favour, allowing them to carry it for him. In fact, he had the audacity to suggest they do it in turns so that it did not look like he favoured one over the other. In any case, they were in awe of him and especially so when he threw around a few heavy words like 'umbilicus', as he had just done. ASAP was another word he used, snapping his finger to get a dramatic effect. He never elaborated on the abbreviations. That would have removed the mystic charm of the word. The less they understood, the more they were enamoured. It was a trick of his. Even if a word was a misfit in a sentence, he used it audaciously, and his gullible sisters would remain blissfully ignorant. They were in total appreciation. I had no qualms about him. He was a survivor. I had to admire the devious rascal. At his age, I had been hiding behind my mother's pallav.

'Save it,' I said, throwing a sidelong glance at him. 'I'm in no mood for your one-liners.'

'Yeh, no one likes the truth. Least of all, Mothers. Someone said "God could not be everywhere and so He made Mothers." Think of that. Mothers everywhere. Up the wall, in the trees, down the well, even in your dreams. Jeez, where can a normal, decent kid hide?'

He pretended to shudder. He had just seen 'Rambo,' and the 'Yeh' was distinctively Stallone. He even twisted his lips to adapt. I ignored him. I was in no mood to get into a fight. Plenty of time during the rest of the day, for that. The two sisters sat in the back. On the edge of their seats, leaning forwards, hanging on to every word that passed their brother's lips. It was fodder for them. They would repeat this conversation, verbatim, to their friends at school. An aura was being created; and the Boy was the chief architect and beneficiary. I was negotiating the busy morning traffic to school. It needed all of my concentration and then some. Everyone was in a hurry – the school buses breaking every rule, other cars ferrying children to school, the motorcyclists weaving to the left and right, and the numerous stray dogs roaming the road. The Boy was twelve and standing on the brink of teenage. He had all the signs and symptoms of oncoming adolescence. Brash, arrogant, conniving, argumentative, and most of all, cocky. But he was a smooth operator and smart enough to cover up all of these qualities with his suave talk and ridiculous one-liners. You never knew when he was using you. His sisters, Elder and Younger, were ten and seven, respectively.

Elder was an outright rebel. She did everything that she was told not to do, just for the heck of it. To see how far she could go before I went mad. If I had wisely used the prudence of my years, I would have told her to do the things that I did not want her to do. Would you call that 'Reverse Parenting?' Nevertheless, what I liked about her was the fact that she was frank about her naughtiness. And if she was caught on the wrong foot, she made no excuses but fought right back. She thrived on harassing her little sister and devising ways to get the better of her brother. She was a little spitfire, and I had a hard job taming her.

Younger was our baby, and she was thoroughly confused most of the time as to whose side she was on. She wanted desperately to be superior like her brother but was enticed by the wanton behaviour of her sister. She spent her life shuttling between the Boy and Elder, and they used her as bait to get things from me. And as for me, I could never deny her anything. But there were times when Younger made up her mind on an issue, and then there was no moving the Sphinx. She was a Taurean and as bullish as they come.

'Change to third. Engine's knocking,' the Boy's curt order cut into my thoughts. Advice from 'His Sonship.' His relaxed body lay nonchalantly on the seat, his hands behind his head. I could not read his eyes behind those farcical sunglasses, but I could hear the unsaid words: 'Jeez Mother, get a move on.' Most of his dialogues were from old Westerns.

'Give me a break. And keep quiet, will ya?' I said with an effort. 'If you open your eyes and remove your blinkers, you might notice the traffic we are stuck in.'

'Hummmm,' he responded.

'Acha, what's the thing you said we had, if we had a mother?' Younger wanted to get it right.

The girls addressed him as 'Acha' or big brother. He acted like the word was an irritant but was secretly proud of the respect it demanded. It was noteworthy how he was a good Suriyani Christiani Achayan in the making. Makes you wonder at how deeply ingrained this cultural heritage is, that it should manifest in a young boy even without his trying or knowing of it.

'Umbilicus, um-bi-li-cus. When are you going to grow up? Learn a few words? Now, get the vocabulary right when you tell your friends. Can't have people thinking I co-habit with illiterates. I have a reputation to keep, you know,' he replied with a sigh. That really made me laugh.

'Will you stop with your superior attitude? Don't give the girls a complex. When they are twelve, they will know as much as you, or more,' I warned him.

'Yes Mummy, maybe more,' Elder put in. She was looking for a fight.

'I doubt that. Anyway, I was just trying to educate the crowd. But if I am unappreciated, I'll just abstain from further dialogue,' the Boy said indifferently and irritatingly.

He used those words to confuse the girls. I just laughed and shook my head. Actually, I paid the kids 50 paise to learn one new word each day. He took advantage of that, and made a tidy sum of money for himself. He would educate himself with up to twenty words a day and collect his money to visit St. Michael's at Pattom for chicken puffs. The girls were yet to appreciate the benefits of this scheme.

He looked at me and raised a quizzical eyebrow, 'I see I amuse you, Mother. That is a change for the better. Better better than bitter.'

'One more word,' I warned, 'another smart-ass comment from you, and you will walk to school.'

'Tut, tut, such words, Mother, and in front of the girls too. What will Fa think if he should know?' he asked, baiting me.

No doubt, it was a veiled blackmail too. I understood that. I was his mother, after all.

'Acha, what will dad say about what?' Elder asked.

'Too farfetched for you, kiddo. Besides, I do not fancy walking to school. Also, just that some people do not like to hear the truth. That's the sum of it.'

I veered the car to the side and hit the brakes.

'Ok, ok,' the Boy conceded, throwing up his hands. 'I am not dense, you know. I get the point. Do not make me walk. You might regret it later, like when I refrain from mentioning you in my thank you speech at the Nobel.' Under his breath, he added, 'Women are so finicky, and how lucky can I get? I have three. Thank you.'

'Did you say something?' I asked.

'No, Mother. Just stating a fact. I was talking to myself. Personal,' he replied.

'Mama, he said women are finicky. Whatever that means,' Elder obliged.

I pretended not to hear.

'I rest my case,' the Boy concluded.

Being a mother and single-handedly bringing up three strong-willed children was an uphill task. The Gulf War had torn apart a way of life that was so comfortable and easy. The Husband had returned to his job in Kuwait. I had opted to stay back with the minions and mould them into worthy human beings. I was aware my bullying days were slowly ending and I was losing control. The babies were growing up, and they were forming a union and cultivating opinions I never knew existed. I had to keep one step ahead if I had to remain in charge of the ship, or shall we say, the Maruti? Or else, there was bound to be a mutiny.

Once, I had a particularly tiring day pacifying Younger, arguing with Elder, and raking my brains for smart rejoinders to the Boy's never-ending observations and wisecracks. I was driving home after dropping them at school. It was early morning, and I was already exhausted. I stopped the car by a paddy field. It was green as far as the eye could see. The air was fresh and crisp. There was total silence. I breathed in deeply and exhaled. *I'll join a Yoga class*, I decided, *or else my hypertension is going to hit the roof.* As I stood leaning on the car, I realized how good it felt to have this small reprieve – to gather my thoughts and devise a strategy. The opposition was getting bolder. It would not be long before they took over. I closed my eyes and said a prayer.

'Dear God, I am at my wit's end here. Give me a plan. Help me. I want to do this Mothering job to the best of my ability. Amen.'

I waited a moment for an answer. God must have sensed my urgency. Or else, He realized I was in deep distress. Whatever the reason, the reply was instant. I opened my eyes and felt the weight lift off my shoulders. A bolt of enlightenment hit me, there was a reverberation in my head, and all was revealed. I was sure that that must have been how Gautama Buddha felt upon attaining Nirvana under the Peepal tree. The word was 'Prayer.' It came to Moi over and over again, ricochetting off the walls of my cranial cavity. That was the answer. Prayer. There was no doubt in my mind that God had just given me a nudge in the right direction. It was up to me to devise a plan using prayer to establish my position and get across my messages, rules, and regulations. No more whats and hows and whys and wheres. The plan had to be carried out through prayer. In spite of myself, I laughed out in glee and congratulated myself for seeking celestial help. What a genius of an idea! How brilliant was I? With The Almighty's help, of course, I quickly added. I did not want Him thinking I was taking all the credit. I was eager to execute the plan.

An opportunity presented itself that evening. Elder had a phone call. The thing with Elder's phone calls were that they lasted a minimum of forty-five minutes to an hour. All the movies were discussed, and the film stars. She drooled into the phone over her current favourite, his dress, and hairstyle. She gossiped on friends and foes. Teachers were thrashed to bits. And of course, endless complaints about parents were exchanged. A lot of stuff was whispered in hushed tones, followed by outbursts of helpless laughing and giggling. We had endless arguments on the length of each call, and I always ended up exhausted and defeated, while Elder rejuvenated with each bout. We would stand like prize fighters in a ring and shout at each other. Younger usually stood helplessly in the middle, trying to decide which side to choose, or stayed neutral till the combat ended. But the Boy had a different take. He would station himself at a safe distance and call out:

'Ladies and Gentlemen, introducing… to my right, weighing in at 63 kilos, the undisputed champion and the winner of all fights until now. An undeniable power to reckon with, "Mother, The Hun."'

I later came to understand the reference 'Hun' was to Attila the Hun and not short for honey as I had thought. And he'd continue:

'And to my left, weighing in at a mere 30 kilos, the charismatic challenger and underdog, who has stood the test of time and risen up after each defeat, like The Sphinx. We salute her persistence and tenacity. I give you, "Whatttacalamity." Ladies and Gentlemen, with this fight we aim to prove that "saaaaize does not matttttter!"' (from *Godzilla*)

That evening, instead of employing my usual tactics, I decided to put my plan into gear. It was a regular thing to have evening prayers. Only this time, I would inculcate all that I wanted to convey, some new rules I had in mind, and a word about telephone usage while we prayed. That night, I implored earnestly of the Heavenly Father:

'Dear God, we give thee thanks for this wonderful day and for all that you have helped us to achieve therein. Help us Lord, to be good children, to help others, and to obey our parents. Give us the strength to tell the truth, no matter at what cost. Teach us to live together in harmony, and with love and respect for each other. Bless our families, teachers and friends. Bless our country and our leaders, and make this world a safer place, where all can live in peace and contentment.'

That was our daily prayer, but then I improvised. Before they could conclude with an 'Amen,' I pressed ahead:

'Also, dear God, help us to control our words and actions. Guide us so we do not argue too much, especially with our elders. Make us understand that the advice of our elders is for our own benefit. Teach us to use all that you have given us with prudence and limitations. I pray that we should not be tempted to use the car unnecessarily, or that we watch too much of television, or use the phone for too long. Sometimes, we are weak and unable to do the right thing. We know that you have appointed mothers to take care of us. Give them the wisdom to guide the family in the right way. All these we ask in Jesus' name, Amen.'

I was aware that I was the only one who said 'Amen.' There was an uneasy silence after the prayer. The Boy smirked because he knew my game, and importantly, he was not the target. Elder stared at me, and she arched her body backwards. A bad sign – it showed she was on the defensive. Poor, sweet Younger hardly knew there was an ill wind blowing.

'Mama, was that about me?' Elder came straight to the point.

'Well, yes and no. It was about all of us,' I replied evasively.

'Ok then, is the phone part about me?' She looked glum.

'Hello dumbo, of course it's about you. Who else hangs on the phone all day?' the Boy stated.

'Well, do you use the phone for a long time?' I asked her after giving the Boy a dirty look.

'You know I do. You always scold me about it,' she pointed out.

'Ok, so try to do the right thing,' I said patiently.

I could see her struggle with herself. Since it was somehow related to prayer, she felt a moral obligation to obey. Better judgment prevailed, and she looked down at her hands, then said softly, 'Ok, Mama, I will try.'

'Good,' I said.

But somehow, I could not rid myself of the feeling that I should have tried this on someone my own size. I felt it was below the belt. She looked so small and defeated. That I was hiding behind God to achieve my goal seemed devious. Then a second opportunity presented itself the next day.

The entire family was engaged in a jigsaw puzzle containing over two thousand pieces. It was a laborious, time-consuming game that we had taken on. All the same, because we had begun the puzzle, it became a matter of prestige to complete it. There was no time limit. The puzzle lay undisturbed on the big table in the centre hall. Anyone was welcome to add a piece at any time. Thus, the puzzle grew, and almost three quarters of it was done. A picture was taking shape, and the anxiety to see its completion was palpable. All of us contributed. All of us, that is, except Younger. Out of the hundreds of pieces, she just could not find one to fit. Her frustration at being excluded from the game was growing out of proportion. I guess my intuition should have warned me of her helplessness and exclusion, and I should have somehow included her. But sadly, I missed the signs. Until one day, Elder shrieked out in horror. The middle piece was missing, making the whole picture useless and grotesque. Without that vital piece, the puzzle was at a standstill, and the picture had no meaning.

I looked at the Boy. 'Not I,' he said.

I looked at Elder. 'Not I,' she said.

I looked at Younger. 'Not I,' she said.

No one had touched it. No one had seen it. No one was responsible. Yet, the fact stared us in the face. Before I go any further, let me introduce you to 'Not I.' This elusive person lived in our home. The gender was unknown, but for convenience's sake, let us assume the person as male. He was everywhere and did everything. He lurked behind the bathroom doors, or else how did you explain wet towels left on the floor, soaps left in the water, and the shower left running? He spilled orange juice on the kitchen counter and did not bother to wipe it. He let the dog out on rainy days and let him back in, making the floor wet and muddy all over. He never finished his glass of milk and hid breakfast or lunch behind the piano to show an empty plate. He scribbled on the wall in the hallway and always left the kitchen tap running. Like I said, he was everywhere and did everything. So, I was not surprised when I received the 'Not I' answer on enquiring about the missing puzzle piece. I simply thought to myself, *Well, who else could it be?* Stupid of me to ask. That night, after our routine daily prayer, I added my scheme.

'And Heavenly Father, give us the infinite courage to speak the truth, face our mistakes, and own up to our wrongdoings at all times. Today, we have faced a difficult situation. The middle piece of our puzzle is lost. We worked so hard on it, and without that piece, all is lost. If anyone among us has anything to do with it, make us bold enough to admit it.'

I heard the Boy snigger and clear his throat, and I prudently concluded the prayer.

'All this we ask in Jesus' name.'

They chorused a subdued 'Amen.'

That night, as I lay in bed, I heard a small sniffle beside the door.

'Mama?' It was Younger.

'What is the matter, darling?' I asked, even as I smiled into the dark.

'Can I sleep next to you, just for a bit?' she asked in a small voice.

'Sure,' I said, as if nothing was the matter.

She crept up next to me and curled into the nook of my arm. She felt so small and adorable. So vulnerable. I felt the wetness on her face. She was crying.

'Love you, Mama,' she said.

'Love you too, honey. No doubts about that. Even if you do something wrong, I will love you just the same. Remember, you are my angel without wings,' I said, as I kissed her ear.

There was a moment of silence.

'Mama, do you think Charlie could have taken the puzzle piece?' she asked hesitantly.

Char lie was our Lhasa apso, just a year old and hardly the size of a big coconut. He was blamed for a lot of things, even leaving the jam bottle open.

'Maybe. But don't you think he is too small for that? He could not have climbed a chair to get to the table.'

She thought over the logic of that.

'Yes, he is small, but he can be naughty,' she said.

'Sure, he can be naughty, and so can you. It's not a bad thing to be naughty,' I said.

'Mama,' she said hesitantly, 'I have been naughty.'

'Hummmm,' I murmured.

'Are you angry?' she asked anxiously.

I noticed she was evasive. I wondered if I should push it. But I thought not. She had come half way. I had a success of sorts.

'You know what? Being naughty is part of being a child. It's not a sin.' She sighed in relief at that, kissed me, and went back to her room. The next day, I found the piece of the puzzle on the kitchen table. It was chewed up and disfigured. I was about to pick it up when the Boy walked in. He saw the piece and smiled.

'Poor unsuspecting things. I can see they have fallen for your new strategy. Attack through prayer. You're heartless, Mother. When will you stop this charade?' he sneered.

'I don't know what you are talking about,' I said, deadpan. His observation confirmed my own suspicion about Moi. Somehow, it left a bad taste.

'Yeh, right,' he said, Stallone-like.

That night, I had other issues I thought to present through evening prayer.

But the Boy beat me to it. 'Please Mother, can I say the prayers tonight?' he asked innocently. I had a bad feeling about that. But I conceded, as there was nothing I could do. I had always encouraged them to pray aloud. He said our regular prayers, then continued thus:

'Dear Father in Heaven, protect us innocent children from the manipulations of the adults among us. Help them to realize it is wrong to take advantage of the little children that you have placed in their care. Deliver us from those who have no guilt about making us work, like washing the car and going out in the dark each night to lock the gates. And Lord, have mercy……'

'Amen,' I said, sensing the Boy was getting carried away with his conversation with God.

The girls were unaware of the undercurrents and looked confused that I had cut short the prayers.

'That was not nice, Mother. I was just getting warmed up,' said the Boy, grinning (Al Pacino in *Scent of a Woman*).

'If you utter another word, believe me, you will live to regret it. I mean it,' I warned.

If he challenged Moi, I had no idea what I would do. I had no options left. We looked at each other, not blinking. Then he laughed, threw his arms around me, gave me a bear hug, and whispered in my ear:

'I won't tell on you because you are the best. And do you know why? Because you take the trouble to think of unique ways to correct us without embarrassing us when we do wrong. You do not give up on us. You take the trouble because you love us so much. That is not lost on me. And for that, we are grateful and so lucky. Thank you, Momma Bear.'

He did not say 'Mother,' as he usually did when he was being sarcastic or flippant. He seemed grateful and sincere. I could not punish him then, could I?

The Union

The Mediterranean Cruise

Very often, late into the night, while I cradled one of the sick children on my lap and nodded my way through the hours, somewhere in the back of my mind, I'd see the blue seas and skies of the Mediterranean and smile to myself.

'Not long now, Lennie,' I told myself. 'Can happen any time soon, ol' girl. Just have patience.'

'Mummai, why are you sitting in the dark,' a voice called out from behind the curtains. It was Elder. Something would have woken her up, and finding her sister missing, she would start a nocturnal search. Now, finding her sister in repose on my lap, she was ready to claim her share of the sanctuary.

Even before I could say, 'Come on and join us,' she had clambered her way up to my lap and snuggled in, deliberately nudging her sick sister to the edge. This would cause a loud, whining protest from the first occupant, which I would need to shush before the unthinkable happened and the Boy woke up. But who was I kidding? Children have inbuilt antennas that keep them informed of everything that goes on around them, even while sleeping. Under two minutes, the little chap would join the group, and seeing that the lap was overcrowded, he would settle in the skirt of my nightgown, which made the perfect hammock for him to spend the night. Both my arms would hurt with the heaviness of the girls, and I had to strain my calf muscles and shin to keep the boy and the hammock in place. I would brace myself and stay awake for the rest of the night, concluding that at least for the present, the reality of the blue seas of the Med were eons away.

And yet, if you dream often enough, the Gods might give in and grant you your wish.

It happened in 1996. Actually, by then, the whole Cruise had become a dead dream. The Gulf War in 1990 took away our way of life. We were displaced, our jobs gone, money was tight, and we were scrambling to get our lives and jobs back on track. There was no time for anything frivolous, much less a dream. We spent two years suspended in purgatory, not knowing which way to turn or steer our lives. The maintenance of three young children, coupled with our daily expenses for basic living, was taking its toll on us. Somehow, we stayed afloat. We were reaching the end of our tether when the Husband's company became functional again, and he was called back. That was a blessed stroke of luck. Unfortunately, my Kuwaiti sponsor had died in the war, and to find another and get the paper work done was a very laborious process. Moreover, the children had joined a prestigious school in Trivandrum, and I was not in favour of unrooting them and starting Arabic all over again. My throat still hurt when I thought of my meeting with the Arabic teacher. So, I stayed back while the Husband left for Kuwait, and the third phase of our life together started to take shape. A long-distance marriage which would last for about fourteen years. I can't vouch for him, but I daresay he took to it like a duck to water, this new phenomenon of being a 'married bachelor.' As for me, without a doubt, it was the best phase of my life. I had the safety of being a respected married woman but at the same time the liberty of living a life of total freedom, time for a discovery of self and self-worth, and a chance to develop any potential I had to the fullest. I opened up a dental practice at the junction near my home and did well for myself. Soon, our money woes were a thing of the past, and life was on an even keel once again.

One day, when the Husband called, I detected an unusual excitement in the tone of his voice. I knew that the incorrigible quirk would accompany such banter. When he was done with his usual teasing, he asked laconically, 'Do you still fancy going on the Cruise, we promised ourselves so long ago?'

I sighed and replied, 'Yeh, when hell freezes over, I guess.'

'Why talk of hell when we could be in heaven?' he countered.

I stayed silent for a minute, then whispered, 'What are you implying?'

'You did not answer my question,' he insisted.

'I'll do anything to go,' I answered, with my heart racing and my thoughts taking flight.

'I'll hold you to that promise,' he said laughing. 'And in the meantime, learn some Greek Cypriot phrases. Might come in handy.'

I don't know what magic wand he had waved, but by that weekend, we were busy applying for visas, making arrangements, and packing bags. Yes, we were taking the brood along with us, even if it might not exactly be the ideal getaway we had promised ourselves. But over the years, we had grown so used to 'the three,' as I loved calling them collectively, that not having them along would seem like we had left some body appendage behind. In order to score some points with the kids, I cunningly camouflaged our secret getaway trip into a gift to the Boy for his excellent performance in the twelfth grade. But he had to be the fly in our ointment and threw cold water on my suggestion. He had set his mind on Miami as a more worthy destination and so, even more cunningly, informed me that if that was the case, then he should be allowed to choose the destination. That sardonic, dry humour that was to be his trademark was taking shape, but as it was in the beginning stages, I was able to curb it and stick to the plan.

Our route was Trivandrum–Mumbai–Kuwait (where the Husband would join us) and on to Cyprus. *Mother of God*, I thought to myself, *just saying it is like having a Mackintosh's Quality Street chocolates flooding the mouth, melting on the tongue, and then drooling onto the lips.* Everything went as smooth as silk, and we landed at Larnaca International Airport on a bright sunny day. I was ready with my first Cypriot phrase, *Kaili Mera* (good morning). It was easy to remember. 'Kaili' was Malayalam for the common Kerala men's wear lungi, and 'Mera' was Hindi for 'mine'. I casually tried it out on the cab driver. He was floored and delighted. After that, we were bombarded with information, jokes that he enjoyed himself, and some serious talk that I guessed was politics. We suffered all the way to our accommodations, and I was properly chastised by the family for my smart talk.

Cypr us was breathtaking. We had rolled down the windows of the cab to drink in the view. The air was crisp and clean, the Mediterranean breeze just the way I thought it would be. Wild flowers grew everywhere, even in the cracks of old broken-down walls. Only the Boy was a bit grouchy.

But even he had to revise his opinion once we entered the town and he laid eyes on the girls. 'Oh well, ok. I guess Cyprus has its attractions,' he conceded cheekily. The people were spectacularly beautiful and friendly to boot. I guess the Greek-Turkish amalgamation worked wonders for them. It made me take a sly look at my unadulterated Syrian Christian self and wondered why Father had not been adventurous enough to take a leap into the great sweltering cauldron that made up the people of the world and got himself a Chinese or European partner. I could have been an exotic product. Then I looked at the Husband and wondered why I had not had the sense to do it myself.

We had rented out a fully furnished flat and planned a week's stay. We thought we'd cook our own breakfast and dinner and try out the local cuisine in the afternoons. That way, we could save a bit of money and use it to avail the bus trips to visit the local sites. On the first day, the Husband woke us up at 5 am. At that unearthly hour, we weren't even sure of where we were. 'Rise and shine! I did not spend a couple of lacs of rupees for the lot of you to come to Cyprus to sleep.' Spoken like a true Syrian Christian Malayalee male. Tired and jet-lagged from the travel, the children were most uncooperative. But that did not deter the father. Soon, we were all dressed and assembled in front of the apartment building. It was a serious cold breeze that now blew in from the Sea. We were all shivering, and we had no appropriate clothes. When Elder's lips turned blue, I turned red and looked at the Husband and had the satisfaction of seeing him turn pale. So, we marched back into the safety of our apartment and stayed there till the sun came out and the shops opened. First off, we got ourselves some warm clothes.

The roads were lined with orange trees that just seemed to sprout out of the ground from everywhere. The branches hung low, heavy with the bright orange fruits, and a thousand vendors sat in the shade, selling baskets of the fruit all along the way. We were so uneducated about oranges that we thought oranges were just oranges. And the Husband, being the captain of our team and a great orange fan, decided to buy a box of the fruits. Later, we found out there were the sweet variety (C. sinensis), the bitter variety (C. aurantium), and a dozen others. No points for guessing which one we'd bought. This box sat in the apartment with no one except the Husband making a brave attempt to eat because he was the one who'd bought them. In fact, after each exhausting day, as we made our way back to the apartment, dragging our feet, the children would plead with me, 'Mama let's not go back. Let's walk the night away. That's better than having to eat those bitter tasteless oranges just because we bought them.' Just then, the captain would try to motivate us, saying, 'C'mon gang, buck up. Once we are at the apartment, we'll have a couple of oranges and refresh ourselves.' Grrrrrr.

The next day, we booked a day trip to the city of Paphos on the southwest coast of the island and it was a breathtaking trip. I enjoyed it and decided to make the most of it, though the Husband and I were not on talking terms. He was miffed that I sided with the kids in the orange business. So much for the Mediterranean Cruise we had waited for with starry eyes. Anyway, it was a two-hour ride by private coach, with a stop at Limassol. What I loved most about these trips were the short stops we made at little villages where old ladies sat on rocking chairs at their doorstep, crocheting. They would call out to each other and chatter away while their fingers played around and created the most exquisite lace. Dress collars, chair backs, table clothes, and so many other beautiful things. I realised I had to make up with the Husband if I wanted to own some of these pieces. Damn!! Maybe even eat a few oranges. But that was a small price to pay.

Arriving at Paphos was like entering heaven. We had the view of the sparkling blue sea from every angle. Younger was unimpressed. 'It looks like the Sea at Shangkumugam beach,' she said, puzzled at my excitement. Elder was in her early teens, and though a bit shy, was showing a marked interest in the male population of Cyprus. *She is on track,* I smiled with satisfaction. I was equally enamoured and thought Cyprus was not a good place to come with your partner if you were planning a romantic getaway, albeit with three annoying kids. The distractions were no less than six feet tall, with sculpted bodies and dreamy eyes. A Zeus, every one of them. As for the father-son duo, for once, food came in second in their lives. We took umpteen photos, posing with the blue sea as the background.

One day, we were just resting in the apartment when the maid came in to clean. She was so knock-dead gorgeous that the Husband spluttered on his tea before jumping up. I asked him what the matter was. 'It's a crying shame,' he gasped, 'to make her work. I'll mop the floor. She's too delicate to be doing it.' *Jesus*, I thought, *the getaway we planned for all these years is not going the right way. I'm raked by my own distractions, and here is the Husband not even able to contain his own. A fine soup this is turning out to be.*

The fourth day, we had the Cruise proper, a day and night on a big, beautiful cruise ship with all the luxuries imaginable. But the cuisine was more European than anything else. By now, having been deprived of a good 'chor, kachi morru, thoran and koddam pulli meen curry lunch' (the traditional Syrian Christian meal of rice, curd curry, a vegetable mix, and the mandatory red, spicy, Malabar tamarind fish curry) for over a week, the Husband was like a lion with a sore paw. He was a slave to his daily quota of traditional spicy curry and rice, but for the greater good of the family, he had made this huge sacrifice. So, when he saw a bowl of rice on the dining table among the items to choose from, he went for it like a man would go for water when lost in the Sahara and heaped his plate. I was not so blind and had noticed that those who opted for rice took only a spoonful. After a while, I spotted the Husband sitting all alone in a corner with a glum look on his face. I went up to him and enquired, and he burst out with indignation, 'Freaking rice is sweet!!' I could not hold back the laughter. I had been wanting to strangle him for ever so long over his uncompromising stand over the fish curry and traditional lunch, that it was satisfying to see him suffer a bit without it. I, at least, was having fun on the cruise. Some scores were being settled. 'And,' he went on, his voice almost a wail, 'don't ask for water. The wine may be free, but we have to pay for the water.' That was the cherry on the pudding. At night, we had a live band playing popular feisty numbers, and the Boy and I danced the night away. The Husband sulked on a sofa somewhere until a bevy of beautiful girls dressed in very little except some flamboyant large feathers did a twirl on the dance floor. That woke him up. We had photos of the same, but sadly, the Boy took them to his school so often, and being an item that was passed around so often, they got lost.

We wound down the tour with an illicit day trip to Israel. Due to the political face-off between the Gulf countries and Israel, we had to surrender our passports and travel using special documents. It was so touching to walk along the 'way of the cross,' visit Gethsemane, see for ourselves where the crucifix was fixed, and touch the stone where Jesus lay. It brought out the latent Christian in Moi.

We returned a week after our adventure. It had not been the Cruise we had in mind. But then, we were older, we had changed, and our outlook on life had altered. Even so, we were happy that we were able to keep the promise we had made to ourselves.

On the cruise ship

Basking in the Cypriot sunshine

Soiree at Midnight

For Sibling, so close to my heart.

Sleep was the last thing visiting me that night. Strains from an old song drifted from the bedside player and filtered somewhere into the recesses of my mind. Elvis cooed, 'Are you lonesome tonight?' An appropriate song, melancholic and haunting. It only made matters worse. Somehow, it wanted to make me cry, and if that should happen, it was goodbye to sleep for that night. It had been unusually hectic that day, and at my age, that should have been enough to make me sleep like a log that night. But what are the rules sleep is governed by? It behaved erratically and was most unaccommodating. Therefore, when sleep decided to be obstinate and refused to oblige, there was nothing I could do but toss and turn. The ache in my legs, the general weariness from the day's chores, and the demands of the clinic did not help. I had discovered from earlier occasions that there was a certain degree of 'nice fatigue' that allowed you to sleep with abandon, as opposed to 'extreme fatigue,' which robbed you of sleep. When I heard the old clock strike twelve, I decided to put an end to waiting for the elusive mirage called sleep. I got up and silently went down to the dining room.

This situation had occurred many times before, and I was beginning to realize with dismay that it was becoming a constant. On previous nocturnal rambles through the sleeping house, I would finally end up at the long French windows that faced the lawns. I would gaze out from the windows into the black sky and remember what Mother had told me when I asked her about what happened to people who died. 'They become stars,' she had said, 'and the really good people become the brightest.' So, if the night sky was splattered with stars, I would count them and make believe the brightest was Mother or Father shining down on me. Communicating, telling me all was fine with them, and that they still watched over Moi. Or, if the moon was out, an eerie stillness prevailed, and she would throw silhouettes of strange designs on the wall. I would try to decipher what they conveyed or just watch her as she coyly peeped and shone through the coconut trees. A slight hint of a breeze would sway the leaves, and the shadows that fell on the wall would begin to dance. I would be so caught up, mesmerised and wondering if there were any rules to the way the shadows changed shape and form. The dancing rhythmic sway of the patterns fashioned by the moon would hypnotise me as a snake charmer would a captive snake. Slowly, these exercises and the solitude of the deep night would soothe me, and my eyes would begin to feel heavy-lidded again. Sleep would beckon, and ultimately, I would surrender willingly.

But that night, as I reached the dining room, I heard a muffled cough and a slight wheezing.

'Ini? That you?' I called out.

Sibling, my little sister. She had just turned fifty that November but was still my adored baby sister, a precious gift from God. I called her Ini, short for Annie.

'Ya it's me, Ini,' she called right back.

Her sound was frail, and it caught at my heart. I was older by nine years, and I took the job seriously. She called me Ini, short for Lennie. It was a funny thing with us. We called each other using this unique moniker. No one else used it except us, between us. It was our own private thing.

'Apa buat?' I inquired. (What are you doing?)

'Tak buleh tedor lah,' she replied. (Can't sleep)

And that was the second thing about us. We spoke the Malay language when we were together, or when we did not want anyone to know what we were saying. Without doubt, this annoyed our children and spouses no end and amused us infinitely. This was because Annie was born in Malaysia, and we had spent our childhood there. The language came naturally to us, and we found it convenient in many situations. But most of all, it took us back to our carefree days with Father and Mother and enabled us to revive our happy childhood. I was concerned that Annie was up so late. She had come to stay with me three years ago. Her health was poor, and she needed all the love and support I could offer as a big sister. But her spirits remained indisputably intact. Even in the face of adversity, brought on by the gradual progression of the illness, she never once complained or let us discern by word or deed that she was ill. She had tremendous courage and a verve that defied logic. She had been an adorable baby who grew up to be a remarkably beautiful woman. Although the disease had robbed her of her fine looks, the beauty from within shone through and gave her an ethereal grace. She sat at the dining table, hunched over and tired from a bout of coughing, her head covered with her favourite white Pashmina shawl. The moonlight lit up her face as she raised her head to look at me, and immediately, she smiled.

'Mari lah, dudok degan saya,' she said. (Come here. Sit with me.)

'Saya pun taboleh tidor lah,' I said. (I too cannot sleep.)

'Bagus. Boleh chakap sikkit,' she suggested. (Good. We can talk a little.)

'Okay. But let me make us some Horlicks. We can have a drink and a chat,' I suggested

'Bagus,' she agreed. (Great)

And so began our midnight rendezvous. A time for ourselves. We sat in our chairs, opposite each other, and visited every place on earth. We went to Hyderabad for the pearls and to Delhi for the Qutub Minar. We went to Mongolia because we were in awe of Genghis Khan, and we walked on the Great Wall of China. We landed in Paris, gazed at the Eiffel Tower, and sat by the Danube. Then, we crossed over to England to hear the Big Ben strike twelve and travel by underground. We skied on the Alps and drank Carlsberg and walked the 'way of the cross' in Old Jerusalem. We crossed the Red Sea and stood by the Wailing Wall. We wanted to visit the United States but felt the journey over the Atlantic would be too long and tiring. That decision was hilarious, but Annie insisted we had to consider her health. We made a long and nostalgic visit to Kangar, Perlis, in Malaysia, the place where Father had settled down when he first went to Malaysia and where Annie had been born. We walked every street and looked at the houses. The places we had known, the friends we had had. The old route to school and the spot where the wild geese had chased us. The field where Father had taught Annie to ride a bicycle. We rediscovered the littlest nuances of our childhood. We gossiped and tore our friends and relatives apart. We spared no one – uncles, aunts, cousins, in laws, and most of all, our husbands and children. We were sad when we recalled the death of our dearest aunty Chinnamma – Chin to us – and how much we missed her custard puddings.

We laughed over unrequited loves and love letters written but never posted. We shamelessly admitted to the number of half-truths we had told and wondered how petrified Mother would have been had she known of them, and her fear that we would be damned to the fires of hell for ever. I narrated how gauche and awkward I had felt over my first crush, Shoukat Ali. When I told her how I had thrown stones at a boy in our neighbourhood – fat, ugly Idris, Annie laughed so hard that she choked over the attack of coughing that followed. We bitched maliciously about our co-workers and ripped apart the fellow who had overcharged us at the car garage. We went over the heartbreak of separation – when I left Annie to go to boarding school – and about the extreme anticipation of reunions. We cried when we sat in silence remembering our beloved parents, who had departed before their time. We were overcome with surreal warmth as we recalled the love and affection they had showered on us, enabling us to become strong, independent women. We recalled proudly how they were instrumental in giving us this strong bond of sisterhood and respect for each other. We wondered if we had ever told them how important they were to us and how much we loved them.

We were positive my neighbour was wearing a toupee and making an extra effort to look young. Annie was sure he was having an extramarital affair, or else why would he wear a wig in the sweltering humidity of the tropical heat? We scrutinized his every movement in the guise of arriving at the truth. His morals were of no interest to us, nor were they the outcome of our analysis. It was the methodical and meticulous conduct of our investigation in which we prided ourselves. Sherlock Holmes was our Guru. I told her of my lonely childhood and how I had longed for a sister. How I had prayed to God in the irrefutable belief that He answered all prayers. I told her sheepishly how I had wanted a flaxen haired, blue-eyed sister. I had been ignorant of Mendel's law and genetics at that time. And I told her how appalled I had been when she arrived, bald and red-faced. Nevertheless, I was her slave forever. She laughed at that and called me a liar. But I could tell she was blushing with pleasure.

We obsessed over John Abraham and ogled shamelessly whenever he appeared on television. We discussed his hair and his height. We agreed on everything concerning him and was proud of the fact that he was a Malayalee even if an apparently spurious one, for his English did not seem to conform with the Kerala English. He was also only a half-Malayalee, but we overlooked that fact. We argued endlessly over Robert de Niro and Sean Connery because I said they were the best things in the West. Annie had a thing for Al Pacino and Hugh Grant. We discussed *God of Small Things* and *War and Peace*. We knew for sure that we could write better than Arundathi Roy. Only, we did not have the time. Leo Tolstoy left us speechless. Selman Rushdie, we concluded was de trop. John Gresham, any old day. Annie told me how, when she first became aware of my existence, she had thought I was so clever and smart and so much bigger than her. She had wondered how I knew everything. She told me how she would wait for me to return from school so she could have the remains of my school snack and the little bit of orange juice left in my drinking bottle. She thought they tasted better than anything Mother made.

In sombre moments, we talked of life and living. Reminisced with a twinge of cynicism and humour of Mother's matchmaking, and how we had met our husbands. How gullible and naive we had been. How trusting and simple. Perfect idiots. And we laughed the whole night when we concluded that Mother had been a manipulating witch who always had her way with us. We giggled at how exasperated Mother was every time we brought up the topic of sex and about how she had become delirious with rage when I cut off my long black hair to look something like Marilyn Monroe. Sometimes, during the monsoon rains, when the air filled with the smell of fresh earth and the sounds of crickets and crocking toads, we fell silent and sat in the stillness of the night. We let the solitude envelop us and basked in each other's company. Such times were more gratifying than others because a lot more communication transpired in silence.

We discussed mundane, everyday things like the cost of fish and recipes. Hairstyles and nail polish. We tore apart the boys our daughters were interested in and expressed relief that my son was a regular guy. He had a healthy roving eye and an ardent admiration for the opposite sex. Like his father, we decided, though he was less blatant about it. And in the dark, hesitantly, we brought out our own sexual fantasies, kept under tight wrap until then, as warranted by decent Malayalee women. We were hilariously aghast at what we discovered about each other and ourselves! However, once we got over our inhibitions, we let our imaginations run riot, and it was one of our best evenings ever. An evening of self-sexual discovery, and Annie said between bouts of coughing, 'Listen Ini, I think I heard Mother turn in her grave.'

Whenever Annie was not doing particularly well, we spoke of God and prayed. I felt bitter and angry with God for making her suffer. But she would smile and philosophise that she was given three years to live after being diagnosed with her malady. She had lived twenty years more, raising a beautiful child and sharing her life with a wonderful husband. 'That is the miracle for those who believe,' she told me.

Most of the plans for Elder's wedding were formulated during our midnight soirees. Whether we should have a gown or a traditional sari. How many guests, whom to invite, and the type of menu. If we should have roses or carnations and if we should reveal to the father of the bride, the full cost of the necklace we had in mind. We bellowed uproariously when Annie suggested wickedly that if we did that, the daughter's wedding would be followed by the parents' divorce.

One night, as we sat and sipped our Horlicks, talking about nothing in particular, much to our delight, two fireflies glowed in the dark outside. We watched them intently, and then Annie said, with an unnatural excitement in her voice:

'Saya ingat ku tatahu apa itu?' (I guess you do not know what that is.)

'Da, saya, tak tahu,' I replied. (No, I don't.)

'Dia dua di sini lah,' she whispered. (They are both here.)

'Who?' I asked, looking around, 'Who?'

'Mother and Father,' she replied.

Then she told me that once she had asked Mother what happened to people who died, and Mother had told her they became fireflies. I looked at her incredulously, then told her that when I had asked Mother the same question, she had told me they became stars. We concluded that Mother must have forgotten what she had told me and had spun another yarn for Annie. Mother would have never thought we would compare notes. A lesson for us!

We enjoyed these midnight rendezvous for a long time, until Annie began to feel the strain. Some nights, she just lay on the bed, too tired to come to the dining room and talk. I sat by her side, and we listened to Neil Diamond or Simon and Garfunkel. I held her hand as I did so long ago when she was so little. It was an effort for her to cross her fifty-first birthday, but she did it gallantly, with panache. She had so often told me that when the time came, she would have no regrets. She had been a dutiful daughter, a hell of a sister, a loving wife, and a devoted mother. Just a month later, she passed away, leaving a vacuum so enormous, it can never be filled. She had lived and left like a lady.

Some nights now, when sleep evades, I stand by the French windows and look out at the night sky. If the stars are out, I scan for the brightest, but if the sky is dark and the night black, then I search for the glow of the fireflies.

Either way, I know Annie would want to keep our midnight soiree.

Treasured moments – Sibling and moi

Love Comes Knocking

I had been married for thirty years, nine months, twenty days, and four minutes precisely when, out of the blue, I fell in love. Now if that is not precise enough for you, I can go even further and give you the exact time that this all-consuming sentiment came over Moi. I will do just that to make it as authentic as possible, this falling in love. It is funny how I even remember what I was doing and what I was wearing when this momentous event occurred. It was just past 11 p.m. I had looked at the clock before closing the book I was reading, Ludlum at his best in *The Icarus Agenda*. I needed to go to the bathroom, and I was there for another ten minutes when the doorbell rang. In a way, it was the love knell, but I was not to know that then. I was dressed in my funny night-suit, all mismatched and worn out; faded and tired-looking. That described both my attire and Moi. It was a good thing that I was oblivious to the enormity of the events that would take place within the next one hour, or I would have been appalled by my uncharacteristic behaviour. Here I was, in my early fifties, three children accounted for, and none of them would approve of their mother falling in love at this late stage in life. They hardly thought of me as a woman, let alone a woman in love. They would have shuddered at the thought of me having any emotional needs, and love, as between a man and a woman, would be last on their mind as something needed by any mother. That was something you did in High School, they would argue in one voice, and I would be the first to agree. You see, they were at an age when they had started questioning the realities of love and the like, same as I had been doing for most of my life now. In short, they were grown up and mature and were cynical to the softer emotions. I had settled down to the mundane routine of being a wife and mother without so much as thinking about it. It seems ridiculous now, but in the old days, what else was a person to do at middle age?

Mine had been an arranged marriage, and when I met the 'suitable boy,' I honestly felt nothing. My mother confirmed that he was from good family stock, and by that, I knew she had checked out if there was even the slightest hint of madness in the family. They were church-goers, she had informed me proudly, and owned about two acres of land. A boy from such a reputable family was a prize find and could easily and effortlessly be put at the top of the list of very suitable candidates. Added attractions were that his house had plumbing and sanitation. A refrigerator and television set increased his worth in the marriage market. My uncle had been quick to point out that there was a huge haystack to the side of the boy's home, which meant there were cows in the shed. That was to be read as sufficient manure for the crops. To refuse the proposal would be blasphemous, they had chorused. Unfortunately, I was not familiar with this line of reasoning, and the different nuances of veiled messages were lost on me. I was yet to learn to read between the lines. That he was healthy was there for all to see. Educated, with a sense of humour. Good looking, but in a rugged, macho sort of way. He was okay if you liked the big, burly, boisterous sort of lads. I personally liked the lanky, artistic sort, but who was asking me? What could I offer as excuse should I dare to rebuff the proposal? I waited for some sign to show I felt something for this epitome of manhood – his haystack, sanitation, et al. So right in every which way. I waited for some tingling, some goosebumps, something, anything to show me this was Mr. Right. But sadly, there was nothing.

Life with the suitable boy later turned out to be life with a suitable husband and then a suitable father to the kids. I was content in a 'Well, I could have been worse off' sort of way. However hard I tried, I could not fathom a 'willing to die for each other' type of passion, the type that Romeo and Juliet shared. Not that I envied their sort of love, because at that point of time, I considered myself too young to die, even for love. The fact of the matter was that at the time of the marriage, I did not know if such a love existed outside of a storybook, and worse still, I never thought there was a way out of my predicament. Ours was a pragmatic sort of relationship from the onset. Strait-laced, austere. We had the children, our share to the continuation of the species, and set about the task of living and contributing our share to society. Still, we had our moments. A flicker of a romance in the making, like when the Husband would suddenly take hold of my hand when we had to make our way across a particularly busy road. And just as I would wonder if the sparks were indeed being ignited, he would drop the hand in question like it was some unwanted appendage and hurry off. He cared, that was for sure, but I craved to taste what hot, burning passion felt like. The type that set you on fire when eye contact was made from across the room. Or did I read that in a book? Whatever said, this obsession only increased with age. Now, don't get me wrong – I did not want out of the marriage. I harboured no such thought. In fact, it would be blasphemy to even think it.

Whenever I was not so consumed with self-pity and felt a little magnanimous, I allowed myself to wonder if the Husband could also be in the same quandary as I. That would have been the greatest joke of our lives together. And our best kept secret. I wondered if he had been persuaded to make a match with me because of certain suitable attributes that I was alleged to have had. Come to think of it, when the proposal was made, my family home did have attached bathrooms for two of our bedrooms, something to genuinely boast about at a time when sanitation per se was shockingly rare! And Mother spoke English. It was no mean feat to have an 'English-speaking mother-in-law,' and if you were really looking for landmark achievements, then she even wrote the language. The very fact that he may be called upon to parley in English would have put off any self-respecting bridegroom, for English was not the common medium of conversation. This frighteningly high benchmark of excellence in itself was a daunting prospect for any groom. And to think he had dared to consider such a prospect put him in a league of his own. But again, he too might not have had the guts to rebuff such a good proposal – even if nothing else, then from the sanitary point of view. I'm sure he would have been tutored on the conveniences of having indoor sanitation, especially during the monsoons. The irony of the whole exercise teaches you to look at unsuspecting areas with respect. Take the role sanitation played in my life. It could perhaps have been instrumental in the way my life took shape. Yet, you cannot blame me for wanting to believe that when the Husband agreed to the proposal, he did so because he found my smile bewitching and because my big black eyes mesmerized him completely out of his senses.

As the sound of the doorbell died down, I left the bathroom and walked across the hall to the door, glancing at the clock again. It was, as I guessed,

11.25 pm. An unearthly hour to fall in love and start on a voyage of adultery, even by the standards set by any liberated Hollywood starlet. It would also be well to inform you that I did not watch the clock because I knew in my bones that something significant was about to happen that night or that I was on the verge of falling in love. It was just a force of habit. The bell rang again, and to my ears, it sounded jarring. Definitely irritating, even angry. It put me on edge and made me impatient. I turned the lock and pulled the door open.

It was the Husband, leaning insolently against the doorpost. His hand was half raised, and I instantly knew he had been in the act of sounding the doorbell yet again. He did that to raise my hackles, and I always fell for it. *Does he have to make a din at midnight, enough to wake the neighbourhood?* And the smug smile on his face told me that he had had one drink too many. This was going to be one long night. He had been to a party hosted by one of the contractors who worked at his site. They went out of their way to please him and so always invited him to the most elaborate parties that served exquisite carte du jour, and the wine and drinks flowed freely. The Husband was not the type to insult his host by his lack of appreciation for the extensive meal served and so would have done justice to both food and drink. And now, I would have to listen to all the stories and the jokes that were so horribly stale and so often repeated after a thousand such feasts. I knew how the next hour would go. So predictably routine, so regular. He would tell me all about the delectably scrumptious items on the menu to the minutest detail and about the different mind-blowing invigorating drinks he had consumed. He delighted in giving me the most agonizing detail of each and every fish, meat, and vegetable served. Their species, genus, and order were categorized so methodically that it would put a marine student to shame. My nocturnal education on such occasions could last for long hours or till I decided I could take no more and went to bed. These were the times when I wondered why I did not get to marry a regular guy who just vomited and blacked out.

I turned around and made my way to the kitchen to put the kettle to boil. It was a forgone conclusion that black coffee would soon be needed. The Husband closed the door and followed me like a tame puppy, all part of the scheme of things after a night out with the boys. As I said, ever so predictable. I glanced at the clock. It was 11.50. While I filled the kettle,

I noticed him out of the corner of my eye. He maintained the smug look and kept standing. Once I had put the kettle on the stove, I turned around and faced him. Strangely, tonight, there were no signs of an educational lecture, just that self-satisfied smile and a hint of something clandestine. I studied him dispassionately, this Husband of mine. The years had been kind to him. At sixty, he could easily pass for forty-five. He revelled in this observation made by all his friends without exception. He even acted the part of the young guy on the prowl, and amazingly, carried it off. My train of thought was suddenly broken when I noticed a stain on his shirt, sort of a yellowish orangish colour. It was a light blue Allen Solly that had cost me a pretty penny when I got it for his birthday. That did it. The fact that he had returned so late in the night, drunk, and I was making coffee at an unearthly hour while he stood with a smug smile, unmindful of the fact that he had ruined an expensive shirt, just got my goat. I gave him the best piece of my mind ever. I got it all out and let it hang there. I told him he snored so loud that I found it hard to sleep, and that he left the bathroom wet after use. Sometimes, the kids were rash and rude and impetuous, and they got it all from him. He never helped with housework, or if he did, it only created more work for Moi. And whenever we went shopping, it never escaped me that he was on silent protest mode. He was never punctual when picking me up from where ever, but he was always early when it was the children. I always planned the schedule and packed the bags whenever we travelled, and it was always my fault even if the 747 was late to land! If I was sick, it was just a cold and would blow over, nothing to fuss about. But if he so much as coughed, it was treated like the Ebola, and all of us were put on red alert, and we had gruel for the rest of the week. It did not matter that I was watching my favourite program on TV – news came first. After a fight, he was always the victim and I the perpetrator. He always told an incident in such a way that the kids adored him and blamed me. He was the Saint and I the Satan. And today was the mother of all days – he had come home drunk and had stained his best shirt with curry. And all this because I had indoor sanitation at the time of the proposal. He had never loved me, just got married to me because of the plumbing. I don't know if I was justified in my allegations, but all through these accusations, he stood silent, insolently, with the smug smile in place.

When I stopped for a breather, he moved. But he still kept his gaze on me and the smug smile in place. I was beginning to worry about him. He opened his shirt, and from inside, he took out what looked like a piece of stained, used tissue. A whiff of garlic and ginger caught my nose. He held it out to me like some peace offering. I was too stumped to react. He took my hand, turned it over, and placed the tissue in my palm. Tentatively, I opened it and curiously peered inside. The thigh of a lobster leg lay within the folds of the tissue. I looked up at him, and he saw the question in my eyes. Sheepishly, he smiled and informed me that he knew lobster was my favourite and he just did not have the heart to eat it without giving me a bit. There was no doubt that the drinks had hampered his inhibitions, or else how could one account for a sane, grownup, cultured individual attending a company dinner party acting so bizarre? But somewhere in my mind, a coin dropped. At a loss for words, unable to respond and overcome by some strange emotion, I glanced at the clock for the heck of it. What else was a person to do? It was four minutes past midnight. Again, I looked at the lobster piece in my hand, then at the man in front of me. He too was studying me keenly. Dishevelled hair, lobster-stained shirt, drunk to the hilt, stupid smug look, disoriented, incoherent, but there was something in those eyes that defied logic. I realized it was no 'big bang,' this falling in love. It grew on you; maybe it took all of thirty years, nine months, twenty days, and four minutes. But it was well worth the wait. I felt the explosion, that spark that I had been waiting for all those years of my life. And yes, the goosebumps came with a vengeance. It did not take a knight in shining armour to finally bring on the rush of adrenaline. Just a piece of lobster and the shabbiest guy possible with the most adorable hangdog expression ever, in the dead of the night, and the air thick with the smell of ginger and garlic.

You never know when love will walk into your life – what age, what hour, or what shape, but when it does, it is all that they say it is and worth dying for.

A lovable guy in spite of his faults

The Family Portrait

Whoever thought that taking a family portrait could incite thoughts of divorce proceedings? A harmless enough arrangement, you'd think, taking a family photo. An attempt at preserving memories. The family brought together in a frame and to remain thus forever. The pride. A sense of achievement – for the parents, of course. To have brought up, or dragged up, the mewling, puking (Shakespeare's words, not mine) infants to this stage. The Boy had done well all along, academically, and was now on the verge of taking flight to follow his dreams to further his studies. He was ready to leave the coop. What better time than now to take a family portrait? Who knew when we would all be gathered together again?

'I'll wear a black tee,' the Boy announced, as soon as the event was fixed.

He was in the 'all black' stage of his life. Black tee, black jeans, black shoes, black shades, black music, and black mood. The girls were not far behind, since aping their brother was their fad.

'No blacks,' I said, firmly. 'No blacks at all. Hello? No one has died here. This is a nice family portrait,' I said with finality.

Then I quickly left the room, as I didn't want to push it.

'Well, a nice family portrait of some reeeeally not nice people,' was the rejoinder.

I heard that, even if it was muttered. I did. But like I said, I did not want to push it. I needed to keep the air light. Not have sulky faces frozen in time and hanging on the wall.

'Mum,' Elder was next.

I knew we were about to get into an elaborate discussion over dress, makeup, hair, shoe, head wear, and whatever else. There was no time for this, as the photographer was due in half an hour and we paid by the minute.

'So, what's the theme here?' she asked. 'Western or Indian or go-with-what-you-want?'

Oi! I mean, where was this coming from? When I was a kid, father would say that we were getting a family picture taken (not portrait, note), and I would wear my Sunday best. That was the only dress I had, and I can still tell you in detail about it. Small red flowers, roses actually, embroidered on a pale blue dress. Satin. Then we would trot off to the studio, take the picture, and trot right back. End of story.

'Make the theme Indian,' I said, just to get her moving.

Younger asked, 'Should I get the pets ready? It is only right to include them. It is a family affair, and they are family.'

I held on to my sanity as I said, 'We will think about that in a bit. But you better get organised and make the theme Indian to go along with your sister.'

'No mum, I'm not talking to her,' she said, darting her eyes at the sister, 'and so I don't want to be in the same theme.'

'Like I care,' retorted Elder. 'So, you go ahead and dress like you came from the planet of the apes. That will suit you.'

'Mother, I don't even want to be in the same portrait as her,' wailed Younger, plopping on the bed.

'It's okay, my dear,' I said to Moi. 'You will be fine. You got through the Gulf War and all that came with it. You are a winner, a champ. Strive on, weave your way through the trials and tribulations of life. Think of the mothers in the war-torn regions of the world. They struggle to get through famine and upheavals. Many have died in the process. They were all persecuted, some even more than you, at all levels.'

Well, maybe the comparison was not fair, as my lot was so much more comfortable, but I needed the boost. By the time I reached the room I shared with the Husband, I was feeling invigorated by the small pep talk I had given myself. He stood in front of the mirror in all his God-given glory.

'Already dressed for the event, are we?' I could not help baiting him.

Ignoring my sarcasm, he asked, while flexing his muscles, 'Well, what do you think?'

'About what?' I asked, feigning ignorance.

'You know,' he said, sizing himself up this way and that and reminding me of a peacock getting ready to mate.

'No, I don't know,' I said, a touch of irritation in my voice. *It's so much easier to face the drought and the desert sands of Sudan*, I thought, *even if it is an unreasonable and unkind comparison.*

'What's the matter with you?' he quizzed, since he was not getting the response, he wanted. And just to bugger me, he added, 'You are looking haggish today. Not so perky, somehow. Shame about the portrait thing. Bad day to schedule it, huh?'

'Can't say you're looking sharp yourself,' I said, while at the back of my head, I kept thinking, 'Easy, easy now.' And yet, throwing caution to the winds, I added, 'Bit of grey in the hair too.' There! I had knocked on his Achilles heel.

'What? You think so?' he croaked. 'I just dyed it the other day.'

And to add insult to injury, I went on, 'Say, I just noticed. Looks like the muscles could do with a bit of toning. Seems age is creeping up on you.' The horror on his face was reward enough. Feeling guilty, I relented and said, 'Hey, I was joking. You're okay.'

But he went on standing there, looking stumped. He made no move to get dressed. By now, I was tired too and began to think that the idea of the portrait was not so brilliant. Finally, when he spoke, he said:

'You know, Hitler was cruel beyond measure. He is the cruellest person I can think of just now. But you have surpassed him. What you just said has cut me to the core. I could go to court with this, and any judge in his senses would grant me a divorce without missing a beat.'

However, we got the portrait done, and I have managed to stay married. I am deeply grateful for life's small mercies. I am thankful that though I might have lost many battles, I have won the war.

The portrait that almost broke up the family

3 Weddings

So, with this three-part series, in which I take you all through the trials and tribulations I faced getting each one of the offsprings married, I've come to the end of a segment of my life.

THE FIRST WEDDING

The slow decline in my physical and mental health, which led me to think I was in dire need of another Mediterranean Cruise, began the day that Elder breezed in through the kitchen door and announced:

'Mummkins, I'm in love, and no matter what you say, I will marry him.'

What is it they say? There is no punishment greater than to give them what they want. Que sera, sera.

'As long as you are sure, I have no qualms,' I replied, 'It's not my life.' Sometimes, we mothers know when not to argue.

'That's decided then. Now I want you to know I will wear a wedding gown. Nothing traditional,' she stated.

She was 5 ft nothing, but it was easier to change the position of the Statue of Liberty than get her to change her mind.

'But the family won't agree. Valichayan (or eldest family member) will be horrified,' I wailed.

'Yeh, I know. That narrow-minded, shoddy ol' toad of a Valichayan will disagree, but that's his job. Work around him, Mummy. Honestly, his monotonous advices kill me a little every time we visit him. It's time someone gave him a jolt in his head,' she said.

'But does that have to be you?' I pleaded.

'Who better,' she laughed.

That got my knickers in a twist. You see, we were an Orthodox sect. A very traditional community. We did not take kindly to change. We did things a certain way or not at all. So how was I going to get the Valichayan to agree to a gown? We certainly needed his blessings. But she might as soon get married in her birthday suit than in a gown. A gown was foreign. Heck, I was sure Valichayan would think if the girl dressed in a gown, she was out to entice not only him but the entire group of older gentlemen in the community, including the priest. And that was profanity of unthinkable proportions. Seriously, we could even be excommunicated. Moreover, I could already hear the malicious gossip that would ensue from the older Chedathies and Kochamma, those stanch, unbending, judgemental matriarchs of the community. But Elder was adamant. I might as well have tried to drain out all the waters from the Indian Ocean. That would have been easier than making her see sense.

So, one cold monsoon day, with the rains pelting down my face, since the winds blew the umbrella in all directions but the right one, I walked up to Valichayan's door. As I trudged along in the rain, I thought back to the time many years ago, how on a wet monsoon day, Mother had walked up to the clinic at the NSS Medical Mission in Pandalam, drenched to the bone to persuade me about my own marriage. In a way, justice was being served. Valichayan met me looking his same old grouchy self. I told him I was there to discuss an important matter regarding Elder's wedding. It concerned her church attire, about a gown she wanted to marry in rather than the traditional sari. He was so still and silent, his face immobile and inscrutable in a frozen frown that I began to think he had died from the shock of my announcement. He just sat there like the mummies of Egypt.

'Valicha,' I implored with atonement in my voice, but he shushed me.

Thank God he's alive, was my first thought. I withdrew, like a turtle would into its shell, and waited in silence. I watched his face, and for want of something to do, I counted the worry-lines on his forehead. There were five. Impressive. What did he worry about? He had God on his side. His nose was bulbous and a dozen hairs stuck out from the left nostril. That was asymmetrical. What had happened to the hairs in the right nostril? *Didn't men have some sort of new pen-like instrument to remove nasal hair,* I wondered. They advertised it on TV. I guessed these old bats did not watch much TV. We sat for a long time like we were mourning the death of King Tutankhamun. Suddenly, for no reason at all, Kylie Minogue got into my head and started singing, the words reverberating through my cranial passages – 'Can't get you out of my head…'

After what seemed like an eternity, he sighed, shook his head, and said, 'The world has gone to the dogs.'

I listened impassively but was nonplussed. I did not know in what context he was saying this. Was it the gown, was it the girl, was it the wedding, was it me, or was it the Monsoon? The possibilities were huge and varied.

Another deep heavy sigh, then, 'A gown?' he growled. 'This is colossal. Unheard of. What about propriety? This will set a precedence. Things will get out of hand. I must refuse.'

'Valicha,' I said in my humble, below-the-sole of my slipper voice. 'That is just what I told the daughter. I told her that we should stick to our rich tradition. But she said I was the obstacle and dogmatic. She insisted that you would understand and agree since you had such foresight and a clear vision for the younger generation.'

I was aghast and proud at how cunning I was. I had not known I had this trait in Moi. This ability to manipulate or lie so smoothly. But as they say, 'All's fair in love and war,' eh? Once again, he entered into his 'Sphinx-like' state. The rain fell heavily outside, and the wind was picking up. The Monsoon was at its peak. I wondered how many more times I would have to make the journey between Muhammad and Mountain with my wayward umbrella before we reached a resolution on this matter and I could rest. Who knew? I might rest in peace for the rest of my life with this one marriage.

Finally, the Oracle spoke, more to himself than me. 'Did she really say that? That I had foresight and a clear vision for the younger generation?'

'O! Yes, Valicha. In fact, she has always told me how motivated she was every time after we visited you. "A man of vision," she would call you. Those were her words. Both you and Kochamma inspire us a lot.'

I thought of how Elder called him a stupid old stick-in-the-mud, but I was more in awe of how I was getting to be splendid at this flattery thing. I was trying my hardest to keep the laughter welling up in my throat from escaping. I wondered if I should add that Elder had often admired his handsome looks and how lucky Kochamma was to have him for a husband. That Elder hoped her own husband would be half the man Valicha was. But I decided against it. There were only so many lies you could tell without provoking The Almighty. And refrain from laughing.

'Well, erm, in that case, I think it will be OK. I hope I will be able to explain all this to the other family elders and persuade them to see this as the correct progressive way. Your daughter is right, you know. We have to take a more open view in these matters, especially if we want to keep the young crowd with us.'

I opened my mouth as if shocked out of my wits and then slowly covered it with my right hand. My eyes were wide with the right amount of surprise.

'You really think so, Valicha? Should we not stick to tradition? We need to keep our values. But I doubt any other family member will oppose you once you take a decision. Everyone knows you have a wise head on your shoulders,' I whispered. Charlize Theron had nothing on me. I deserved an Oscar.

'Come now, my dear,' he said magnanimously, with a short, embarrassed laugh, though he accepted all the adulations I offered like a King. 'You should also learn to be progressive, get in with the times. Be more receptive. Accept change. The gown will be fine. But a word of warning. It should be modest, giving importance to decorum and modesty. Nothing offensive, you understand.'

I rushed home and gave the good news to Elder, glad I was still alive and the problem solved. She looked at me and smiled as she announced:

'That's good then, Mother. Though how you got the stupid old ape to agree, I will never understand. Have you ever felt he looked like a gorilla? Anyway, here's the design I have in mind.'

I stared down at the model wearing a strapless wedding gown and ample amount of cleavage on display. I think I blacked out and suffered a cardiac arrest.

The Second Wedding

Three years after riding the tide over the incident with the Elder and her gown, I turned my attention to the Boy. He was getting long in the tooth and was no longer a little boy. But you know mothers – we believe our kids never grow up. However, when the Boy began to inch past his thirtieth birthday and yet showed no interest in the opposite sex, or even the same sex, there was reason for grave concern. It is the right of any parent to be concerned, and so, I began to address the issue as any mother worth her salt would, before the community and the church considered it their duty to get to the bottom of the problem.

I shifted into first gear when he came home for a short spell. I caught him on the phone in the backyard and eased myself into the range of his conversation, hoping to overhear some romantic 'goings-on.' All I got were some 'grunts' and 'guffaws,' and 'hums' and 'ah-has,' followed by a 'seriously' and a 'not bad.' What kind of chit-chat was that? We sent him to the best Schools and Universities and you will forgive us for thinking that he would have picked up a little more vocabulary along the way. Learn to form a complete sentence.

'So, who was on the phone?' I ask, nonchalantly.

'Say what, momma?' he asks innocently.

'Just asking who it was on the phone,' I ask, like I'm not interested.

'Aww. You know these freaking calls,' he says dismissively.

Moi (sly): 'Anyone in particular?'

He (slyer?!): 'Oh no! No one in particular.'

Moi (shamelessly): 'Got to be someone.'

He (flippantly): 'Oi, fishing, momma?'

Moi (determinedly): 'Maybe.'

He (cunningly): 'Well, it's a girl.'

Moi (hopefully): 'So, give.'

'Your daughter, momma, my sister,' he roared.

I didn't speak to him for the rest of the day and for two more days, for effect. He begged and cajoled and apologized and tailed me about the house. There's something to be said about a big-muscled fellow following you around, begging for forgiveness. I imagined him to be his father doing the begging and got a kick out of that. That's as close as I'll get to the Husband begging me for anything. Anyway, the Boy continued to plead with me to forgive him, that he was helpless about these repartees, and that his DNA was to blame, for it carried the humour gene from me. As if that was consolation. If that were true, then he got his cynicism from me too, enough cause for me to hate Moi! Finally, I told him I would relent on one condition. As he was willing to do anything to placate me, he agreed at once. I knew that he hated for me to be angry or sad, so I played up a bit on the emotional card. He took my hands and sat by me and reassured me that he would do anything to put the smile back on my face.

Now I shifted into second gear. I got him to agree about considering marriage. I told him about Mrs. Aye's daughter. Convent-educated, doctor, an accomplished pianist who taught Sunday School at church. He feigned horror and said that he was a healthy, normal guy with no complications in his life and didn't need an in-house doctor. Then he let it be known that he would look favourably on a girl who could play the drums and accompany him on his guitar. Undaunted, when I pressed on about Mrs. Aye's daughter, he asked me if she played football or ever watched the 'World Cup.' He told me his partner should be able to discuss Watergate and NASDAQ, appreciate music by Meatloaf and Iron Maiden, and watch rugby. Most of all, she should be able to pack for a journey in twenty minutes flat and keep shopping to a minimal. The prospective should be partial to black colour in general and clothes in particular. I had a feeling 'the biter was being bit.' I sulked and told him to find his own partner, since he insisted on being snide. I told him he should go to all the football games and maybe he would find someone appropriate on the field. At once, he retorted triumphantly, 'There! See, that is where I get my humour from.'

Our telephone conversations from then on were strained. He tried to charm his way back into our mother-son status-quo, but I remained cold and distant. It was a plan, of course, to get him to come grovelling back once more so I could state my terms again. And try a new strategy. All this was getting to my health and wellbeing. The Husband was blissfully ignorant to all that was going on beneath his very nose, in spite of my warning him that I was being driven to an early grave. In fact, he advised the Boy to play the field and not get hitched until after forty. Grrrrr. Some people have nothing between the ears when it comes to parenting. After about two weeks of trying to win me over and getting nowhere, he admitted unconditional defeat.

'Go on Mother, you have me where you want me. En tout. Do with me as you wish,' he said in a low voice.

I shifted into third gear. The sarcasm was still lurking just behind those words, but I ignored it and seized my chance. I told him I would register him on a dating site. He insisted he was not that desperate. That those sites were sort of porn sites, and he did not want to be exposed. That he would not be put out on the stock market to have his worth valued and worry about his ratings. But when I pouted, I could see him roll his eyes and raise his hands.

'You will remember for ever that I did this for you, Mother,' he said theatrically, and added with a wry smile, 'Greater love has no man than this, that he lay down his life for his mother. John 15:13, with appropriate corrections, of course.'

I registered him right away and spent hours, days, and months on the dating site, scouring for the right person. Meticulously, I'd read through the personal data of attractive girls to discern those with similar interests. No one mentioned football or NASDAQ. However, those who came nearest to his interest, I forwarded to the Boy for his perusal and final say. I developed a crick in my neck from the constant use of the net. The Husband even accused me of having an online affair with 'some old goat,' as he put it, or else what was I doing surfing the net so late into the night? Through all of this, I kept on, hoping the end to this conundrum was near. So, I was gutted to the core when the girls called me one day and let on that the Boy forwarded all the details I was forwarding him, to them. He had not looked at any of them. Not one. In fact, he told the sisters that 'Mother was showing an unusual interest in young girls.' I ask you!! I had suckled a viper at my bosom. I left him alone after that. You know when you are beaten. I think he was a little disappointed that I never pestered him on the topic any more. There was no tongue-in-cheek banter between us anymore, and I knew he thrived on that. I kept up the charade, hoping, perhaps, that he would come around and do the right thing. My silence was my winning move, although it tore me apart when we were not nagging each other, and I felt a heaviness in my heart. The phone rang late one night.

The Boy (with enthusiasm): 'Hey, momma.'

Moi (evenly): 'Hey.'

He (with more enthusiasm): 'Guess what?'

Moi (pretending to smother a yawn): 'What?'

He (with an embarrassed laugh): 'I think I'm in love!'

I stayed silent.

He (with slight panic in his voice): 'Momma, you there? Hello?'

Moi (in a whisper): 'Yes, I am here.'

He (sounding a little hurt): 'Well, aren't you happy? That's what you wanted, right?'

Moi (my heart starting to hammer): 'I'm happy. Yes. So, what are the details?'

He (back to cheeky): 'Well, to begin with, it's a girl,'

'Really? I thought it would be a cat,' I chuckled.

'Mother, what would I do without you?' He said with a sigh.

'You are not joking, are you?' I was sceptical.

'No, Momma Bear. I promise. Don't think me that cruel. You can plan your wedding,' he laughed.

I put the phone down gingerly. I started to smile slowly. I looked upwards.

'Yeh God!' I said, raising a fist into the air. 'We hooked the big fish. We did it again! Together.'

The Third Wedding

Of the kids, 1 thought, *Two down, one more to go.* The preparations for the third and final wedding in the family was a whirlwind of activity. For starters, we had just two weeks to put it together. Arranging the trousseau, the ornaments, the invitations, the reading of the banns, the wedding menu, the flower decorations, the music – they all had to be decided and finalised in fourteen days. No points for guessing who had to shoulder all this. The phone rang incessantly, and no one answered it unless I did. It came to a state where I did not know if I were here or there. It was at a time like this that the Husband breezed in with four suspicious looking characters and prowled around the house, paying special attention to the room which was to act as the bridal suite. I was alarmed, but before I could protest, the Husband assured me that he had everything under control. So, when Younger came running to the kitchen looking distressed and demanding to know who the men in her room were, I could tell her nothing, as I knew nothing.

'Fa, what's happening,' she turned on her father.

'It's a wedding present, darling,' he said, grandly.

'What? Those four peculiar looking "boodos" in my room? You gifting them to me?' she asked, incredulously.

Oh, my poor ganglions, they are going to be excited beyond belief, I thought. They will start acting up in some way, and I'd have no control. I'll admit I'd never heard the term 'boodos' before; but somehow, it seemed correct and right on target. And I can show you a fifth! I am married to him; God save the me from murdering the man.

'Kochu kalli (little minx), I didn't mean the chaps, you know,' he said, laughing. 'I meant I'm doing up your room as a gift. I'm doing the ceiling in particular so that when you guys use it after the wedding…. erm…. (clearing his throat here), you can look up and admire the beautiful false ceiling I'm putting up, and with dimming lights too.'

'Fa,' the daughter wailed, 'why don't you just buy me a diamond something or other like every normal father? Don't you think the ceiling will be the last place I would be looking...?' she stopped, looked aghast, turned red, and then burst into loud sobs.

'It's all your fault, Mama. Why couldn't you marry a Dentist or some such lame fellow? You had to find an Engineer who has a penchant for false ceilings of all things.'

There it was, full circle. The ultimate Villain, Moi. It did not matter that my own mother was at fault. She was the one who had found the man that was the Husband and the father of the bride-to-be. But Mother had made the Great Escape, and I was left to face the music. *After I die*, I thought, *I'll seek her out and put her to death again, if it is possible.* She still owed me for that telephone conversation at the post office in Ayroor.

'What's wrong with you?' I demanded of the Husband. 'Why did you have to upset her? She needs her room to dress and organize, and you have got workmen in there? How will she have her privacy?'

Without missing a beat, he came right back, 'So she can have her privacy in another room. She can share the room with us. You know what? You spoil the kids. You are putting these ideas into her head. I don't know why you have to be so anti-me. You were the one always saying I do nothing around the house. See what I get when I do? And why does she have to have the room to herself anyway?' he argued.

'Well, have you ever been a bride?' I ask, exasperatedly. 'Have you?'

He shook his head like I was mad and making a mountain out of nothing, not even a mole-hill.

'Who can understand women? Not any man in the world. They never appreciate anything you do for them,' he said, shrugging his shoulders and walking away.

'So then don't talk if you've never been a bride,' I shouted after him.

Then I went to find Younger and pacify her. This, when I had a thousand things to do and a thousand places to be at. *Oh God*, I thought. Like for the other two weddings, I should have asked him to come down from Kuwait just two days before the nuptials. Just to show I had a Husband and the kids had a father. More fool me, for thinking his coming early would ease my burden. Now, though the daughter was getting married, it looked like the parents were heading for Splitsville. Or worse. Work progressed in the bedroom. Younger cried and sulked and said no one really loved her. The Father reassured her that he was doing the work on the wedding suite because he loved her to 'thithereens.' Now, how much love is that? You figure it out. The banging and grinding in the room kept us all on edge. The dust was everywhere. Only one person was oblivious to the fact. He called over a couple of friends, and over copious cups of tea and hearty laughter, they discussed the merits of an excellent false ceiling in the bridal room. I heard the Husband tell his friends in an undertone how 'the "girls" don't understand.' And they came right back and reassured him that 'women never get it, no matter what.' And 'how we poor men have to put up with all their paranoia.' More laughter and clinking of glasses.

The wedding trousseau was delivered two days before the big day. I got it wrapped in layers of thick plastic to stop the dust from getting to it. We laid it carefully on the bed in the master bedroom, and I left for my appointment with the florist. When I returned two hours later, there was a turmoil of unimaginable proportions in the house. As I ran indoors, I heard Younger call to me with panic in her voice. I rushed up and saw her standing in the middle of the room, pale-faced and shaking. She was crying like her heart would break.

'What's the matter?' I asked. I felt the vomit rise in my throat.

'I can't find the wedding dress anywhere,' she whispered. 'You know we left it on the bed.'

'Relax, relax,' I told her, more to pacify Moi than her.

In undertones, as usual, I mollified myself. I kept saying, 'Lennie you're all right. You faced the life at the boarding school with panache, survived College and took the moniker "maidanum" in your stride, was undaunted by Kallu Mathai, endured the ragging at the Professional College, took the plunge to share your life with a total stranger, survived the Gulf War, and single-handedly brought up three exceptional human beings, bringing them this far. And you're still standing. Now is not the time to doubt yourself. This too, shall pass.'

'It will be here, somewhere. It can't have just walked out,' I managed, with a hysterical laugh. Then we searched the room, the cupboards, and the bathroom (odd place to look, I know, but we've got to look, right?). Well, actually, we had laid it nice and proper on the bed, so I had no idea why we were searching at all. After about two hours, the Husband sauntered into the room to rest, tired from all the ceiling fixing, I guess. He caught us searching desperately and asked us what was happening. We told him of the missing item.

'Was it on the bed?' he asked.

'Yes,' I said. I was getting a bad feeling.

'Wrapped in thick plastic?' he queried.

'Yes,' I whispered, glaring at the Husband, and as a dreadful feeling crept up on Moi, I felt myself turn into Medusa, with a stare that could turn him into stone.

'Erm… I thought it was a lot of waste plastic. I was going to take a nap and the bed was littered. So, I just gathered the whole thing and stuffed it into a cardboard box in the garage. Good show I did not burn it,' he added.

Lord, give me strength, I prayed, as I kept my clenched fists steady by my sides. It would be so easy to strike out and box his ears. But if word got around that the bride's parents were engaged in a boxing match, we'd never live it down. We searched the umpteen boxes in the garage, retrieved the wedding dress, and the day was saved. In the end, in spite of all the turmoil, the wedding went off resplendently – the bride was gorgeous in her sari and jewellery and looked like a princess. As she walked down the aisle on her father's arm, no one would have guessed how close she had been on the previous day to a total nervous breakdown. As for the father, he puffed out his chest and held up his head, and I'll bet he was thinking of the ceiling he had installed for his precious daughter.

The nest is empty now. There will be no more weddings. Everything has become a memory. Every once in a while, the Husband goes into the room that was the wedding suite. He will lie on the bed and gaze up. His sense of achievement at creating the masterpiece obliterates all else. The ceiling of a Maharaja's palace would not seem as magnificent in his eyes.

Without doubt, master-minding the three weddings and carrying them out with such aplomb made me a doyen of success in the eyes of many. But in reality, I was drained and spent and tired by the gargantuan amount of effort I had put in to achieve that scale of success, what with a husband who tried to hijack the events at each turn. Getting the main players to participate and organizing the whole process had taken the ultimate toll on my health and life. It is a wonder that I'm not dead due to the exertion and stress of making a success of each endeavour.

And yet, if you ask me how the ride was, I'd say it was good. It was worthwhile.

Appreciation

In all of the hats that I've worn in my life, I think the most precious and the one I've enjoyed wearing the most is my 'mother hat.' It has been the most stimulating, frustrating, bewildering, satisfying, and the one closest to my heart. I'd say 'The Offsprings' are my 'raison d'etre.' There is no doubt about it. The weekend banter with the Boy, which keeps my wits sharp, the quasi arguments with Elder, which keeps my adrenaline pumping, and a treasured poem that Younger gifted me on the day she got married, is proof I did three things right.

And best of all, later in life, the Husband and I gifted ourselves many holidays to many exquisite places, only this time, sans the children.

I started a story. It has to end somewhere. So, here we are. But that does not mean there are no stories left.

Gods Precious Gift To Me

from the first breath
as a little child
all i have ever known
is you mother

the first sound
of a syllable
i have spoken
is you mother

even as a teen, rebelling
against the strength of your guidance
only to find a stronger friend
in you mother

every moment, every thought
morality and deed
all the lessons learned
is from you mother

who i am to who i will be
my tone, control and humility
are inherent traits
of you mother

an infant to an adult
life has passed but
i met no finer woman
than you mother

Mother you are who i am
as i am who you are
as my children will be me
and in them will be you.

Poem by Younger

Epilogue

Dear readers,

This is my first attempt at authoring a book. My greatest achievement will be to have entertained you; my greatest fear that I might have bored you. Either way, I'm satisfied I started something and saw it to the end. Only, don't be indifferent to it. That, dear friends, will hit where it hurts.

Every time I proofread, a new memory would pop up, and I'd feel the need to add it. Until I realised if I don't stop, this book will never get done. So, I stopped the corrections and additions. Hence, there may be some hiccups and inconsistencies. Mea culpa.

I am glad you have journeyed with Moi from my childhood, school days, and college to marriage, motherhood, and beyond. In writing this, I have been lucky to have had the chance to revive and relive precious old memories. Some happy, some painful, either way enabling me to walk the old roads and visit forgotten places. I, for one, have enjoyed the experience.

THANK YOU

About the Author

I'm a dentist by profession, so everything I speak is the tooth, or should I say 'truth?' I own up to the fact that I have not, as yet, written a book. Nor have I made a publication or sent in an article to any newspaper. Hence, there is nothing of significance to boost my ego except for the fact that I dared to remove my father-in-law's tooth once. Not many can boast of that. Even so, I now dare to swim with the sharks and publish this work among well-established writers and literary giants, hoping to hold my own.

I like to think I'm cosmopolitan – born in Kerala, childhood in Ceylon, and early girlhood in Malaya. In my teens, I was shipped back to a boarding school in India, where I gathered ample fodder for my later writings. I studied dentistry at The Govt. Dental College, Trivandrum, and later worked in Malaysia for a stint. After marriage, I imparted my dental expertise to the people of Kuwait until Saddam Hussein put an end to it. I returned to India, and since then, have had my own practice and have also been associated with a private dental college.

I am retired and live in Trivandrum. Oh, I still have the Husband of 46 years to remind me that life is a challenge, no matter the time or the age. I'm enjoying the empty-nest syndrome, though I do a lot of e-nagging. Why else do we have children?